Data-Driven Campaigning and Political Parties

JOURNALISM AND POLITICAL COMMUNICATION UNBOUND

Series editors: Daniel Kreiss, University of North Carolina at Chapel Hill, and Nikki Usher, University of San Diego

Journalism and Political Communication Unbound seeks to be a high-profile book series that reaches far beyond the academy to an interested public of policymakers, journalists, public intellectuals, and citizens eager to make sense of contemporary politics and media. "Unbound" in the series title has multiple meanings: It refers to the unbinding of borders between the fields of communication, political communication, and journalism, as well as related disciplines such as political science, sociology, and science and technology studies; it highlights the ways traditional frameworks for scholarship have disintegrated in the wake of changing digital technologies and new social, political, economic, and cultural dynamics; and it reflects the unbinding of media in a hybrid world of flows across mediums.

OTHER BOOKS IN THE SERIES

Journalism Research That Matters
Valérie Bélair-Gagnon and Nikki Usher

Reckoning: Journalism's Limits and Possibilities
Candis Callison and Mary Lynn Young

News After Trump: Journalism's Crisis of Relevance in a Changed Media Culture
Matt Carlson, Sue Robinson, and Seth C. Lewis

Borderland: Decolonizing the Words of War
Chrisanthi Giotis

The Politics of Force: Media and the Construction of Police Brutality
Regina Lawrence

Imagined Audiences: How Journalists Perceive and Pursue the Public
Jacob L. Nelson

Pop Culture, Politics, and the News: Entertainment Journalism in the Polarized Media Landscape
Joel Penney

Democracy Lives in Darkness: How and Why People Keep Their Politics a Secret
Emily Van Duyn

Building Theory in Political Communication: The Politics-Media-Politics Approach
Gadi Wolfsfeld, Tamir Sheafer, and Scott Althaus

Data-Driven Campaigning and Political Parties

Five Advanced Democracies Compared

KATHARINE DOMMETT, GLENN KEFFORD,
AND SIMON KRUSCHINSKI

OXFORD
UNIVERSITY PRESS

Oxford University Press is a department of the University of Oxford. It furthers
the University's objective of excellence in research, scholarship, and education
by publishing worldwide. Oxford is a registered trade mark of Oxford University
Press in the UK and certain other countries.

Published in the United States of America by Oxford University Press
198 Madison Avenue, New York, NY 10016, United States of America.

© Oxford University Press 2024

All rights reserved. No part of this publication may be reproduced, stored in
a retrieval system, or transmitted, in any form or by any means, without the
prior permission in writing of Oxford University Press, or as expressly permitted
by law, by license, or under terms agreed with the appropriate reproduction
rights organization. Inquiries concerning reproduction outside the scope of the
above should be sent to the Rights Department, Oxford University Press, at the
address above.

You must not circulate this work in any other form
and you must impose this same condition on any acquirer.

Library of Congress Cataloging-in-Publication Data
Names: Dommett, Katharine, author. | Kefford, Glenn, author. |
Kruschinski, Simon, author.
Title: Data-driven campaigning and political parties : five advanced
democracies compared / [Katharine Dommett, Glenn Kefford,
and Simon Kruschinski].
Description: New York : Oxford University Press, [2024]. |
Series: Journalism and political communication unbound series |
Includes bibliographical references and index.
Identifiers: LCCN 2023039561 (print) | LCCN 2023039562 (ebook) |
ISBN 9780197570234 (paperback) | ISBN 9780197570227 (hardback) |
ISBN 9780197570258 (epub)
Subjects: LCSH: Campaign management—Data processing—Case studies. |
Internet in political campaigns—Case studies. |
Data mining—Poltical aspects—Case studies.
Classification: LCC JF2112.C3 D66 2024 (print) | LCC JF2112.C3 (ebook) |
DDC 324.70285—dc23/eng/20231018
LC record available at https://lccn.loc.gov/2023039561
LC ebook record available at https://lccn.loc.gov/2023039562

DOI: 10.1093/oso/9780197570227.001.0001

Paperback printed by Marquis Book Printing, Canada
Hardback printed by Bridgeport National Bindery, Inc., United States of America

Contents

Acknowledgments   vii

1. Introduction   1
2. Theoretical Framework   20
3. Data   43
   Practitioner Perspectives on Data   66
4. Analytics   71
   Practitioner Perspectives on Analytics   99
5. Technology   104
   Practitioner Perspectives on Technology   131
6. Personnel   136
   Practitioner Perspectives on Personnel   163
7. Explaining Variation in Data-Driven Campaigning   167
8. Conclusion   191

Notes   207
References   211
Index   241

Acknowledgments

This book is the product of many years of data collection and analysis. Like parties themselves, we have drawn upon a variety of sources and would like to acknowledge and thank all those who have made this book possible. We would like to thank the hundreds of interviewees who gave up their time to speak to us at length about their experience of data-driven campaigns. While not named within this piece for reasons of anonymity, we want to recognize and deeply thank each and every one of you. In particular, we want to recognize the contribution of each of our named practitioners who offered a short vignette. These reflections provide a vital glimpse of practitioners' perspectives of campaigning and offer an important and enduring resource for future study.

In preparing the manuscript, we have also benefited from the support and advice of numerous colleagues. We would like to particularly thank Joshua Marsh, Andrew Barclay, and Chris Steer for supporting the research for this book. In addition, we thank Chris Jones, Duncan McDonnell, Ann-Kristin Kölln, Jesse-Baldwin Phillipi, Sanne Kruikemeier, Tom Dobber, Sara Bannerman, and Erica Rzepecki for feedback and discussion on the topic of data-driven campaigns. We also want to acknowledge the particular support and encouragement we received from Daniel Kreiss and Nikki Usher as editors of this book series.

This research would not have been possible without the funding of several funding agencies. We would explicitly like to acknowledge the support of the NORFACE Joint Research Programme on Democratic Governance in a Turbulent Age and co-funded by ESRC, FWF, NWO, the European Commission through Horizon 2020 under grant agreement No. 822166, and the Australian Research Council for funding through grant DE190100210. Furthermore, we would like to thank Marcus Maurer, who provided funding and support as political communication's research lab head at the Department of Communication at the Johannes Gutenberg-University Mainz for conducting the research in Germany.

Finally, we would like to thank our families and friends for their unwavering support of our academic endeavors.

1
Introduction

Election campaigns represent a key moment when political parties around the globe reach out to the electorate to gain support. The leaflets, posters, doorstep conversations, and messages that parties disseminate have long been seen as an essential and laudable part of democratic practice. And yet, over the past 10 years, such virtuous depictions of campaigning have been challenged by a new, more sinister account. Political parties are seen to have amassed vast databases of highly personal information. They are seen to be using complex analytical techniques to profile and gather unprecedented insight into our personal lives. And they are perceived to be deploying these techniques to manipulate voters and elections (Rubinstein 2014, 879). Such practices paint a particular image of modern campaigning and the role that data plays in elections today that has raised a range of democratic anxieties. Journalists have accordingly highlighted privacy concerns (Cadwalladr 2017a) and data breaches (Murphy 2019; Jones & Cinelli 2017; Scally 2019). Scholars have documented threats such as voter suppression, manipulation, exclusion, deception, privacy violations, and a fragmentation of the public sphere (Bennett 2016; Jamieson 2018; Moore 2018; Taylor 2021; Zuiderveen Borgesius et al. 2018). And policymakers and civil society organizations have sought to mitigate risks associated with data-driven practices such as microtargeting (Cicilline 2020; European Commission 2021; IDEA 2018; Kofi Annan Foundation 2020).

Within this book we suggest that the world of data-driven campaigning (DDC) is more complex and diverse than these (often sensationalized) accounts suggest. At present, however, the breadth and nature of data-driven campaign activity are not fully appreciated because of a focus on US practices and the risks of DDC. What is needed, therefore, is greater empirical understanding of how data is used in campaigns around the world, with more attention paid to whether (and why) usage varies internationally. Only with this insight is it possible to engage in a more empirically grounded discussion of the impact of DDC on democracy.

At present, when thinking about modern campaigning, US practices are commonly evoked to proclaim the routinization of DDC. There is extensive evidence available to support this idea. Senior officials in US presidential campaigns from both the Republican and Democratic parties have spoken about the importance of data and analytics. Catherine Tarsney, analytics director at the Democratic National Committee (DNC), for example, has discussed the need to build up a "360-degree view of voters by routinely incorporating data from new sources" (Data Council 2019). Elsewhere, the annual Reed Awards (2023), handed out by the US-based *Campaigns and Elections* magazine, now recognizes and celebrates the best data analytics solution, the best use of machine learning in online fundraising, the most sophisticated targeting in direct mail fundraising, and the best application of AI (artificial intelligence) technology to optimize targeting. There are also numerous examples of companies that offer data and analytics services to support US campaigns, ranging from the Republican group Data Trust (n.d.)—who advertise themselves as "the leading provider or voter and electoral data to Republican and conservative campaigns, parties, and advocacy organizations" (n.p.)—to fundraising platforms such as the Democrat-supporting Act Blue, which describes its process of "constantly A/B testing our contribution forms" to maximize donations (Act Blue n.d., n.p.). US parties are also reported to be investing in data personnel and systems. The DNC, for example, hired a chief technology officer to oversee a staff of 65 employees, and increased investment in a new data system and new data points by purchasing 65 million cell phone numbers in 2020 (Ryan-Mosley 2020). Data is therefore a well-established component of campaigning in the US context.

Looking beyond the United States, there is some evidence that these practices are found elsewhere. In Australia, for example, the former national secretary and campaign director for the Australian Labor Party, Noah Carroll, argued that "[t]he interconnectivity of field work, data, analytics, research and messaging is the clear systems requirement of current and future campaigning" (quoted in Bramston 2016, n.p.). There is also evidence of international parties purchasing data lists for campaign purposes, with Canadian parties working with Environics Analytics, which breaks down the population into lifestyle clusters (Delacourt 2012), and UK parties hiring Experian and Data8 to access, analyze, and store data (Information Commissioners' Office 2018). Moreover, LinkedIn shows an international job market for data analysts and statisticians within party campaigns, with vacancies advertised in Australia, Canada, the United Kingdom, and Germany. Such examples suggest that data has become a central component of modern campaigns and is playing a key role in guiding electoral strategy.

And yet, while there is some evidence of campaigners' increased investment in data, there are also signs that the data practices of many parties are not as extensive, sophisticated, or concerning as often depicted. In many parties outside the United States, campaigners are highly curtailed regarding the type of data they can collect and store. In Germany, for example, there has been coverage of the way in which data protection law fundamentally restricts the type of personal information that parties are able to collect (Dachwitz 2017; Jaursch 2020; Kolany-Raiser & Radtke 2018), and of the strong cultural norms that reduce public acceptance of data collection and targeting (YouGov 2017: Völlinger 2017). In that regard the Berlin Data Commissioner (2021, n.p.) concluded in their annual report that:

> parties can certainly use modern digital technologies for party work and election campaigns if this is done in accordance with data protection regulations. In Germany, however, it is not permissible to create profiles of voters, as is the case in the US, for example. By and large, the parties adhere to this. However, less comprehensive data about supporters and voters also needs protection. Therefore, political parties must exercise due diligence and consistently implement data minimization and anonymization.

Similarly, there are signs that in many countries, parties do not possess reliable systems to facilitate the use of data. In Canada, for example, a post-2021 election review published by the New Democratic Party reported that two of the party's data systems—CallHub and Dandelion—"crashed when they were needed most," leading to calls for tools to be capacity tested ahead of Election Day (National Democratic Party 2021, 7). In the United Kingdom, even the most highly resourced parties reported limitations with their databases, with the Labour Party's post-2019 General Election review noting that "vital systems and platforms were frequently unreliable, slow, hard to use, glitch-ridden, or tied up by complicated access restrictions," with the party's database, Contact Creator, in particular, reported to "not have the capacity to cope with high levels of data input" (Labour Together 2019, n.p.).

Meanwhile, in terms of data analytics and targeting, there is evidence that many international parties are restricted by data-protection rules. In Germany, for example, the Social Democrats published a campaigning fairness code which explains that the party will only use voter targeting which is exclusively within the framework of the high European and German data-protection standards (SPD-Parteivorstand 2021). There is also evidence that some parties lack the resources to invest in developing and updating sophisticated models (Kefford et al. 2022). In the United Kingdom, for example, the Liberal Democrats' post-2019 General Election analysis suggested that the party did not invest in ongoing and continually updated modeling, but rather relied on a single multilevel regression and poststratification (MRP) model conducted in June, meaning that their strategy was based on data that quickly went out of date (Kearns & Alexander 2020, 6). Such contrasting pictures of campaign practice suggest there are important questions about the way in which data is being used in modern campaigning. It indicates that far from there being a single manifestation of DDC, data is used in a variety of ways. This has important implications for any attempt to understand the use of DDC and suggests that concerning practices are not an inherent feature of DDC, but may be present to different degrees. At present, however, three things are lacking: first, a framework for understanding what we mean when we refer to DDC; second, empirical insight into the variety of ways in which data is presently being used in campaigns internationally; and third, an explanation for that variation that pays attention to the contexts in which DDC occurs. Only by addressing these three gaps is it possible to fully appreciate the role of data in modern campaigns and consider its impact on democracy.

Contribution

In this book we provide the first internationally comparative study of DDC. We do so by exploring DDC across five advanced democracies: Australia, Canada, Germany, the United States, and the United Kingdom. Studying practices within 18 parties, we offer unprecedented insight into the reality of modern campaigns. Seeking to move beyond the prevailing emphasis on extensive data collection and concerning data analytics practices, we clarify what we mean by the term *DDC*, unpacking the spectrum of ways in which parties can utilize data, conduct analysis, deploy technology, and staff data-driven campaigns.

Adopting this approach, we combine conceptual mapping with empirical analysis to show not only that data can be gathered and utilized in a variety of different ways by political parties and campaigns, but also that specific parties in different countries vary in their precise engagement with data. Mapping variations, we also demonstrate that the vast majority of parties' data-driven practices are mundane, predictable, and removed from the hyperbolic accounts that dominate popular commentary, but that there are differences in how certain parties behave.

These conclusions are drawn from fine-grained qualitative research, and in many ways the book is unashamedly descriptive. As scholars who draw on a variety of methods in our research, we believe that any effort to understand DDC must begin with the provision of detailed "thick" descriptions of contemporary practice in order to generate new theories and accurate diagnoses of problematic practice. We therefore utilize qualitative methods to contextualize DDC practice with a view to advancing this body of scholarship.

Adopting this empirically grounded qualitative approach, our analysis is well-placed to explain different practices, and we do so by introducing an original theoretical framework that shows the relevance of systemic, regulatory, and party-level factors for any attempt to understand variations in DDC. Moving beyond the prevailing tendency to cite the importance of a country's data and privacy regulation in shaping DDC activity, we explain the significance of factors such as the electoral system, campaign regulation, and party ideology for DDC practice. Adopting this approach, we reveal why actors in the same jurisdiction use data differently, and how country context makes a difference in what is possible. Together, these insights help us to understand not only what is happening in political campaigning, but also how a variety of contextual factors can inform how and why data is used. These insights are likely to be highly significant for regulators or other actors seeking to respond to perceived challenges presented by DDC, revealing the very different factors that could be altered to change data practices.

In tracing the components of DDC and seeking to map and understand its contemporary practice, we argue that it is important not to overstate the novelty of this phenomenon. Data, as one form of information, has long been used to shape strategic decision-making. Whether gathering feedback from customers, conducting focus groups to test messages, or simply recording the demographics of people spoken to, the process of gathering and looking at patterns in information or data is a long-standing component of much political and commercial activity. As a result, in studying DDC, we engage with the rise of new tools and capacities, but we also spell out the many long-standing practices which remain core to data collection and analytics today.

We show that rather than representing a radical new activity, over recent years DDC has evolved. Understanding this heritage is vital in the context of growing concern about the democratic implications and consequences of these activities, as it suggests that the use of data can be a valued component of democratic contact and should not, therefore, be universally condemned.

Cumulatively, these insights lead us to contend that:

- DDC is not a uniform practice, but can appear in a range of different forms;
- DDC is not inherently problematic, but can be used in ways that may be more or less acceptable to citizens;
- DDC is not new, but is the latest evolution of a long-standing practice of gathering and analyzing data in efforts to secure electoral success;
- Systemic, regulatory, and party-level factors affect the form of DDC.

What Do We Actually Know?

In making these contributions, we build on an emergent academic literature on DDC that, while expanding in recent years, so far lacks a detailed, comparative analysis of practices in different countries. The role of data in politics has long been recognized, with studies of, for example, parties' use of polling to gather insights into voters in the 1960s (Abrams 1963) and voter-segmentation techniques (Phillips et al. 2010, 311; Webber 2006). However, the most recent work on political campaigning suggests that there has been a substantive shift in attitudes toward, and use of, data.

Diagnosing the emergence of a new fourth era of campaigning (Römmele & Gibson 2020), scholars have directed attention to "an organizational and strategic dependency on digital technology and 'big data'; a reliance on networked communication, the individualized micro-targeting of campaign messages, and the internationalization of the campaign sphere" (Römmele & Gibson 2020, 595). While scholars often fail to define or characterize this activity in precise terms (Dommett et al. 2023), it has been widely suggested that there has been a "big data revolution" (Hersh & Schaffner 2013, 520), and a growing reliance on microtargeting for "every aspect of modern elections" (Rubinstein 2014, 883). Beyond these broad depictions, however, there have so far been few attempts to pinpoint the precise indicators of DDC or to explore the degree to which similar practices are found in different parts of the world.

Reviewing scholarly depictions of DDC, what emerges is therefore a relatively homogenous account of the role of data in modern campaigns that mirrors the popular focus on US practices (described above). Hersh (2015, 24), for example, offers a detailed study of data use in the United States that explains:

> In an effort to win an election, campaigns seek to mobilize supporters and persuade undecided voters. In order to contact these voters and transmit mobilizing or persuasive messages, campaigns must predict which voters will be responsive to their appeals, and they must decide which voters should get which kinds of appeals. To make these decisions, campaigns gather data and form impressions about the voters.

He goes on to detail how data can derive from a range of sources, but "in more recent years, campaign organizations develop statistical models that generate a score for each voter, which estimates the probability that they support a particular party or candidate or that they will be likely to vote" (Hersh 2015, 28). This depiction of data-driven targeting and modeling has been widely replicated. Indeed, Chester and Montgomery (2017, 3–4) describe how campaigns "can now take advantage of a growing infrastructure of specialty firms offering more extensive resources for data mining and targeting voters." This includes:

> data about individuals from a wide variety of online and offline sources, including first-party data from a customer's own record, such as the use of a supermarket loyalty card, or their activities captured on a website, mobile phone, or wearable device; second-party data, information collected about a person by another company, such as an online publisher, and sold to others; and third-party data drawn from thousands of sources, comprising demographic, financial, and other data-broker information, including race, ethnicity, and presence of children.

In line with such accounts, it is common to see descriptions of political databases that "hold records on almost 200 million eligible American voters" wherein:

[e]ach record contains hundreds if not thousands of fields derived from voter rolls, donor and response data, campaign web data, and consumer and other data obtained from data brokers, all of which is combined into a giant assemblage made possible by fast computers, speedy network connections, cheap data storage, and ample financial and technical resources. (Rubinstein 2014, 879)

While offering a range of valuable insights into the dynamics of modern campaigning, this literature has several shortcomings that we argue warrants a new approach.

Particularly notable is the lack of comparative international analyses of DDC. While a small number have emerged in other contexts—with studies of practice in Canada (Bennett 2016; Munroe & Munroe 2018), Germany (Kruschinski & Haller 2017), and Australia (Kefford 2021)—for the most part our understanding of DDC reflects norms and practices found in US presidential campaigns, and is rarely comparative (cf. Kefford et al. 2022).

Although it is of course valuable to understand the dynamics of US campaigning, particularly given the influence that these practices can have on campaign activity elsewhere (Vaccari 2013), we argue that US practices should not be equated with general practice across advanced democracies because they are not simply diffused around the world through processes of "modernization," "imposition," and "imitation" (Pasquino 2005, 4; t'Veld 2017, 3). Rather, we argue that there are important systemic, regulatory, and party-level factors which mean that DDC practices found in the United States will not be replicated elsewhere (Kruschinski & Haller 2017).

Whether thinking about variations in data-protection law, party finance, or even electoral systems, the boundaries of legally and socially acceptable behavior are not consistent across advanced democracies. Indeed, even within the United States, there are reasons to think that this depiction may not accurately describe all DDC activity. The focus on well-resourced campaigns supported by expert data professionals can, for example, overlook the data practices of grassroots activists and lower-order (or down-ballot) campaigns that may not have the resources to cultivate large-scale data collection and analytics operations (Kefford et al. 2022). It also overlooks the potential for state-by-state variation where different local regulations and practices can cause DDC practices to vary. At a very basic level, therefore, we need to interrogate what we mean by DDC and how and why this practice might look different in different contexts and circumstances.

We also note that while there has been a growing interest in DDC, there have been relatively few empirical studies of the actual practice of this activity. Due to a range of challenges in securing access to observe campaigns in practice, and widespread reticence (especially among conservative parties) to give interviews about campaign activity (Dommett & Power 2021), many studies have based their depiction of DDC on claims made by companies selling DDC services. These assertions about campaign capacity can be easily located. Taking just one example, the C|T Group, an international consultancy company led by Lynton Crosby—an Australian political strategist who has advised on election campaigns around the world—claims it can gather "reliable, high-quality data to shape and influence behaviour in the desired direction by targeting the motivations of key actors and utilising identified pressure points to achieve the desired outcome" (C|T Group n.d., n.p.). Such sources can provide *some* insight into the objectives and goals of campaigns, but social scientists need to be wary of such assertions, which are often self-serving. As the Cambridge Analytica scandal has demonstrated, companies often make significant claims about their capacities that are not reflected in actual practices (ICO 2020).

For these reasons, there is a need to study the actual practice of DDC cross-nationally to ensure that our understanding reflects the real rather than potential use of these techniques. Pursuing study at this level, it becomes possible to understand how parties' use of data varies in different countries, or even varies between or within parties in the same context. It is also possible to ask whether we can observe one form of DDC in all countries, or whether there are different types of this practice in different contexts. Furthermore, consideration can also be given to why DDC appears more sophisticated in certain contexts, and more basic in others.

To generate these insights, this book reacts to the existing literature by posing three interlinked questions. First, we ask at the most basic level: What is DDC? Offering a definition that distinguishes four components of this practice—data, analytics, technology, and personnel—we outline how activity can differ at each level. Second, and operationalizing these frameworks, we ask: How does DDC practice vary? Presenting empirical data gathered from our five case study countries, we show exactly how parties are using data in different countries, highlighting variations and similarities exposed through our data collection. Finally, we ask: What explains different DDC practices? In doing so, we consider the relevance of systemic, regulatory, and party-level factors as drivers of campaign practice. By posing these questions, we offer unprecedented insight into modern campaigning, and demonstrate through detailed descriptive accounts of the mechanics of DDC cross-nationally that the drivers and potential responses to DDC are multifaceted.

In writing this book, we rely not only on our own academic analysis; we also integrate the voices of leading campaign professionals. At the end of each of our four substantive chapters (on data, analysis, technology, and personnel), we ask practitioners from across our countries to reflect on the logic of prevailing narratives around DDC, providing more direct insight into the way that campaign professionals understand the dynamics of the modern campaign. This book accordingly provides an important juncture from much previous work, helping scholars, practitioners, and those concerned about these practices to better understand the subtle nuances and influences upon parties' use of data.

What Is DDC?

Within this book we define DDC as a mode of campaigning that seeks to use data to develop and deliver campaign interventions with the goal of producing behavioral or attitudinal change in democratic citizens. We see DDC as composed of four central components: data, analytics, technology, and personnel. In offering this definition, we depart from much existing scholarship. Many academics have tended to avoid defining this phenomenon, with a recent systematic review (Dommett et al. 2023) showing only a handful that have outlined the traits of DDC (for example, Baldwin-Philippi 2019; Munroe & Munroe 2018; Kefford 2021). This tendency has allowed certain implicit and untested assumptions to become endemic and leaves many unanswered questions about the boundaries of this activity.

In our previous work, we have asserted the need to recognize variations in *what* data is being used, *who* is using data, and *how* data is being mobilized as part of a campaign (Dommett 2019; Dommett et al. 2021; Kefford et al. 2022; Kruschinski & Bene 2022). And we have demonstrated the potential for parties to simultaneously exhibit data analytics and targeting practices that are highly complex in some communication channels and simple and mundane in others (Kefford 2021; Kruschinski & Haller 2017). Spotlighting these different possibilities, we argue that there is limited utility in characterizing one set of (the most sophisticated) practices as indicative of DDC. Instead, we argue that there is a spectrum of types of data and mechanisms for data collection, as well as a range of different analytical techniques that can be deployed by different personnel to engage in DDC.

Our definition reflects this argument, meaning that we do not reify particular forms of DDC, but rather focus on the different ways in which data can feature within, and be used by, different organizations. By considering our four key elements of DDC—data, analytics, technology, and personnel—in turn, we distill the range of different possible practices that can be observed in each area of campaign activity. This approach allows us to move attention beyond US presidential campaigns and the handful of international instances in which US-style practices appear to be evident, to offer a more encompassing picture of the way data is being used by political parties across advanced democracies.

Why Do We Need to Understand More about DDC?

DDC is, if we believe much of the commentary, a serious threat to the effective functioning of liberal democracy. Though DDC is only one component of a far wider debate about the capacity of technology to revitalize or undermine democratic practice, numerous scholars and policymakers have raised concerns about the impact of data-driven practices (ICO 2020, US Senate 2018). These prognoses are significant because they are not confined to academic discussion (Harker 2020, 157; Jamieson 2013; Nadler, Crain, & Donovan 2018, 34; Rubinstein 2014, 886; t'Veld 2017, 3), but have begun to inform wide-ranging proposals for democratic reform. In countries around the globe, proposals have begun to be made by policymakers for improved data-protection law, increased transparency, and regulatory oversight of data-driven practices (Kuehn & Salter 2020, 2600–2601). These proposals have the potential to dramatically shape what constitutes acceptable (and legal) practice, and yet they are based on limited empirical evidence. In providing more insight into DDC, this book seeks to facilitate more sophisticated debate around the democratic implications of these practices, and appropriate responses to this activity. It also provide a template for thinking about the study and analysis of new technologies in politics more generally. As exemplified by new debates around the use of AI in politics (Kapoor & Narayanan 2023; Robins-Early 2023), there is a tendency to focus on the negative potential and to rush to regulate concerning practices, but our analysis suggests the need for a more empirically grounded and nuanced approach (Jungherr & Schroeder 2023).

First, at the most basic level, we argue that in order to appreciate the threat that DDC poses to democracy, there is a need to have a clear conception of the problem DDC poses. As Nielsen (2020, n.p.) has argued, "whenever we deal with any large public issue that requires a societal response, we've got to get the problem right otherwise our responses will be at best ineffective and at worst counterproductive." At present, the dominance of the US case has elevated concerns around particular practices which are deemed problematic. This includes voter-suppression activity (Kim 2018) and political redlining (Harker 2020, 155–156; Judge & Pal 2021; Kreiss 2012). However, it is not clear the extent to which these practices are found elsewhere, or whether other "problems" may be perceived in different contexts. With decades of scholarship showing variations in public attitudes toward privacy and democratic expectations, it is by no means to be expected that citizens (or policymakers) in different countries will perceive DDC practices in the same way (Kozyreva et al. 2021). In one context, it may therefore be deemed completely unacceptable to purchase information about citizens without their consent, while in another it may be relatively unproblematic. These possibilities make it vital to more fully appreciate what is happening in different countries in order to facilitate more informed discussion of the type and extent of democratic threat posed by DDC. Only when equipped with such knowledge can we determine which potential responses are most likely to produce the changes sought by democratic citizens in different contexts.

Second, and related to the point above, we draw attention to the current tendency for policymakers to propose data and privacy regulation as a means of curtailing problematic DDC practices. While an important type of response, we argue that this is not the only means of influencing the nature of data-driven campaigns. Indeed, our analysis shows that variation in DDC can be a product of a complex interplay of systemic, regulatory, and party-level factors. As such, efforts to shape DDC can usefully recognize the influence of a range of different factors, making it informative to examine how particular contextual factors affect the way DDC is manifest if seeking reform.

For these reasons, we argue that while it is reassuring to see action taken that is designed to protect the democratic system, there is a danger that without a clear understanding of precisely how data is being used and what is driving these practices, regulatory interventions will either tackle the "wrong" problem, or tackle the "right" problem but in ways which do not produce the desired result. As such, our book not only is important for academic understanding, but also has serious implications for democratic practice.

Our Cases

Our analysis of DDC by political parties focuses on practices in five advanced democracies: Australia, Canada, Germany, the United Kingdom, and the United States. These cases, while similar in many ways, exhibit significant variation on key systemic and regulatory dimensions that underpin our theoretical framework. These differences allow us to explore why DDC looks different in alternative country contexts, and yet we also seek to explain variations within each of our cases. As Vaccari has argued, "[e]ven within the same political context, campaign techniques are adopted in different ways by different political actors" (2013, 11). For this reason, we study a range of different parties within each of our case studies, considering how party-level factors exert an influence on the practice of DDC.

As outlined in Table 1.1, our five cases vary across many of the key variables commonly associated with campaigning, especially that of political parties. In terms of systemic variables, this includes variations in the electoral systems (mixed; majoritarian), systems of government (federal; unitary), party systems (multi-party; two-party), and hybrid media systems (high, mixed, low). Further, our five case study countries offer a balanced selection of weak, medium, or strong party, and campaign, data, and privacy, as well as media, regulations. While there were an infinite number of variables we could have presented to demonstrate the variation among our cases, we argue that the differences highlighted in Table 1.1—and discussed in more detail in Chapter 2—provide sufficient justification to draw generalizations from these five cases to other advanced democracies. We, of course, would have liked to extend this analysis to explore cases that varied even further, but ultimately, we chose cases that would provide sufficient generalizability while ensuring that we were able to gather the required empirical insights to fully understand the manifestation of DDC in each context.

Across the five country case studies, our analyses detail the practices of 18 political parties. As outlined in Table 1.2, within each country we include the major parties, as well as a selection of minor parties. The explanation for

Table 1.1 Key Systemic and Regulatory Variables

	Systemic Variables				Regulatory Variables			
	Electoral System	System of Government	Party System[a]	Hybrid Media System[b]	Party Regulation	Campaign Regulation	Data and Privacy Regulation	Media Regulation
Australia	Mixed: Alternative Vote and Single Transferable Vote	Federal	Multi-party	Mixed	Weak	Weak	Weak	Weak
United Kingdom	Majoritarian: Plurality	Unitary[c]	Multi-party	Mixed	Medium	Medium	Medium	Medium
United States	Majoritarian: Plurality	Federal	Two-party	High	Weak	Weak	Weak	Weak
Germany	Mixed: Plurality and Party list	Federal	Multi-party	Low	Strong	Strong	Strong	Strong
Canada	Majoritarian: Plurality	Federal	Multi-party	Mixed	Medium	Medium	Medium	Medium

[a] While there are numerous ways to classify party systems, for our purposes here we have simply used a two-party/multi-party distinction to highlight the number of "relevant" parties in the party system (see Sartori 2005, for more on this).

[b] To provide a sense of the level of hybridity in each of the media systems, we have considered the ways that old and new media are combined, which provides opportunities for grassroots participation and that new media and old media shape each other and are integrated with one other so that new media logic emerges. To assess this variable, we distinguish between systems as displaying "high," "mixed," or "low" levels of hybridity. In particular, we draw on the work of Mattoni and Ceccobelli (2018) here to outline what we consider to be of most interest for DDC.

[c] The UK here is classified as a unitary state, but due to devolution of certain powers to Scotland and Wales is technically an asymmetrically decentralised unitary state.

Table 1.2 Party Variables and Parties Included in Analysis

	Party Variables			
	Resources[a]	Structure[b]	Ideology[c]	Attitudes to DDC[d]
Australia				
Australian Labor Party	Medium	Stratarchical	Social Democrats	Enthusiasm
Liberal Party	Medium	Stratarchical	Christian Democrats/Conservatives	Enthusiasm
Australian Greens	Low	Federated	Greens	Mixed
United Kingdom*				
Labour Party	Medium	Stratarchical	Social Democrats	Enthusiasm
Conservative Party	Medium	Hierarchical	Christian Democrats/Conservatives	Enthusiasm
Liberal Democrats	Low	Stratarchical	Liberals	Enthusiasm
Green Party of England and Wales	Low	Federated	Greens	Mixed
United States				
Democratic Party	High	Stratarchical	Social Democrats	Enthusiasm
Republican Party	High	Stratarchical	Christian Democrats/Conservatives	Enthusiasm
Germany				
Social Democratic Party (SPD)	Medium	Stratarchical	Social Democrats	Enthusiasm
Christian Democratic Union (CDU)/Christian Social Union (CSU) (together: Union parties)	Medium	Stratarchical	Christian Democrats/Conservatives	Enthusiasm
The Greens	Medium	Federated	Greens	Mixed
Free Democratic Party (FDP)	Medium	Stratarchical	Liberals	Enthusiasm

(continued)

Table 1.2 Continued

	Party Variables			
	Resources[a]	Structure[b]	Ideology[c]	Attitudes to DDC[d]
The Left	Low	Stratarchical	Democratic socialism/Left-wing populism	Reticence
Alternative for Germany (AfD)	Medium	Stratarchical	Nationalism/Right-wing populism	Mixed
Canada				
Liberal Party of Canada	Medium	Stratarchical	Liberals	Enthusiasm
Conservative Party	Medium	Hierarchical	Christian Democrats/Conservatives	Enthusiasm
New Democratic Party	Medium	Federated	Social Democrats	Enthusiasm

[a] Resource was calculated based on Political Party Database Data (2022). Due to inconsistencies in other possible resource metrics (i.e., a lack of available data on total party income for our cases), we looked at data on campaign spending for Australia, Canada, and Germany. For the United Kingdom we used data from national spend from the database. US data was gathered from the FEC website. The most recent available data was utilized, and we converted all national currencies into US dollars to ensure comparability. In reporting this data, we distinguish between low (less than $10 million spent), medium (between $10m–$100m), and highly ($100m+) resourced parties.

[b] To assess this variable, we applied the framework provided by Bolleyer (2012, 320), in distinguishing between parties as being hierarchical, stratarchical, or federated. This framework suggests that while hierarchical parties see power held centrally, in stratarchical parties power is held across levels, whereas in federated parties it is held regionally. An assessment was made across each of the variables specified by Bolleyer in reaching a classification. For Canada, there is debate about the best way to characterize the party structure (see Carty 2004; Coletto et al. 2011). Likewise, for the German parties, there is some debate, however, we have used Bolleyer's assessment of their structure here as a way of highlighting organizational differences.

[c] This coding was based on the Political Party Database Data from 2020. The United States is not included in this database, hence entries for this country were produced by the authors.

[d] Attitudes toward DDC vary across parties and there is no preexisting measure to monitor variations. Accordingly, we drew on our existing research and the secondary literature to differentiate between "Enthusiasm," "Mixed," or "Reticence."

*The parties within the United Kingdom were the national party. Interviews were not conducted within devolved parties (such as the Scottish Labour Party).

this relates squarely to issues of access. Within many of our case study countries, we were unable to secure sufficient numbers of interviews, or to identify documents for analysis to ensure we were able to verify our insights for each party in the party system. In such instances, we chose to exclude these parties rather than risk misrepresenting practice. The 18 parties covered in this book provide a cross section of major and minor parties and, reflecting our theoretical framework (outlined in detail in the next chapter), capture a variety of differences related to party resources (high, medium, and low), structure (hierarchical, stratarchical, federated), ideology (social democrats, conservative, greens, liberal, left, right), and attitudes toward campaigning (enthusiasm, mixed, reticence). These cases accordingly allow us to generalize about political parties across advanced democracies and not only to point to the variations we identify, but also to theorize about the drivers of variation by using our framework.

The focus of this book is on DDC by political parties. However, our view is that it is essential to recognize that data is used by a wide range of organizations and individuals. Whether thinking about governments, universities, civil society organizations, or businesses, data is a valuable currency. This is because, in reflecting the well-known adage that "information is power," data provides actors with insights about the world that can be collected and mobilized to deliver a range of outcomes. Whether helping to identify an audience for a desired product, to enable targeted messaging to "nudge" a recipient into a desired action, or to test audience reception to specific initiatives, data is integral to the way a whole range of actors work today. Parties are therefore by no means unique in collecting and analyzing data, meaning that the findings of this book resonate far beyond these organizations. Although we focus on these actors as key institutions within liberal democracy (Bartolini & Mair 1990), we recognize the potential to expand this study to reflect on the activities of other institutional types.

Our Empirical Data

DDC often reaches the public consciousness via the sales pitches of campaign professionals and companies (such as Cambridge Analytica)—painting a distorted picture of the capacities and uses of these techniques. In contrast, this book promotes the voices of other actors within the system, offering unique insight into the experiences and views of those who engage in DDC. We do so in two ways. First, we draw on 329 interviews[1] that we conducted with party operatives, campaign consultants, pollsters, and data brokers to contextualize developments. Undertaken between 2017 and 2022, we spoke primarily to senior party officials working within campaign headquarters, as well as grassroots campaigners (most often at a regional level) and to actors within external campaign organizations who were supporting party campaigns.[2] These interviews focused on the use of DDC, how usage had developed over time, how DDC was viewed, and the conditions under which it was (and was not) deployed. All interviews were recorded and transcribed where consent was given, or interview notes were taken and approved. This formed a corpus of documents that were then coded and analyzed by the researchers to identify recurring themes and ideas. This interview data offers unprecedented insight into how we understand DDC, as well as its variation both within and between different parties around the globe. We use these interviews to understand not only what is happening, but also why these practices have come about.

In relying on interviews, it is, however, important to note that our ability to gain access to interviewees within different parties was not uniform. In many cases we found that parties simply lacked a large staff base, curtailing the available number of interviewees, but we also encountered overt unwillingness to engage. Evident most prominently in ideologically conservative parties, there were instances in which we were unable to secure interviews with current staff. In addition, we encountered the widespread use of non-disclosure agreements (often in major political parties), which meant that party staff and consultants were limited in their ability to be interviewed, or in what they could disclose. Encountering these varied issues, we used alternative sources of data to gather insight and to verify claims. Specifically, we collated a wide range of documentary evidence, including internal party reports, post-election analyses, regulatory reports, media coverage, and firsthand accounts of election campaigns. We also conducted reviews of party websites and social media archives, and we drew on analyses and reports from civil society groups and nongovernmental organizations. These documents were used to build up a rich picture of how data was talked about by different types of actors in different contexts. While most of these sources were publicly available, we also gained access to a small number of internal party documents that were used to help us understand the actual practice of data use. Triangulating multiple data points, we used these sources to build up a rich picture of practice in hard to access campaigns. While our data collection was not, therefore, unproblematic, we have nevertheless compiled the most comprehensive account of DDC practice offered to date.

To augment our analyses of DDC, we also provide practitioner perspectives that allow us to give voice to those directly involved in DDC.

While academic analysis can help us to unpick the common themes and ideas that run across our cases, we also want to give readers the chance to hear directly from practitioners themselves. For this reason, between chapters we provide opportunities for campaign professionals and regulators to offer their own perspective on the different aspects of DDC that we discuss. These perspectives are intended to provide tangible examples of the kind of practices we observe, offering a more extended glimpse into the perspectives we uncovered in our interviews. Moreover, they allow often behind-the-scenes practitioners to go on the record to communicate their own ideas about the use and significance of DDC in their own voice. Valuable not only for general readers, these interventions are intended to be of use to those teaching political communication, providing stimuli for students to consider the form and implications of this type of campaign activity.

Structure of the Book

The remainder of this book is structured as follows. In the next chapter we introduce our original theoretical framework to explain variations in DDC. Building on extant scholarship in political science and political communication that has utilized multilevel frameworks to understand the drivers of organizational change or political practices (such as Barnea & Rahat 2007; Esser & Strömbäck 2012; Gauja 2017), we develop a three-level framework which consists of systemic, regulatory, and party-level variables. We then move through the four central components of DDC that are especially significant for understanding variation. These are: data, analytics, technology, and personnel. Within each of these chapters we classify existing practice and then, presenting empirical evidence from our five cases, map variation in the form of each particular aspect of the data-driven campaign. In Chapter 7, we apply our theoretical framework to explain some of the variations outlined in previous chapters, showing the importance of considering systemic, regulatory, and party-level factors when seeking to understand and explain the existence of different data practices. In our final chapter, we discuss the conclusions that can be drawn from our analysis and consider the significance of our empirical evidence for debates about democracy.

2
Theoretical Framework

Data-driven campaigns can come in very different forms. As suggested in the last chapter, both familiar and more novel data can be gathered, analyzed in different ways and for different goals, employed and managed using different technologies, by a range of different personnel. DDC can therefore be mobilized in a variety of different ways to promote many goals, making it possible to characterize and observe this activity in alternative forms. Within this book we attempt to demystify the different manifestations of DDC (a task we predominantly undertake in Chapters 3–6), yet we are also interested in explaining why different forms of DDC emerge in different places, and what causes more or less sophisticated practices to be adopted by political parties.

In this chapter, we build on existing work that has begun to describe and theorize DDC (Bennett 2015; Hersh 2015; Anstead 2017; Dobber et al. 2017; Kruschinski & Haller 2017; Kefford 2021). In particular, we aim to build a framework that can explain not only differences between parties in a single country, but also differences across national contexts. In doing so, our aim is to understand how and why practice may not be replicated elsewhere, and why we might expect DDC to look different in specific national or party contexts. In this chapter we therefore provide the first comprehensive theoretical framework to date for explaining DDC, offering a framework that can be applied to a range of different national and international contexts, not simply our five case study countries. Our framework advances a party-centered, multilevel approach, highlighting the relevance of systemic-, regulatory-, and party-level variables for DDC. Specifically, we identify 12 variables across our three levels that help account for the different manifestations of DDC cross-nationally. In this chapter, we first introduce our approach to developing this framework, and then outline each of our variables. In Chapter 7, we return to apply this framework to explain the variations cataloged in our chapters on data, analytics, personnel, and technology within and across the five democracies under study.

Theoretical Foundations

In seeking to explain why DDC may vary, it is possible to draw attention to a range of different traditions in political science and political communication. We focus on a number of these to highlight the importance of actors, structures, and ideas to the operation of DDC. Our framework's underlying approach is rooted in three intellectual traditions: rational choice theory, institutionalism, and constructivism. In drawing on these three intellectual paradigms, our goal is not to "prove" that one approach is more correct than the other, but instead to blend insights from these alternative traditions to build a rich and multifaceted account of the drivers of party campaigning.

The theory of action underlying our model at the individual level is the rational choice approach, which assumes that political actors behave in a utility-maximizing manner and choose those alternatives that promise them the greatest benefits (Downs 1957). In the context of election campaigns, this means that political actors will behave in a manner likely to best achieve their electoral goals (Schoen 2015; Krewel 2017), resulting in gradual modifications of campaigning techniques and strategies (Swanson & Mancini 1996; Plasser & Plasser 2002).

The degree to which political elites have the capacity to adapt their election campaigns to changes in media, technology, and political participation depends on the party contexts in which they are integrated at the system level. Thus, our model postulates, recalling Gibson and Römmele (2001), Schoen (2015), and Epstein (2018), that the party context is another cost or benefit in the calculations of political elites. This party context and the party level of our model draw on institutional and constructivist traditions in political science, meaning that while political actors may seek to maximize their capacities to achieve electoral goals, the institutional realities and exogenous shocks, as well as dominant ideas, norms, and cultures within parties, can inhibit or facilitate the ways in which DDC can manifest within organizations (Gauja 2017, 4). In this sense, party actors' conception of rationality is affected by many events and influences within and beyond their control, ranging from relatively small concerns, such as a local party scandals, to more seismic disruptions, such as a global pandemic. These theories direct our attention to the ways in which actors' responses are affected by conditions.

Finally, we also seek to recognize the role that global debates and the spread of ideas and information can play. Far from existing in isolation, many changing campaign practices can be seen as part of a transnational pattern of influence and learning (Negrine & Papathanassopoulos 1996; Plasser & Plasser 2002). For example, the Obama campaigns drove a wave of campaign innovation globally (Bimber 2014; Lilleker 2016; McKenna & Han 2014), while more recently innovations and a focus on AI have changed the focus on political debate (Jungherr & Schroeder 2023). Such examples highlight the role that ideas about what is possible can play in shaping political action (Gofas & Hay 2010). For this reason, it is important to pay attention not only to the ideas that individual actors hold, but also to the ideational contexts in which they are located in order to understand how and why new ideas emerge and come to be seen as viable (or not).

In line with this thinking, we propose a three-level theoretical framework of DDC, identifying explanations at the *system*, *regulatory*, and *party levels* for why data, analytics, technology, and personnel are used differently by parties within and across countries (Figure 2.1). This approach builds on work by Esser and Strömbäck (2012), Krewel (2017), Gibson and Römmele (2001), and Vaccari (2013), who use multilevel frameworks to analyze the empirical conditions under which party campaigns in the same or different country contexts adopt certain communication practices.[1] Our model builds on this approach by introducing a regulatory level, as we expect political campaigns' use of data, technology, analytics, and personnel to be dependent on different regulatory variables (Bennett 2016; Kruschinski & Haller 2017; Dommett 2019). Therefore, our model's system- and regulatory-level variables can explain why we see cross-country differences in DDC, while variables on the party-level give insights as to why "we see parties in the same system that are more or less developed in their use of these techniques" (Gibson & Römmele 2001, 32). Our framework can thus be used to explain not only intra-national differences and similarities of DDC practices between parties, but also cross-national differences and similarities.

We introduce four explanatory variables each on the system, regulatory, and party levels that can help to explain the constraints and opportunities for political parties engaging in DDC. To identify these, we reviewed existing scholarship on parties' technological innovation, including variables identified by Kruschinski and Haller (2017), Kreiss (2016), Vaccari (2013), Esser and Strömbäck (2012), and Lamprinakou (2010). For the system level, our key variables are the *electoral system*, *system of government*, *party system*, and *hybrid media system*. At the regulatory level, we identify *party regulation*, *campaign regulation*, *data and privacy regulation*, and *media*

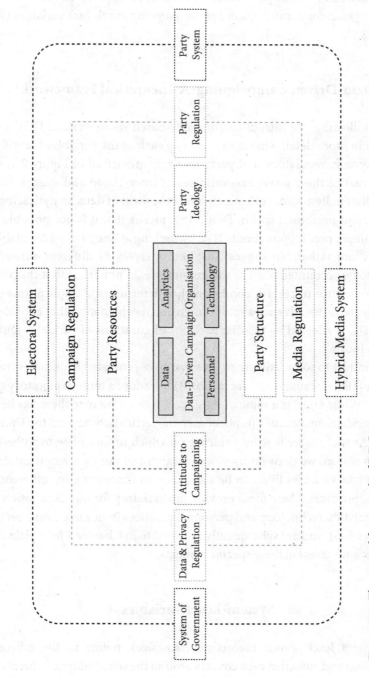

Figure 2.1 Theoretical framework of DDC.

regulation. Lastly, at the party level, we identify *party resources, party structure, party ideology*, and *attitudes to campaigning* as relevant variables (see Figure 2.1).

Data-Driven Campaigning: A Theoretical Framework

In the following, we introduce our party-based framework of DDC and explain in more detail what is captured by each of the variables identified at the system, regulatory, and party levels. Summarized in Figure 2.1, we conceptualize these levels and variables as interrelated and suggest they can individually and/or collectively affect the form of data, analytics, technology, and personnel within DDC. This means that it is not possible to make simple predictions about DDC by looking at one of our 12 variables in isolation; rather, we suggest that the interplay of different variables needs to be accounted for. For this reason, we do not argue that the presence or absence of certain conditions has deterministic implications for DDC; instead, we advance a multidimensional explanation that considers how DDC is affected by the distinctive configurations of variables found in each locale.

In contrast to some existing studies that have generated hypotheses from their multilevel framework (Vaccari 2013), we adopt a more exploratory approach. While DDC is a topic of significant interest, to date there has been little empirical analysis of this phenomenon, particularly beyond the United States. As such, there is scant evidence on which to formulate hypotheses. For this reason, we draw on previous research and our own empirical data to highlight variables likely to be significant in accounting for differences in DDC practices. These ideas provide the backdrop for our exploration of data, analytics, technology and personnel practices in our five countries (in Chapters 3–6), and are subsequently returned to in Chapter 7 to explain the variations we reveal in these specific contexts.

System-Level Variables

The system level of our theoretical framework points to the different institutions and rules that each country around the world adopts. It directs us

Table 2.1 System-Level Variables and Indicators That Can Explain Variation in DDC

Variables	System-Level Indicators	
Electoral system	Type of electoral system (e.g., plurality, majoritarian, proportional, mixed)	Compulsory or voluntary voting
System of government	Unitary vs. federal system	Presidential vs. parliamentary system
Party system	Number of "relevant" parties	Competition and cooperation between parties
Hybrid media system	Type of media channels available	Conditions under which media channels can be accessed

to consider the systems by which we choose to elect and run government and also the dynamics of the media system. The four specific variables we focus on are the electoral system, the party system, the system of government, and the hybrid media system (for an overview, see Table 2.1). Discussing each of these factors in turn, we highlight the different types of system that can exist in alternative national contexts and reflect on what this may mean for the way in which DDC is conducted and employed. Systemic variables therefore help us to understand how and why data-driven campaigns differ from country to country.

By thinking about the systemic variables that affect DDC, we are able to demonstrate that the use of data, analytics, technology, and personnel is not uniform, but is shaped by the specific conditions found in different contexts and different institutional, social, and political environments. This aligns with modernization theory and its underlying contention that changes in society, politics, and media are major causes for adaptive behavior by rational political campaign elites (see Esser & Strömbäck 2012; Krewel 2017; Plasser & Plasser 2002). System-level variables are therefore seen to shape the system within which DDC is organized and conducted, allowing us to better theorize the way institutions do or do not shape campaigning. To date, the effect these system-level variables have on DDC practices has received very little attention. Indeed, it is the regulatory and party levels of our framework which have been focused upon most (Bennett 2016; Kreiss 2016; Dommett 2019; Kefford 2021).

Electoral System

The electoral system can be understood as the method used to translate votes into seats (Renwick 2010). Often defined by a country's constitution or electoral law, different democratic ideals and electoral specificities can be observed around the world (Farrell 2011). These differing features can be significant for parties' use of DDC. While it would be possible to focus on a range of attributes, we consider the type of electoral system and aspects of electoral law as likely to be significant in causing variation in political parties' use of data, analytics, technology, and personnel for their campaigns.

Beginning with the electoral system, we suggest that alternative electoral configurations create different incentives for the use and form of DDC, often encouraging political campaigns to focus on particular groups of voters. Majoritarian electoral systems—especially single-member plurality—are, in theory, designed to produce strong majorities, strong governments and, often, strong major parties that dominate legislatures. Thus, there is an incentive for parties to adopt individualized and decentralized campaign strategies in heavily contested voter districts or battleground states (Farrell 2011; Esser & Strömbäck 2012). Under such systems, a party may practically abandon a district where it sees no chance of winning or where victory is seen to be guaranteed and intensify its efforts in electorally significant areas or communities. This dynamic has been recognized in some existing research on data-driven tactics, which shows the utility of data-driven techniques for targeted voter communication and resource allocation (Harker 2020, 155–156; Judge & Pal 2021). In such contexts DDC is therefore likely to be characterized by the use of, for example, analytics techniques devoted to identifying particular types of voters, as opposed to optimizing a message with broad appeal across the entire populace.

In contrast, proportional party-based electoral systems, theoretically, have different functions and are based on a different set of democratic ideals which increase representation and diversity in legislatures (Renwick 2010; Farrell 2011). In these contexts, parties campaign beyond the districts in which they are strong in order to increase their overall vote share, meaning that data-driven techniques such as segmentation and targeting are less likely to be used to concentrate attention on only certain groups of voters, and message testing may be used to develop wide-ranging appeals may be more widely utilized.

In many electoral systems, candidate-based and party-based elements are mixed. Hence, in these contexts it is possible to observe campaigns combining nationwide engagement with some activity focused on more electorally significant districts. These differences suggest that parties may encounter different incentives to utilize each component of DDC, resulting in differential uptakes of specific techniques and a focus on collecting different types of data.

We have also included electoral laws related to voting under the umbrella of the electoral systems variable and see it as potentially significant in accounting for variation in DDC. This is because certain requirements—such as compulsory voting in Australia—create different incentives for DDC. The particular electoral system and laws related to voting found in each context can therefore incentivize different types and extents of engagement with particular audiences, prompting parties to exhibit alternative forms of data, analytics, technology, and personnel.

System of Government

Another area that has received scant attention in the scholarship on DDC is the system of government. We understand this variable to describe the political institutions that are directly or indirectly relevant for political decision-making. In a narrow sense, the system of government is the part of the political system which generates binding decisions for the rest of society (Elazar 1997; Riker 1964). This system-level variable therefore relates to regulatory and party-level variables, including campaign regulation, media regulation, and party structure, and can affect practices at each of these levels. Specifically, within this section we discuss the potential for the unitary or federal, or presidential or parliamentary structures of a system to induce variation in DDC practices.

First, depending on how a constitution organizes power between the central and subnational governments, a country may have a unitary or a federal system. In a unitary system, local or municipal government is combined with national government, meaning that political sovereignty is concentrated (Elazar 1997). In federal systems, there is an intermediate level of governmental authority—often states or provinces—between the national and local levels of government which has its sovereignty constitutionally protected (Riker 1964). Therefore, state and provincial governments share sovereignty with the federal government and have at least some power over a wide range of issues in a federal system. These differences have potential consequences for how power is wielded and, as such, for party organization and campaigning.

In unitary systems, power is often wielded through hierarchical or core-peripheral models (Elazar 1997). In hierarchical models, authority and power tend to be concentrated within a single actor and imposed in a top-down manner on lower actors, with varying degrees of bottom-up influence (Eldersveld 1964; Bolleyer 2012; Kefford 2018). In the center-periphery model, central actors are more or less influenced by actors at the periphery (Katz & Mair 1995), often displaying oligarchical tendencies as power becomes concentrated in the hands of those at the center (Michels 1966). In these contexts, the central or core actor is pivotal to the activity of the organization as a whole. Applying these ideas to consider DDC, it appears that the dynamics of power distribution in unitary systems may affect the way that DDC is adopted. If, for example, elites wield significant power, then they are likely to be influential in conditioning the adoption of DDC, resulting in top-down implementation and standardized adoption patterns. If, however, those at the center distribute power more widely or lack central control, then adoption may vary and be less standardized.

Turning to federal systems, in these contexts power is distributed more formally between different actors, with states characterized by separate "arenas held together by common framing institutions" aimed at "the deliberate coming together of equals to establish a mutually useful governmental framework" (Elazar 1997, 239). Within these systems we therefore tend to see power distributed more evenly between actors, with coordination or oversight at least partially shared (Kefford 2018). In these contexts, DDC is therefore less likely to be directed by central authorities and be uniform in nature, but is rather likely to exhibit local variation within the context of certain common practices. Within these systems we may therefore expect to see greater local innovation in relation to the use of data, fewer centralized personnel, and more decentralized data collection systems and technologies.

The second aspect of this variable is whether a case employs a presidential or parliamentary system, as these systems create different incentives for campaign organization and messaging. As outlined by Samuels (2002), under presidential systems, it is possible for an individual and their associated party to capture control of the executive branch directly, whereas under parliamentary systems parties organize to win legislative seats and capture executive power indirectly through the election of legislative representatives. These dynamics mean that parties organizing to win elections "will develop different organizational forms and adopt different electoral strategies" (Samuels 2002, 462). Within presidential systems, for example, there is an incentive to focus funds, message, and strategy on individuals (Farrell 2006), resulting in single candidate-centered campaigns in which compelling (tested) messages stressing the candidate's capacity to act as a strong leader are articulated (Poguntke & Webb 2005). Such campaigns can often have limited longevity, being constructed around a particular candidate and having limited life span after the election ends. Applying these ideas to DDC, it is likely that in presidential systems—especially those without strong party organizations—campaigns will rely on external expertise, will need to purchase data insights, and will rely on externally provided technology to facilitate campaigns as they will lack ongoing infrastructure and capacity.

In contrast, in parliamentary systems, greater emphasis is often on party attributes and appeals, concentrating on the common aims and objectives of multiple candidates. Parliamentary systems also tend to exhibit more enduring campaign organizations, with many parties having significant numbers of members, and the party organizations developing their own infrastructure and expertise that are maintained over time. Applying these ideas to DDC, it is likely that in such systems data collection is done by party members and staff, with a more limited role played by external actors. In such campaigns, technology and expertise may also be more likely to be developed in-house, leading to long-standing investment in databases and staff. Such differences once again suggest the potential for different manifestations of data, analytics, technology, and personnel, with different practices deemed more or less likely in each systemic context.

Party System

While clearly related to the electoral system and system of government, the party system needs to be understood as a significant variable shaping DDC practices in its own right. Based on the classic definition of Sartori (2005, 44–45), we understand the party system "as precisely the system of interactions resulting from inter-party competition [and] [. . .] the relatedness of parties to each other." While a range of party system attributes can be examined, we focus on the explanatory significance of the number of "relevant" parties and the degree of competition and/or cooperation between parties, seeing these factors as important influences on the way in which parties campaign to win votes and seats, and in turn utilize data, analytics, technology, and personnel differently.

The number of parties active within a given political system can have a range of implications for the strategies any individual party may pursue. In the main, less fragmented party systems—often where there are two parties of government—encourage vote-maximizing behavior whereby these parties compete to win the support of voters who may cast their ballot for either party by converging on the "center-ground" (Downs 1957). In contrast, in multiparty systems, parties are often seen to diverge, seeking not to win the same votes, but to develop distinctive policy agendas and identities that allow them to win differential pockets of support (Budge et al. 2010). In these contexts, there can also be a need for greater cooperation between parties, as coalitions and alliances may be more significant for securing electoral success (Laver 1989).

These differences may result in alternative DDC practices. In less fragmented systems, campaigns may be more focused on identifying and appealing to supporters and "floating" or "undecided" voters, leading them to test and adapt campaign messages to boost appeal. In more complex party systems, attention is likely to instead focus on mobilizing their supporters and may also focus on understanding the dynamics of possible coalition formation.

Hybrid Media System

The final systemic variable we consider is the hybrid media system (Chadwick 2017). We understand the hybrid media system to describe the wide variety of media that exist for communication (Blumler 1980). This term encompasses traditional and legacy media, such as television, radio, and newspapers, and new or online media, such as social media, instant messaging, or online political advertising. Political parties draw on a wide variety of communication channels for electoral campaigning and engage in hybrid media strategies (Magin et al. 2017). Identifying possible influences to explain variation in the manifestation of DDC, we note the potential for countries' media systems to vary considerably in terms of hybridity (Hallin & Mancini 2017; Mattoni & Ceccobelli 2018), distinguishing between media systems with high, mixed, or low levels of hybridity. In particular, we focus on possible variation in the number of media channels available and differences in accessibility, differentiating "high" systems as those with multiple channels and easy accessibility, "low" as those with few channels and low degrees of accssibility, and "mixed" as those with both high and low.

At the most basic level, countries differ in their number of traditional and digital media providers. While some countries have established public broadcasting (Hallin & Mancini 2017), a diverse range of private providers, and numerous online and offline news sources, this is not always the case (Reuters 2022). Such differences are likely to be significant for DDC as they affect the number of different channels parties may want to invest in. Campaigns in contexts with a range of digital and traditional media channels and non-partisan news providers may therefore invest in data, analytics, technology, and personnel able to thrive in online and offline media, while those with access to only certain news channels may invest more particularly in certain types of data or expertise.

An additional factor characterizing the hybrid media system is media accessibility. Overlapping to some degree with media regulation, here we are particularly interested in the degree to which media channels advance a particular partisan agenda. The presence of a partisan agenda can affect the degree to which parties may want to engage with certain channels, leading those in an unfavorable partisan media ecosystem to use unmediated forms of communication (Jackson & Lilleker 2007; Zaller & Hunt 2007). The impact of such dynamics for DDC may therefore lead parties to invest in data, analytics, technology and personnel designed to optimize different media and communication techniques. A party in an unfavorable media environment is therefore likely to invest in forms of DDC such as email lists or peer-to-peer texting technologies to enable unmediated communication.

Regulatory-Level Variables

At the regulatory level we focus our attention on regulatory frameworks that have the capacity to affect the manifestation of a data-driven campaign. To date, efforts to highlight examples of campaign variation have focused

Table 2.2 Regulatory-Level Variables and Indicators That Can Explain Variation in DDC

Variables	Regulatory-Level Indicators	
Party regulation	Restrictions on sources or amounts of donations	Rules around registration, membership, or coordinated activity
Campaign regulation	Campaign finance limits	Access to media provisions
Data and privacy regulation	Exemptions to privacy legislation and regulation	National or supra-national regulation about the collection of personal data
Media regulation	Media concentration and competition rules	Restrictions on particular media practices

particularly on data and privacy regulation, but within our model we highlight the significance of four variables: party regulation, campaign regulation, data and privacy regulation, and, finally, media regulation, which come with different sets of indicators for explaining variation in DDC (for an overview, see Table 2.2). Introducing these variables, it is important to note that regulation can come in a variety of forms, including direct government regulation, mandated partial self-regulation, mandated full self-regulation, and voluntary self-regulation (Rees 1988). Depending on the configuration, these can result in strong, medium, or weak regulation in different countries, having consequences for the precise form of data, analytics, technology, and personnel.

Party Regulation

At the regulatory level, we begin by differentiating party regulation and campaign regulation. While these are highly connected ideas, for our purposes we draw a distinction between these two, seeing the former as describing the standards and controls that govern the form and activity of political parties within any given context, and the latter concerned with the rules that are applied specifically to election campaigns. Engaging first with the idea of party regulation, Van Biezen and Rashkova (2014) have shown that party regulation can vary dramatically (see also Karvonen 2007; Van Biezen & Borz 2012). Of relevance to DDC, we consider variation in party finance and party organization rules as evidence of party regulation.

In terms of party finance, Van Biezen and Rashkova (2014, 894) show that parties can be subject to different requirements in regard to "the regulation of direct and indirect public funding, as well as the regulation of private sources of funding, expenditures and requirements of reporting and disclosure." This means that parties in some countries have public funding, while others offer limited state support. There are similar variations in the extent and type of reporting and disclosure that parties are subject to. In terms of DDC, these laws reveal differences not only in the ease with which parties are able to access finance, but also in different degrees of oversight (Power 2020). In countries with extensive financial regulation, available resources are restricted, meaning that parties' abilities to spend on data, analytics, technology, and personnel are curtailed.

Similarly, differences in how party organizations are regulated are likely to affect DDC. Some countries exhibit strong or "stringent registration requirements" for parties (Van Biezen and Rashkova 2014, 7), while others impose strong, medium, or weak restrictions on membership requirements or coordinated activity. Applied to DDC, in the more stringent regimes, parties are likely to be curtailed in their ability to build an extensive membership, share data, or work with external partners. In comparison, parties that are subject to less regulation are able to act without such external fetters, leading to different manifestations of DDC.

Campaign Regulation

Turning to our second regulatory variable, campaign regulation, we distinguish this form of regulation as pertaining directly to the rules and procedures governing parties' electoral campaigning practices. Campaign regulations tend to focus on the "regulated period" that precedes Election Day, a period in which campaigners are subject to specific forms of oversight not evident outside elections (Mendilow & Phélippeau 2018). As with regulation outside of election periods, campaign regulation can cover a wide range of party practices (Zipkin 2010), and can be weak, medium, or strong, but we focus on the significance of particular provisions relating to campaign finance and media access for DDC.

In regard to campaign finance, in addition to general constraints on party activity, countries can impose particular restrictions on activity in election periods. Limits on spending by candidates and/or parties (often at a local and national level), or on donations, can therefore be observed and additional spending transparency requirements can be imposed. Such campaigning regulations have been shown historically to affect campaign practice (Power 2020). In terms of DDC, the existence of additional restrictions can particularly hinder campaigns' ability to perform the costliest aspects of DDC within electoral periods. Evidence of randomized controlled trials (RCTs) or Multilevel Regression and Poststratification (MRP) modeling is therefore likely to be curtailed in contexts with strong campaign finance regulation.

In addition, within campaign periods, regulation can stipulate the conditions under which campaigns can access and utilize different media. Connected to media regulation, restrictions can be imposed, for example, on access to television for electoral broadcasts, or on other forms of media such as political advertising. Indeed, Kaid and Holtz-Bacha (2006) show that while political advertising is heavily regulated or even banned in some countries (e.g., Ireland, France, Belgium, Portugal, Switzerland), it is relatively unrestricted in others (e.g., Australia and the US). Such different regulatory provisions affect parties' ability to access different media channels within campaign periods, having implications for the type of audience identification and targeting they can undertake.

Data and Privacy Regulation

Our third variable is data and privacy regulation. While data protection and data privacy are often used interchangeably, there is an important difference between the two. While data protection focuses on how data can be used, data privacy defines who can have access to data (Bennett 2015; Harker 2020; Judge & Pal 2021). This form of regulation has perhaps been the most commonly cited as significant in existing attempts to understand variation in DDC, as it affects the data that can be collected and the type of analytics that can be performed in a particular jurisdiction (Bennett 2016; Dobber et al. 2019).

Data and privacy laws vary from country to country, but can cover areas including transparency, purpose limitation, data minimization, accuracy, storage limitation, and confidentiality, to name but a few. Once again, these laws can be more or less restrictive (i.e., weak, medium, or strong), affecting not only what data parties can collect, but also how it can be used (Hersh 2015). Existing research has suggested that these variations have significant implications for DDC. In particular, Bennett's (2015, 371) work suggests the significance of "the absence of any comprehensive data privacy law" in the United States as important to understanding campaign practices, noting also that "[t]he extent to which voter surveillance will be engaged in is, at one level, related to structural conditions, legal requirements and cultural practices within different countries" (Bennett 2015, 381). Elsewhere, Baldwin-Philippi (2019, 2) has suggested that "lax regulation around privacy and data use" means data campaigning in the United States far outpaces that in other countries. Kruschinski and Bene (2022) also describe the European Union as a terrain which is heavily regulated when it comes to the use of data and analytics, limiting the analysis that is possible for parties themselves to perform. However, they conclude that social networking platforms such as Facebook or Instagram can be used by parties to circumvent national restrictions, as these platforms make data and targeting capabilities available that parties themselves could not collect or perform (see also Dobber et al. 2019; Dommett & Zhu 2022). Such examples demonstrate that data and privacy legislation can prompt campaigns to engage in different practices around data, analytics, technology, or personnel, either limiting their ability to conduct DDC, or prompting them to identify work-around solutions.

Media Regulation

We understand media regulation to describe any efforts to restrict or shape media practices evident in the hybrid media system (Chadwick 2017; Lunt & Livingston 2012). Applied to govern these practices in traditional legacy media and/or online media, this form of regulation can be imposed by the state, but can also emerge from self- or co-regulatory practices whereby the media industry develops codes of conduct and governance that define acceptable practices (Puppis 2010; Lunt & Livingstone 2012), either year-round, or within campaign periods. Media regulation can cover a range of media activities and be evident in weak, medium, or strong forms. We suggest that competition law and restrictions on specific media practices have particular implications for the form of data, analytics, technology, or personnel.

Regulation governing competition on media has emerged in many national and international jurisdictions, and frequently aims to exert control over market concentration in order to ensure media pluralism (Bania 2019). In many contexts, strict competition law exists to prevent single actors from dominating the media market, but in others such concentrated ownership is not prohibited. Such different environments—as suggested in our discussion of the hybrid media system—have implications for DDC by affecting the availability of media channels open to different campaigners. While parties in countries with strong media competition laws have access to a range of different media outlets that they can use to communicate their targeted messaging, in countries with weaker systems, it is possible for single actors to dominate (Chadwick 2017; Mattoni & Ceccobelli 2018). In these different contexts the incentives to invest in different aspects of DDC can vary, leading to alternative manifestations of this activity.

In addition, media regulation can also restrict specific media practices, affecting the conditions under which different media can be utilized. These regulations can be imposed by companies, by campaigners themselves, or by the state, and they range from content regulation that restricts the type of claim that can be made (or the conditions under which specific claims can be made), to limits on actors' ability to use media affordances such as targeting (Dobber et al. 2019; Dommett 2019; Harker 2020). One such recent example is the proposal made by the European Commission (2021) to restrict the data that campaigns can utilize for targeted messaging, a change that would curtail the incentive for parties to invest in data collection and analytics techniques. Once again, the precise restrictions on media affordances vary in accordance with national rules, but so too do the restrictions imposed by multinational companies, as changes made by platforms such as Facebook or Google are not always imposed in every jurisdiction. This means that the same media can often be used in different ways, depending on the precise media regulation in evidence.

Party-Level Variables

In developing our party-level variables, we have drawn on existing party scholarship which have discussed different factors to influence campaign practices (Gibson & Römmele 2001; Schoen 2015; Kreiss 2016; Krewel 2017). Here we identify four variables as likely to be influential for DDC. These are: party resources, party ideology, party structure, and attitudes to campaigning (for an overview, see Table 2.3).

Table 2.3 Party-Level Variables and Indicators That Can Explain Variation in DDC

Variables	Party-Level Indicators		
Party resources	Financial resources	Activist and staffing resource	Links to civil society and third-party actors that the party can draw on
Party structure	Organizational configuration of party	Distribution of power between components of party	
Party ideology	Ideologically acceptable practices	Ideological ties to other actors and sources of expertise	
Attitudes to campaigning	Elite and grassroots attitudes to data-driven techniques		

Party Resources

The first variable on the party level is party resources, which can be defined as assets that a party wields to function successfully as it works to structure competition, govern, represent, and shape public opinion (Poguntke et al. 2016). According to Ware (1996), there are two main generalized resources that can be used in an election campaign: money and labor, both of which we argue are significant for data-driven campaigns. Parties' ability to gather and access both of these resources can be influenced by variables on our model's systemic and regulatory levels (i.e., electoral system and party or campaign regulation), but is also affected by specific party-level attributes such as size, history, and the demographic characteristics of their support base. Noting these differences, parties can have high, medium, or low financial and personnel resources.

As with data and privacy regulation, existing research has strongly pointed to the influence that inequalities in money exert on DDC. Hersh has therefore argued that one reason campaigns rarely use consumer data directly "is simply that most campaigns do not have the resources to buy commercial data and link it to their voter file" (Hersh 2015, 170; Kruschinski &

Haller 2017, 8). Moreover, financial resources can often be focused on election campaigns, making it challenging for parties to invest year-round in campaigns.

In addition, it's important to recognize differences in available labor. Previous work has highlighted parties' differing numbers of campaign staff and volunteers (Poguntke et al. 2016), showing that parties have different types and numbers of personnel resources to draw on in support of their campaign. In addition, parties can have differing amounts and types of connections to affiliated organizations (such as trade unions or businesses), sister parties (Dodsworth & Cheeseman 2016), or companies (Dommett et al. 2021). The extent to which parties possess such ties can mean they are able to draw on high, medium, or low levels of expertise and capacity when it comes to DDC.

Party Structure

We introduce party structure as the next variable on the party level. Two indicators, in particular, are likely to influence the manifestation of DDC: organizational configuration, and the distribution of power. Thinking first about organizational configuration, existing scholarship has demonstrated that parties can come in a variety of different forms. While often containing a leader, executive, and membership (Scarrow 2015), the precise configuration of parties can vary significantly. Some parties may be small, nationally focused operations with a central office clustered in one location. Others may be sprawling organizations, with large subnational regions, especially in federalist countries like Germany, Australia, and Canada, exhibiting regional party leaders and regional party members in addition to national membership and leadership. Parties can therefore dramatically vary in terms of organization, creating different challenges in terms of coordination and mobilization that can affect DDC.

In addition, party structures can vary considerably in regard to mechanisms and processes of autonomy and control. Existing scholarship has shown that power can be exercised in parties in very different ways (Bolleyer 2012). Though some organizations can concentrate power in a central office (hierarchical parties), or in their regional chapters (federated parties), others can distribute it across the party organization (stratarchical parties). There can accordingly be significant differences in the degree of autonomy and control that different actors can exert in a campaign (Kefford 2018). Within existing scholarship on party campaigning, Stromer-Galley (2019) has pointed to the potential for "controlled interactivity," whereby local actors are granted limited autonomy to implement centrally determined goals.

Thinking about the consequences of these structures for DDC, it is likely that the approach to each element of DDC will reflect preexisting power structures. Parties exhibiting "controlled interactivity" are therefore likely to see elites providing centralized data collection and analytics techniques and technologies. Those with more limited central control may allow more autonomy in relation to data collection, analytics, and the use of technology—giving members greater power. Interestingly, some scholars have suggested that the adoption of digital technologies is likely to facilitate more decentralized activity among grassroots activists (Gibson 2015), suggesting that different power structures may exist in relation to different media forms. These alternative theories hint at the potential for parties to approach the adoption of DDC in different ways, depending on their preexisting power structures and processes.

In observing the significance of power and control within party structures, it is notable that the organizational configuration of parties is also relevant here, as organizations can possess more or less centralized infrastructure. In the United States, for example, political parties have no formal organization at the national level that controls membership, activities, or policy positions. Parties are weakly institutionalized (Crotty 2009). This contrasts to parties in other contexts, where centralized systems exist and allow a degree of central organization and control. Such capacities accordingly appear significant for parties' DDC activity, affecting who is responsible for the uptake (or otherwise) of these tools, and how wide their sphere of influence may be.

Party Ideology

Party ideology is the third variable and is understood as a set of ideas or beliefs that parties hold about how society should be organized (Ware 1996). Political ideologies are one of the most important organizing features of political parties, but when it comes to DDC we suggest that they can play a particular role in determining acceptable campaigning practices and fostering ties to other actors and sources of expertise.

Party ideology can have potential influence on the use of data, analytics, technology, and personnel because it can affect the type of activities that parties are willing to undertake. As Lamprinakou (2010, 345) formulates: "party electoral behaviour [. . .] is dependent on the innate characteristics of a party's political identity [. . .] developed through a long-term process of organizational and ideological fermentation, internal and external stimuli, formal and constitutionally defined principles as well as informal rules, values and traditions that define intraparty dynamics and the leadership's course of action." This means that parties will not be equally amenable to the use of certain practices and techniques, suggesting that DDC tools will not be uniformly embraced. Speaking to this point, one existing study has suggested that some parties may indeed reject DDC practices on ideological grounds, a possibility observed in the Netherlands (Kefford et al. 2022).

Ideology can also provide an important tie between a party and other actors who share similar principles and agenda. Often present in the form of long-standing ideological families—such as traditions of conservative or social democratic thought (Freeden 1996)—shared ideological affiliations can provide a common bond between parties and external actors. Highlighted in previous work on consultancy, these ideological ties can be important to party operations as they help identify like-minded actors who share certain views and ideals (Kolodny & Logan 1998; Sheingate 2016)—ties and loyalties that are valued in the context of partisan competition (Martin & Peskowitz 2018). In the context of DDC, ideological ties are likely to have particular implications for data analytics and personnel.

Attitudes to Campaigning

Our last variable on the party level is attitudes to campaigning. Underpinning our party-centered multilevel theoretical framework is the idea that individuals matter in shaping, interpreting, and enacting strategies for electoral success (Downs 1957; Krewel 2017; Schoen 2015). In line with this idea, this variable suggests that political actors within parties may approach the use of data, analytics, technology, or personnel with enthusiasm, with reticence, or with a mixture of enthusiasm and reticence.

Previous research has focused on the way in which elites, and specifically elite politicians, exert significant influence over the attitudes of others, shaping voter preferences (Holcombe 2021) and party positions (Cross & Pilet 2015). They are also seen to play an important role, as Gibson and Römmele (2001, 35) have argued, in the process of adopting new, professionalized campaign practices, which is seen to require "extensive senior-level decision making, organizational reform, and financial muscle." Such dynamics mean that, in terms of DDC, elite attitudes can exert an influence over the degree and type of investment a party makes in data. Specifically, we suggest that where elites perceive data to have value for a campaign and are enthusiastic about DDC, parties are likely to exhibit higher levels of investment in data and data infrastructure, resulting in additional resources channeled toward data collection, analysis, technology, and personnel. In contrast, where there is more reticence, data-driven decision-making is not likely to prevail and there will be limited investment. This raises questions about the backgrounds of elites and whether individuals in positions of power have experience or understanding of data and its value.

Elites are not, however, the only actors within parties (a point discussed further in Chapter 6); members and activists also play a key role in shaping campaign practice, making attitudes toward campaigning at these levels also significant. Previous research has shown that grassroots actors can ignore elite strategies around campaigning and engage in rogue campaigns (Dommett et al. 2020). It has also shown that local parties can be innovators and entrepreneurs in adopting new campaign strategies—revealing the potential for grassroots actors to pioneer new approaches or to embrace new methods and ideas before elites. Such possibilities suggest that grassroots actors may display different degrees of reticence or enthusiasm toward data-driven techniques, affecting their approach to data collection, analysis, technology, or personnel.

While neither of these groups is homogenous, and it can be possible for more enthusiastic or reticent attitudes toward DDC to occur simultaneously, we suggest that the attitudes of those in positions of power—either at the national or local level—can impact the shape of a data-driven campaign.

Conclusion

For all the popular commentary on DDC and the emerging work from scholars, systematic comparative analyses have remained remarkably absent. This has left a dearth of theoretically grounded explanations of the phenomenon, limiting our understanding of why this practice can vary. In this chapter, we have developed the first comprehensive theoretical framework yet advanced, highlighting 12 variables at three levels that we suggest affect the form DDC takes in different parties across different countries. Having provided this framework, in the chapters that follow we catalog and illustrate the variation that can occur in DDC activity, exploring how data, analytics, technology, and personnel can manifest in different circumstances. Then, in Chapter 7, we return to explain these variations, applying this framework to consider why DDC by parties does not look the same in each of our case-study countries, and why different countries and parties engage in this practice in (often subtly) different ways. In moving beyond single case-study analyses, and especially the dominance of the US case, the remainder of the book therefore offers a more sophisticated understanding of DDC that encourages scholars, electoral regulators, and political actors to reconsider the conventional wisdom on DDC, and to engage in a more nuanced debate about contemporary campaign practices in the twenty-first century.

3
Data

For what seems like decades, the idea that personal data has become a commodity has been widely reported on (Zax 2011). The collection of "big data" is widely perceived to lead to competitive advantages that determines "winners" and "losers" in areas across commercial marketing, professional sports, and electoral politics (The Economist 2017). The acceptance of data practices has thus become standard fare in many industries, and for electoral politics data has come to be seen as increasingly central to political parties' campaign activities. It is therefore common to encounter the idea that "elections are becoming increasingly 'datafied,' with advertising and marketing techniques being offered by a network of private contractors and data analysts, offering cutting-edge methods for audience segmentation and targeting to political parties all over the world" (Bartlett et al. 2018, 26).

There remain, however, a number of questions—both normative and practical—about the role of data in electoral politics. It is particularly unclear what types of data parties collect, and where this data originates from. These fundamental questions are often unanswered within existing literature, making it difficult to grasp exactly what is occurring internationally.

Within this chapter we expand our empirical knowledge of data as an independent variable that shapes campaign practices and shine a light on the diversity evident within our cases. First, we will provide an overview of scholarship on the collection of data in electoral politics, outlining existing accounts of this element of DDC. Second, we draw on our empirical case studies to offer a detailed description of the different types of data found within our five cases. Providing a schematic framework that identifies specific kinds of data points, we clarify the types and sources of data that can be collected by political parties. We show that data is used in different ways in different country contexts and that there is no uniform manner in which data is collected for electoral politics across our cases. This descriptive exploration serves as the basis for the detailed analysis of the influencing factors for these variations in our explanatory Chapter 7.

Data-Driven Campaigning and Political Parties. Katharine Dommett, Glenn Kefford, and Simon Kruschinski,
Oxford University Press. © Oxford University Press 2024. DOI: 10.1093/oso/9780197570227.003.0003

Existing Accounts of Data Use by Political Parties

Given that it is widely accepted that DDC practices have increased across many advanced democracies over the past decade (Bennett 2016; Anstead 2018), the dearth of studies which clarify exactly what data is used, and where it comes from, is problematic for scholars and electoral regulators alike. Equally, there are almost no conceptual or theoretical frameworks that seek to explain the drivers of data collection. And, certainly none of those that exist does so on the basis of a cross-national analysis. This obscures and limits the insights we have into the practices of political parties as critical democratic actors, specifically in terms of the type of data that is being gathered and utilized by a range of actors in democratic politics.

Much recent academic scholarship on DDC has focused on the emergence of prolific amounts of new and more personalized data. Concentrating on the affordances of digital technology, it has been argued that "[v]oters can, through the digitisation of personal lives, be monitored and targeting *(sic)* continuously and in depth, utilising methods intricately linked with and drawn from the commercial sector and the vast collection of personal and individual data" (Hankey et al. 2018, 11; Tactical Tech 2019). The collection of information disclosed on (or inferred from) social media profiles, the use of browser history, and information such as "most-visited websites, which soda's in the fridge" are therefore seen to be gathered by modern campaigns and used for data analytics (Rubinstein 2014, 865).

While this work plays an important role in spotlighting the latest forms of available data and parties' data-collection efforts, what is lacking is a systematic cross-national analysis that details the different types of data that parties can gather in different contexts. While it is therefore commonly claimed that parties possess vast databases of information that contain, as Barocas (2012, 32) has suggested, "anywhere between 300 and 900 individual data points for each individual that appears in the database," we have limited understanding of the nature of these precise data points, and of how the same type of data—such as information on the electoral register—can vary by region or country. This makes it challenging to assess what information is being utilized and whether specific data points or collection methods are common.

In addition to this issue, current accounts also tend to paint a rather ahistorical picture of data use which is divorced from wider discussion of the communication strategies and organization of political parties (Panebianco 1988; Katz & Mair 1995). Accounts originating primarily from scholarship on party organization (as opposed to communication) have traced the history of data collection by parties for decades (Mills 2014). This includes in the United States (Hersh 2015), Germany (Kruschinski & Haller 2017), Australia (Kefford 2021), and the United Kingdom (Johnston et al. 2012). Building on this work, we suggest that it is important not to see DDC as something inherently novel or only connected to new data sources and collection practices, but rather as a long-standing practice that has evolved over time to incorporate new data forms. While it is true that DDC—broadly defined—has become pervasive across many advanced democracies (Bennett & Lyon 2019; Dommett 2019; Stromer-Galley 2019), the fundamentals of campaigning remain the same. Mobilization, persuasion, and engagement are the key goals, and the tools used to drive these behavioral responses—canvassing, broadcast and narrowcast advertising—are long-standing features of campaigning.[1]

We also argue that it is important to gain a more detailed understanding of the sources of data that parties utilize. Notably, the existing literature provides incomplete evidence on these fronts. There is extensive coverage of the US case (Kreiss 2012, 2016; Nielsen 2012; Hersh 2015). There are also useful contributions from outside the United States, including in Australia (Kefford 2021), Germany (Jungherr 2016; Kruschinski & Haller 2017; Clemens 2018), Canada (Munroe & Munroe 2018), and the United Kingdom (Anstead 2017; Dommett 2019). This work has tended to outline how, in Kreiss's (2017, 1) terms, "[s]ophisticated voter databases now contain everything from political party data gleaned through millions of interactions with the electorate, public data obtained from state agencies, and commercial marketing information that is bought and sold on international open markets with a significant number of new variables having become available over the past few years." Others have pointed to the importance of information provided by the state (Hersh 2015), by volunteers' canvassing efforts (on the doorstep or telephone), by commercial companies (such as polling insights) (Kreiss & Howard 2010, 1035–1037), and by data brokers (Bennett 2015; Bennett & Bayley 2018). This literature makes clear that parties are not acting alone. In other words, political parties in many advanced democracies do not have the capacity to collect and analyze data at the scale and sophistication often required for the types of functions they want to perform. In reflecting upon US practices and whether these are transferable, Jungherr et al. (2020, 204) point to the fact that US campaigns, which are highly financed, have access to a "rich environment of specialized vendors skilled in developing data-driven services." While the level of external vendors that political parties in other advanced democracies have access to does not come close to that in the United States, they can play a significant role in helping political parties collect and analyze data. This means that political parties can usefully be understood as being part of a broader ecosystem populated with a diverse set of actors who work with political parties on a range of functions (Dommett et al. 2020), a point we discuss further in Chapter 6 on personnel.

Thus, when it comes to our understanding of data, there are a number of important gaps within current understanding that have allowed particular, often sensationalized accounts to dominate and to be perceived as the norm. Reacting to these tendencies, we argue that there is a need for a more in-depth engagement with the question of how data features in data-driven campaigns.

Data: Types, Sources, and Utility across Our Cases

In this section, we identify four types of data (distilled in Figure 3.1) that are utilized by different parties to varying degrees. As this figure reveals, in classifying these types of data, we do not suggest that different types of data are

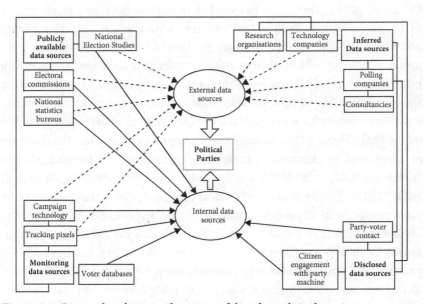

Figure 3.1 Internal and external sources of data for political parties.

comparable to each other in type or source. Indeed, some data involves party labor and is gathered through canvassing activities undertaken by party members and supporters. Other data is provided freely to parties by the state. Some data is collected by parties in raw and unfiltered forms, using cookies to collect tracking data, for example, from party webpages, while other data comes via intermediaries, with research firms, polling companies, or analytics organizations providing raw or modeled data for a fee. Beyond this, we also observe tech company data, which parties never actually possess, but which is accessed through a social media interface that allows parties to identify and target users online, or through data brokers where parties often do not access the underlying data. This *potential* wealth of data is not, however, always utilized by parties. Hence it is important to understand which different types of data parties utilize, and how they are integrated to inform party activity. By doing this, we can better contextualize whether there are different types of data used across our advanced democracies and what causes variation.

The first type of data is *publicly available data*. This data can be paid for or can be free. It often comes from sub-national or national electoral commissions, national statistics bureaus or authorities, and can come in the form of an electoral roll, marked register (a list of who cast a ballot), or census data. The types of data source available in each jurisdiction vary, as do the particular data points provided within each source. Commonly encountered, however, is data such as age, gender, postal code, and marital status. Publicly available data can come from national election studies, which provide survey data on public attitudes and voting intentions. This type of data can also be collected by parties themselves, or come from data brokers and other intermediaries, who either repackage data from these sources to generate inferential insights, or who curate lists of data such as phone numbers or email addresses that are in the public realm. In many advanced democracies, publicly available data is critical to political parties, and often forms the foundation for their DDC activity.

The second type of data is *disclosed data*. While in previous analyses, disclosed data and what is referred to as publicly available data were collapsed into a single category (Dommett 2019), for our purposes we have split these to deepen our understanding of the diverse sources of data. Disclosed data here, as shown in Figure 3.1, refers to data freely given by citizens. This is commonly provided directly to parties via direct voter contact activities such as door-knocking, phone-banking, email, online and offline surveys, or direct mail. Yet information can also be disclosed by citizens to other actors such as polling companies or commercial organizations, who may then pass on or sell that data to parties. While this type of data may appear mundane or antiquated in the digital age, it remains critically important to the types of campaign activities that parties in advanced democracies are focused on. We observe common data points collected by parties, examples of which are included in Table 3.1. Often gathered using standardized scripts that are specific to each party, there is a recurring interest in vote intention, attitudes to key issues, and demographic characteristics. Contact details such as email addresses and phone numbers also remain important so that voters can be targeted online and offline. For example, using email addresses, parties can create "custom" and then "lookalike" audiences on platforms such as Facebook.[2]

The third type of data is *monitoring data*. This type of data is usually the product of tracking data online or from parties or other organizations seeking to understand public behavior. This data often provides limited utility to political parties as the data is not easily applicable to campaign goals (Nickerson & Rogers 2014), with some notable exceptions. For example, parties attempting to mobilize donations or to prompt supporters to volunteer may trial competing campaign messages and use monitoring data— such as when emails were opened, and websites visited after an email was

Table 3.1 Examples of Data Points That Parties Possess

Publicly Available Data Points	Disclosed Data Points	Monitoring Data Points	Inferential Data Points
Age	Age	Email open rate	Age
Gender	Gender	Event attendance	Likelihood to be persuadable
Marital status	Phone number	IP address	Likelihood to be a supporter
Address	Address	Geographic location	Income
Party registration	Party identification	Internet service provider	Psychometrics
Turnout history	Attitudes to key issues	Browser information	Attitudes to key issues
Postal code	Vote intention	Liked pages	Vote intention
Location voted at	Email Address	Purchase history	Likelihood to have children

opened—to assess how engaging the competing interventions were. Often this data, as shown in Figure 3.1, comes from tracking cookies that parties may embed on their websites, pixels embedded into emails the parties distribute, or it may come from third-party data brokers.[3] This can include data points such as IP addresses, geographic location, or browser information. Monitoring data can come from the party itself, as internal data can be gathered on, for example, how many contacts the party has had with voters in a specified area. It can also come from external organizations and, regardless of source, can be collected online and offline.

Finally, there is *inferential data*. This is data that is interpreted; in many instances, inferences are drawn about larger populations from a smaller sample of citizens. For example, a nationally representative sample of citizens is often used to derive aggregate-level inferences about vote intention. As is common in the analytics process used by many parties—discussed more in the next chapter—modeling is undertaken on a small training set to measure how persuadable voters may be, the correlates of persuadability or vote intention, or how likely individuals are to be supporters. These measures are then applied to a larger dataset, and inferences are drawn about these voters from the initial sample. As with monitoring data, inferential data can come from commercial organizations and data brokers who may use the data points they have collected to develop segmentations or voter types or personas. It can come from social networking platforms, which draw inferences about users based on their online activity, or from sources such as national election studies. These kinds of data can prove particularly valuable for parties, especially when their ability to gather disclosed data is limited. In addition to these more sophisticated forms of inferential data, parties can also collect data on more routine inferences. A volunteer may therefore make an inference about a voters' political preferences without them directly *disclosing* their views, or alternatively a simple piece of software can be used to guess the ethnicity or age of a voter based on their name. Inferred data can therefore come in a variety of different forms. Whilst often a valuable form of data, there are certain risks and legal constraints on the use of inferred data, particularly where campaigners are subject to regulation emphasizing the need for accurate data or direct consent (Naik 2019).

It is important to note that across our four types of data, some are individualized, while others are at less granular levels, such as geographic, postal code, or electorate level. Moreover, as explained further below, some data points—especially monitoring data points—are those most directly affected by the legislative and regulatory regimes in place around data privacy. This is especially true for the European Union's General Data Protection Regulation (GDPR). Thus, the relationship between some of the data that parties can collect and acquire is heavily affected by the role and regulation of third-party actors, whether these are tech companies or data brokers.

Understanding Variations in Data Use across Our Five Advanced Democracies

In this section, we demonstrate that the manifestation of these data points is not consistent, as available data points, data-collection practices, and sources can vary depending on context and by party. To be clear, our aim is not to describe and compare every data point used by our case study parties, as these are too numerous and diffuse to be covered comprehensively. Rather, our goal is to highlight important trends and differences in party practices. Looking ahead to our explanation (Chapter 7), we begin to point to some possible reasons for these differences, suggesting, for example, that some data can only be collected by parties who invest significant resources in personnel or technology. What will become clear from the next section is that, despite claims that data-driven practices provide parties with unlimited insights into citizens' lives, practice within our cases suggests that parties do not uniformly have access to all types of data (Margetts 2017). Moreover, we note that much of this data provides limited (if any) insights about voting behavior, and data sources are often not easily synchronized or combined.

Publicly Available Data

Despite sensationalized accounts of the way campaigns have drawn on data from tech companies such as Meta to supposedly transform campaigning, publicly available data remains an essential component of the data that parties in many advanced democracies draw on. While there is variation in the type and availability of this form of data in our case studies, it remains a critical component of the databases that almost all the political parties in our case study countries maintain.

In Australia, parties have easy access to substantial amounts of publicly available information. Registered political parties are given access to the electoral roll from the Australian Electoral Commission, which contains details such as the names and addresses of all citizens registered to vote, which is roughly 90% of the adult population. Beyond this, Australian parties can access a wealth of data from the Australian Bureau of Statistics which is not individual data, but its granularity is at a geographic area commonly containing 200–800 people, what is known as a Statistical Area 1 (SA1) (Kefford 2021). After an election, political parties are also provided with information such as at which voting booth citizens voted, which can, at times, be of use to parties. While this data is valuable for parties trying to understand sub-populations, it is also useful for organizing campaigns, as volunteers are often given a list to door-knock which is half or an entire SA1. As one Labor interviewee discussed:

> For field campaigns most parties in Australia divide up electorates by SA1s and then choices are made about which SA1s are the most valuable to put resources into. This might not be entirely scientific and can be as simple as, "well that end of the electorate is strongly for us and the other end is strongly against us, so we will door-knock this end first, or vice versa." Obviously that is just for doors, the phones are based on our modeling about who are the best targets, but these all work in unison with one another.

Political parties in Australia also frequently purchase publicly available data. Often this is to acquire datapoints such as phone numbers or email addresses to augment the other data they have on voters.

In the United Kingdom, the situation is similar. One interviewee from the Conservative Party reflected, "Political parties have always had full access to the electoral register for a constituency. They used to have it on paper." Enshrined in the Representation of the People Act (2001a 497, reg.105; 2001b 341, reg. 106),[4] parties are legally entitled to access. The data contained in this file is basic, providing household addresses and age of maturation (i.e., when first eligible to vote). In addition, parties can purchase the marked register, which contains information about who did or did not cast their ballot at the last election, and UK parties append this information to the electoral roll within their own databases. The collation and integration of this data is often not straightforward, and commonly requires significant time from party staff and volunteers to input this information into their own voter databases. This information is nevertheless seen to be particularly important because, as one interviewee described, it provides:

nine to ten million individual-level records of whether or not an individual voted . . . at that specific general election because that's massively powerful in predicting how they'll vote in the past and in targeting future activity. If you know somebody votes at general elections but doesn't usually vote in local elections, they're an obvious target at local election time because they're not going to vote unless you go and bother them.

Similarly, it is helpful in identifying those not to target because, as another interviewee noted:

If we know somebody hasn't turned out in three or four successive general elections or local elections, we're not going to target them in a local election. You know, it would be pointless. But without that information, we kind of risk targeting the wrong people who are unlikely to turn out.

The electoral register is then routinely appended with other forms of freely available information. Additional sources, such as census information, national statistics, and the British Election Study, can also be accessed without charge, although certain data brokerage companies charge parties to access services that aggregate these forms of publicly available information (often pairing it with privately gathered insights). Historically, some of our interviewees also talked about harvesting insights from social media profiles. Although now not practiced due to restrictions imposed by GDPR—which imposes requirements around consent—one interviewee from the Liberal Democrats spoke about harvesting data from "people's Twitter handles" and "their Facebook profile" to gain "a better idea about what their interests were." This kind of contextual data was seen to be exceedingly valuable to parties. Indeed, one Labour Party interviewee described how adding data on the number of Catholic schools in an area within Scotland was insightful because data analysis revealed that "simplifying massively, areas where the Labour vote is very Catholic are areas where the shift to the SNP in the period 2013 to 2019 happened."

The public data available to Canadian parties may not be as extensive as that in the United States, Australia, or the United Kingdom, but it is also not as limited as that in Germany. The Canadian *Elections Act* contains provisions whereby political parties are provided with a copy of the electoral roll each year, and an updated list after the writs are finalized. The information provided includes the first and last name, address, and the unique electoral identifier code used by Elections Canada (Patten 2017). Interviewees also mentioned that they can get access to home phone numbers as well, but, in an era of predominant mobile phone usage, these are not as valuable as they once were. Importantly, in Canada you can register to vote at the same time as casting a ballot, so data about registration status is of less value than it is elsewhere because it is not always available ahead of an election. However, after Election Day the list is again provided to political parties, which allows them to update their own databases (Bennett & Bayley 2018). Elections Canada assigns each individual a unique identifier that follows a voter even if they move, allowing parties to match up voters even if they have changed location. The significance of different forms of data for parties in different contexts, and especially compared to the United States, can be highlighted by an example provided by an interviewee from the NDP:

> So a really simple example is that in the US, I think zip codes are a lot more powerful than postal codes are in Canada because for me in my own riding, my postal code or the first three digits of my postal code can be very different from the person across the street. You don't get as much information out of a postal code. . . . So even if I move within my riding, I'm probably not going to have the same postal code. But in the States the zip code is . . . it could be statewide or it could be for a whole region. It's a lot more indicative of where people are located. So when, for example, a lot of tools are using zip codes to derive some sort of useful information, whatever that may be, you can't do that with postal codes.

Publicly available data in the United States varies by state but often comes from "individual-level records from the voter registration system, but also data from the Census Bureau and state licensing agencies" (Hersh 2015, 3). One prime example are voter files, which are lists of all registered voters in a given state or district, compiled by the local and state election authorities. These files are often depicted as the starting point for all data operations in a modern US campaign, and both US parties have invested considerable resource in building data operations that gather state files into a single national database (Therriault 2016). The precise datapoints available in the voter files vary in accordance with local law, meaning that "in some states, campaigns can obtain public records of individual voters' race or party affiliation; in other states they cannot" (Hersh 2015, 4; see, for an overview, Barberá 2021). It also varies in format and availability, meaning that unlike in the United Kingdom where a single file is available, US campaigns have to check state data to ensure that it is consistent. This is vital, as states can often take different amounts of time to implement redistricting guidelines and may therefore not be wholly up to date (Black, quoted in Wilson 2022; Van Duyn 2021, 171).

The voter file is combined with numerous other pieces of publicly available data to build up a multifaceted picture of individual voters, but it can also be used to profile addresses. For example, a newly developed tool created by the DNC—the Geographic Address Dataset—gathered 260 million addresses by compiling data from multiple sources, including the voter file, Postal Service data, and records from private vendors, allowing the party to identify a reported 25 million new addresses that were never before included in the DNC's records (Lapowsky 2022). Such data-collection exercises also often draw on census data that provides information on trends over time, mapping, for example, the characteristics of electoral support in particular congressional districts. A number of universities and research centers also provide datasets that can be utilized by parties, meaning that in addition to the American National Election Study, databases are curated and made publicly available by groups such as the MIT Election Lab or Open Government Data Initiatives (e.g., Data.gov).

In Germany, financial resources for political campaigns are comparatively small due to a strict party financial regime which is based on public funding and geared toward transparency (Federal Ministry of the Interior and Community n.d.; Bundestag 1994). This manifests in German parties relying heavily on publicly available data (statistical offices of the state, voter data from the Federal Election Commissioner) or data which costs relatively little to access (such as the register of residents or the population register). Moreover, in Germany, only some data is available, and certain information can only be purchased six months before an election, including names, addresses, and educational qualifications, if a party asks for data on a clearly defined population group of a certain age (Weitbrecht 2019; § 50 Abs. 1 of the Federal Act of Registration). In comparison to the other cases, the data that German parties can access is further circumscribed by regulatory requirements. For example, the country's data-protection rules forbid parties from the collection, combination, and long-time storage of personal data on voters without their consent (Hessian Commissioner for Data Protection and Freedom 2023). This means that information cannot be collected on individual voters, or even on households, for more than one campaign. One

German party strategist from the Christian Democrats explained how this affects both publicly available data and disclosed data as follows:

> It is true that data may be acquired for senior citizens or first-time voters for the elections from the residents' registration offices. However, these merely state "Max Mustermann, Musterstadt." Unprofiled data without any additional information which we are not allowed to combine or keep after the election without the voters' consent. Thus, we are very reserved to use it since cost and also the approach are out of proportion. The smallest level of aggregation we are allowed is six households. So, the information that canvassers collect with our app is linked to an exact GPS coordinate, but we are not permitted to record voters' names or addresses, so the party can only build files on general locations and geographical regions rather than individual voters. This means that the data we are collecting will only be useful for targeting people at their homes—not over email or by telephone, as in the United States. So, all in all what we do has nothing to do with a "big data" campaign.

Disclosed Data

The acquisition of disclosed data is a well-established and critical aspect of data collection within our countries, with parties in the United States (Wielhouwer 1995), the United Kingdom (Butler 1995), Australia (Mills 2014; Kefford 2021), and Canada operating canvassing activities for decades. Yet in Germany, until 2019 it was only the two major parties who canvassed strategically to collect data (Kruschinski & Haller 2017). When it comes to disclosed data, major parties are often advantaged, as they have the capacity to employ capital and labor resources to collect and acquire data (see Chapter 6).

In Australia, interviewees spoke extensively about the way they collected data via direct voter contact, such as door-knocking, phone-banking, or through online petitions. They also spoke about using survey methods, including from national or local-level polling, online mailing lists, or methods such as robo-polls or interactive voice response (IVR) polls. This is largely in line with the US experience (Hersh 2015). The key data points that parties in Australia seek to collect are past vote; vote intention; issues that the voter feels especially strongly about; issue positions; and a range of demographic variables. The parties all work with various polling and social research organizations to produce qualitative and quantitative insights into the electorate; this includes YouGov, Essential Media, and C|T Group. While Australia is the only one of our cases that uses compulsory voting, there was little difference in the types of data points that parties in Australia collect compared to the other cases.

Interviewees in the United Kingdom suggested that they gathered disclosed data from different sources. In terms of internally procured data, parties drew heavily on doorstep and phone canvassing, but differed in the precise data they collected. The Conservatives used a series of 0–10 scales to assess party identification that one interviewee described as providing a "richer quality of data" by overcoming variance in the data previously gathered by activists. Labour, in contrast, experimented with question wording to advance campaign goals. One interviewee reflected on the value of:

> asking people, have you voted or are you going to vote? Those have very simple closed answers and voters not being fools, they also know that the closed answer that makes you fuck off and never come back again is the answer yes. If however you give them a question where they have to think, the idea in Kahneman and Tversky[5] world is that having thought it then becomes more likely that they execute that action without subsequent reflection. So the question on the script was always about what time do you plan to go and vote? And we would make a great show of capturing that information. But actually, the purpose of asking the question isn't to capture the information, it's to elicit an action in the respondent.

In addition, all our UK parties drew, to varying degrees, on polling commissioned from external providers, with interviewees emphasizing its importance. As one Labour interviewee said: "I mean, polling data is sort of key for our team. Obviously, we wouldn't have the capability to collect that. So yeah, we have working relationships with people at YouGov, Opinium . . . at different times, we've used different polling companies, to be honest. I mean, those relationships were key." Minor parties were, however, limited in how much polling they could conduct. Parties also gathered disclosed insights online. Indeed, between 2010 and 2017 the Conservative Party invested in online data collection to increase their email list from 500,000 emails in 2010 to 1.4 million by 2019 (Wallace 2017). UK parties therefore used a range of different methods to capture alternative forms of disclosed data insight.

In Canada, as in our other cases, disclosed data is seen as extremely valuable for parties to collect. One interviewee from the NDP, for example, said:

> The best data you can collect is data that people give you . . . which 60 years ago would have been primarily door-to-door canvassing, knock on someone's door, hey, I'm from the NDP, this is what we believe, do you believe that? . . . Certainly now in a digital world, that exact same exercise is done in different ways. We instead of knocking on people's doors, we call them and we say, hey, exact same pitch.

Interviewees also pointed to the rise of peer-to-peer texting and the significance of online (and offline) petitions for acquiring disclosed data, especially around individual issues the citizen may be interested in. One interviewee noted how they used specific questions, asking:

> Do you want to ban hate symbols? If you do, sign up to the petition, add your voice. And the people who do that, there you go, they've taken an action to say, yeah, we believe what you believe and they put in their name and their email address and their postal code so we know where they live. And maybe their phone number, maybe not their phone number, and now we're going to follow up with those people and say hey, you believe in banning hate symbols, what do you think about fighting climate change? Oh? You're down with that too? Cool, awesome. Well, we should continue this conversation. Then when it comes to an election, we can go back to them and say, Oh, you remember how you wanted to ban hate symbols and fight climate change? And we want to ban hate symbols and fight climate change, well, now is our opportunity to do that. So if you vote for us, then we can do those things.

The secondary literature also pointed to the importance of disclosed data collected by constituent offices (Patten 2017) as a means of identifying local issues and concerns—something that was not common in all our cases. Polling and focus groups were also used by all our Canadian parties to gather insight on public attitudes and voting intention (Delacourt 2012; McGregor 2014; Delacourt 2019).

In the United States, disclosed data is collected via a multitude of methods. First, US parties rely heavily on data collected via doorstep and telephone canvassing using scripted conversations in congressional (Nielsen 2012) and presidential elections (Bimber 2014; Issenberg 2012b; Jungherr et al. 2020). Campaigns also gather information about public attitudes, using polling (with internet polling receiving growing attention in recent years; Kusche 2020; Ruffini 2016, 15; Voigt 2018) and focus groups (Newman 1994, 20; Kusche 2020; Stromer-Galley 2019). In addition, US parties use online petitions on social media platforms, with many advertisements within the Meta advertising archive showing parties to be using surveys and email signups to gather further information about voters (Wong 2020). Furthermore, US campaigns use mobile applications to gather data such as mobile phone numbers and email addresses (Stromer-Galley 2019, 169). While the methods for gathering disclosed data were common to the United States and our other countries, the scale of this activity in the United States and parties' ability to buy data disclosed to other (often commercial) actors were more prominent.

Interviews with German party strategists show that parties gathered disclosed data from different sources and thereby encountered obstacles. All parties spent money on national and constituency-level polling and put an emphasis on disclosed data collected through focus groups. For both data sources, however, parties' financial capacity to commission polling and conduct focus groups varied dramatically. Thus, resources influence how disclosed data can be bought or collected. As one interviewee from the Left noted: "Of course, we would like to conduct weekly polls like the bigger parties to get a better picture about the thoughts of the voters. However, money is missing on all ends so that we need to look at polls which are published by the media and then run selected polls if we need detailed information about important aspects of the campaign."

Disclosed data about individual voters is also collected by German parties. Especially, the bigger parties collect voter information about issue positions; and a range of demographic variables via canvassing, by collecting signatures on petitions on- and offline, or online mailing lists or social media. However, disclosed data is legally restricted to be collected and processed only with explicit consent by the voters to do so. Thus, in comparison to our other countries, disclosed data is a rather difficult terrain for all German parties and especially the smaller parties due to a lack of financial resources and strict data regulation.

Monitoring Data

Monitoring data, similar to inferred data which is discussed in the following section, is less prevalent across the parties we cover for the simple reason that this type of data, whether it comes from third parties such as social media companies, market research services, or data brokers, often requires higher budgets and is in some cases connected to higher regulatory barriers. The technology behind it will be discussed in more detail in Chapter 5.

In Australia, monitoring data from digital channels contains information such as how long those being tracked spent on certain sites, as well as what sites they visited. This replicates what most commercial organizations do when trying to understand their current customers and to identify to whom they should market their goods or services, including where they should place that marketing material (Tactical Tech 2019). One of the most important ways that parties collect data online is through their websites. As outlined in Kefford (2021), party webpages for each of the Australian parties had tracking cookies from Google and Facebook, among others. In contrast to some of our other cases, the Australian parties placed far less emphasis on understanding their membership and their supporters, including their geographic dispersal. This relates to the use of compulsory voting which renders get-out-the-vote (GOTV) strategies of limited value (Kefford 2021).

In the United Kingdom, we found some evidence of the form of digital monitoring evident in Australia in the privacy statements of political parties. Our interviewees were often unwilling to discuss their use of these practices, but one interviewee from Labour gave more insight. Reflecting on practice pre-GDPR, they described how in 2017:

> what we could do was create a custom audience list driven from the voter database but then use the Facebook pixel to tell that they'd reached the website, that they'd maybe signed something so there was a conversion event. That they maybe donated, what the value of that donation was so that we could track a positive ROI. But at the same time if they'd come from Facebook and hit the page, they'd then maybe pick up a Twitter cookie, or maybe pick up the Google Adwords cookie and vice versa. We'd have people come in on Adwords and then maybe we could add them to a different targeting pool in Facebook. That kind of interplay was really important.

Most other interviewees were more willing to talk about a different kind of monitoring data and spoke about collecting data that allowed them to monitor campaign interventions. One interviewee within the NDP, for example, spoke about their efforts to "collect election results and know how many volunteers we've got door-knocking... building a model to understand what campaigns outperform similar areas and underperform. And for us that allows us to understand where best practice might be. So, it's very much data informing learning and evaluation of what we've done before." In this sense, data about the impact of campaigning was gathered by parties, allowing them to test and evaluate the success of different interventions. It was noted, however, that the capacity to conduct this kind of testing and evaluation was limited, especially during election periods.

In Canada, we found evidence of both forms of monitoring data. Once again, major political parties admitted to using tracking pixels from Facebook—yet again there was reticence to speak in detail about this activity. The use of metrics and campaign monitoring was, however, more readily spoken about, and our interviews showed that parties were increasingly interested in gathering data on their campaign interventions (Munroe & Munroe 2018, 147). Some, for example, spoke about looking at email-opening rates, or at click-through rates on social media content. And yet, in many parties we heard that current efforts to gather this data were lacking. One interviewee within the NPD, for example, spoke about their current efforts to identify "what metrics we have and what KPIs we can measure" to keep track of the success of campaign interventions in prompting activist engagement, noting that historically "we didn't have enough capacity to track that."

Due to the domination of Silicon Valley in the tech industry, US campaigns have frequently been well advanced in comparison to our other cases in their collection and use of monitoring data, and especially tracking data (Zeng et al. 2021). Despite this, there remains a lack of empirical studies which have documented the use of this data in the United States, like elsewhere. According to Gorton (2016, 68), in the United States "lifestyle information can be purchased from private firms such as Acxiom, Claritas, and Experian," which is gathered "by monitoring the data trail individuals create through their Internet activity, such as website visits, online purchases, and interactions on social media sites, including status updates and 'likes' on Facebook." There is also a proliferation of digital listening companies selling services in the United States, which provide what Karpf (2012) describes as "passive democratic feedback" on online behavior.

There is more insight on campaign monitoring, as US campaigns routinely gather data on contact rates, email-opening rates, and financial donations (Walker & Nowlin 2021). Unlike our other cases, there is evidence that campaigns in the United States have begun utilizing location data from mobile phones as an important data source that is being collected and utilized (Schleifer 2019). US campaigns also use experimental research to gather data on voters' responses to campaign interventions, to tweak call scripts or canvassing protocols (Bimber 2014; Gorton 2016; Issenberg 2012b; Voigt 2018)—with these methods used more extensively than in our other cases to gain feedback on interventions.

In Germany, parties are more hesitant about the use of monitoring data, often because of a lack of know-how, resource limitations, and concerns and uncertainties about possible breaches in data regulation. Almost all parties use tracking cookies on their homepages; however, email and Facebook pixel are only used in experimental ways. One strategist from the Christian Democrats explained this as follows:

> On the subject of Facebook pixels on websites, I have to tell you quite honestly that I started to work on it last year in 2017, but didn't finish it since there are now complicated regulations coming with it, we simply didn't take into account. However, our main problem is that we can't install them on each candidate's website, because we would have to check back with like five internal teams again. And there I lose time that I don't have in the election campaign.

Despite these barriers, all German parties showed interest in the use of monitoring data for measuring the effectiveness of campaign interventions, with campaign strategists particularly emphasizing the possibilities of using new technologies to conduct evaluations. Interviewees from all parties therefore described the collection and analysis of monitoring data for their offline communication, such as canvassing, or their online communication, such as homepage visits, search results, engagement on social media, or return on investment (ROI) of social media advertising. However, interviewees from the Left described these practices as "cherry on the cake" and "only feasible if enough time and personnel is [sic] available."

Inferential Data

Inferential data was evident across all our cases; almost all the parties we examined possessed such data, and this was commonly produced either from the application of analytical techniques to other forms of data, or through simple human judgments.

In Australia, the process of generating inferential data involved transforming publicly available and disclosed data into more sophisticated forms of data points (Kefford 2021). One example of how parties in Australia do this comes from a Labor interviewee:

> We run phone surveys and we try and find people who are not committed to one of the two major parties or the two major candidates in their seat, so it might be that they were unsure or maybe they were leaning towards one of the two major candidates, but they weren't really sure yet. Maybe they were planning to vote for a minor party, but they were not willing to put one of the two major candidates first. We would identify that group of people from our phone surveys and say, Okay, these are the kinds of people we want to be targeting our persuasion efforts to. As we run our phone surveys on a relatively small number of people, we need a way to extrapolate from this group to the rest of the population. So, we ask, who else in the population looks like these high persuasion targets from our phone surveys? We use this as the training set, we then validate the model on a separate dataset.

Inferential data, however, was not always gathered. While some state-based Greens parties said they had used this in small quantities, others avoided it for reasons such as a lack of resources and broader discussions within the party about data privacy (Kefford 2021).

In the United Kingdom, inferred data comes in different forms. The Information Commissioners' Office (ICO) reported that the Labour Party, the Conservative Party, and the Liberal Democrats paid for commercial data about individuals or groups, either factual, estimated, or a combination of both, from suppliers under commercial terms (ICO 2020). Experian is a major provider of data to UK parties, and provides categorization of broad groups of voters to aid targeting. While no longer available (due to GDPR), one interviewee from Experian spoke about the company providing data about inferred ethnicity, with an interviewee explaining how they:

would have looked at surname, Christian name combinations and . . . infer something about their likelihood to be non-white or that sort of stuff. . . . Experian have got some very, very clever modelers who can begin to build a suite of models that estimate age by household. They estimate ethnicity, they can estimate social grade, they estimate life stage. Are you a married couple, likely to be a couple with children or not, are you likely to be retirees, that type of thing. They basically build a load of demographic-type models derived from these thin data files.

UK parties also gather inferred data through their own canvassing activity, with activists themselves making and recording judgments that often end up in voter files. Interviewees therefore recalled how canvassers often code hostility to canvassing activity as evidence of a lack of party support, without verifying this assumption (Stratton 2022).

In Canada, the Liberals also purchased commercial data to identify the likely ethnic and cultural backgrounds of voters based on their names (Delacourt 2013). There is also some evidence of inferred insights about demographic groups and voter attitudes being purchased from external providers. The precise information being gathered from these companies is, however, opaque, meaning that we have limited insight into the kind of inferential data gathered in Canada. As in our other countries, more observational inferences are commonplace in canvassing activity, with comments about likely party support, household composition, and ethnicity sometimes recorded without being directly disclosed.

As has become evident throughout this chapter, the US Democrats and Republicans have been engaged in a data "arms race," which also includes the collection of various inferential data to furnish their voter files (Kreiss 2016; Therriault 2016; Voigt 2018). This use is especially based on the analytical capabilities of US campaigns. Both parties draw inferences from their wide variety of data sources, which provide several individual pieces of information about the millions of registered voters in the United States (Benle & Papatla 2021). In 2016, for example, an internal strategy memo within the Republican National Committee (RNC) described using data to "predict possible outcomes as well as develop more customized voter contact programs with a true ROI analysis for every dollar spent or contact made" (RNC quoted in Voigt 2018, n.p.). This kind of strategy was highlighted by Voigt (2018), who described how the 2016 Trump campaign developed scores which helped to identify voters who require issue-related persuasion or a "nudge" to turn out and vote. Aside from parties' own inferential analysis, US campaigns also have numerous companies to draw upon who offer inferential data. Tunnl, for example, provides voter segments based on inferential data, allowing parties to target "Hispanic persuadables" or those who oppose or support the "Respect for Marriage Act" (Tunnl n.d.). Inferential data is therefore widely collected and available to US campaigns.

In Germany, parties also draw on inferential data but encounter challenges, namely resources and data-protection laws, which forbid them from collecting, combining, and long-time storage of personal data on voters without their explicit consent. The Christian Democrats, Social Democratic Party, the Greens, and the Liberals conduct their own inferential analysis for vote potentials in geographic areas, mostly based on publicly available and disclosed data (see Chapter 4). Parties also buy inferential data from data vendors. However, this was done only by a few parties and was used in experimental ways. For example, the Christian Democrats and the Liberals "rented" inferred data (so-called geographic potential analyses) during the 2017 federal election from an external data vendor (Deutsche Post Direct GmbH), where the statistical probability of party affinity is calculated for so-called geographical microcells (6.6 households). Other forms of inferred data are less prominent, and this is often seen as a product of the resources required to acquire such data, as well as regulatory drivers.

Conclusion

In this chapter, our first central component of DDC—data—was unpacked so that we can better understand the types of data collected and the sources of this data. In particular, we identified four types of data, distinguishing between data that is publicly available, disclosed, monitored, and inferred. Reviewing empirical evidence as to the use of each type of data in our five case study countries, we found that while there was a degree of commonality between our cases in terms of the types of data collected, there was significant variation within countries and among parties in the exact form of information that parties possess. We therefore found that while almost every party collects public, disclosed, monitoring, and inferential data, the specific data points they gather and the way they collect data are often different.

In discussing each form of data we have offered a more detailed picture of the type of information that parties collect, but it is also important to note that these pieces of information are often not linked together and are difficult to compile into a single, unified voter profile. While most parties, as will be discussed in Chapter 5, do invest in voter databases that attempt to combine many of these data points, it is common to rely on a variety of systems to store and manage data over time. This renders data management and protection an increasing concern for parties around the globe.

Characterizing practice in our five countries, it is clear that US activities are not uniformly replicated. US parties draw extensively on all four of our types of data. While their public data is often poorly formatted and requires extensive processing, it nevertheless forms the basis of voter-contact strategies and is appended by disclosed data, monitoring data, and inferred data to build up a rich understanding of voters' preferences and behaviors. The variety of different data points observed in the United States is far more extensive than in our four other cases, reflecting a more developed industry for buying data and comparatively weak regulatory oversight.

In Australia, Canada, and the United Kingdom, public data is essential to parties' data-collection efforts, with the publicly available data file the core source to which other forms of data are appended. In Germany, these data sources are also important, but access is more restricted. Interestingly, whilst both the United Kingdom and Germany are subject to the GDPR, in Germany the pre-existing cultural and legal landscape creates a more restrictive regulatory environment, resulting in stricter constraints on the data parties can collect.

As within the United States, parties in our other countries all invested heavily in offline and online activities designed to gather disclosed data. They also made efforts to gather inferred and monitoring data, but these data-collection efforts were less extensive. We particularly found that institutionalized major parties have an advantage over their smaller competitors, who have fewer resources, in gathering these forms of data (Gibson & McAllister 2015).

Cumulatively, these findings reveal parties' differing ability to gather different types of data. Rather than replicating practice in the United States, across our other cases parties' use of different data types varies, with the specific data points gathered from different sources not always consistent. Importantly for our explanatory framework, it appears that parties are not operating on a level playing field, with cross-national differences reflecting particular regulatory dynamics and party-level variations Our findings accordingly show that the data used for DDC is not uniform around the globe.

Practitioner Perspectives on Data

Data, as outlined in the previous chapter, can come in a variety of different forms and can be gathered in a range of different ways, many of which are long-standing and widely accepted. The precise type of data evident in any specific context can vary considerably, but certain core pieces of information are routinely found within campaigners' databases. In order to understand more about the types of data utilized and the risks of different data-collection techniques, we asked two practitioners to respond to the following provocation:

In recent years, a number of influential accounts have suggested that political parties and other campaigners have acquired enormous amounts of highly personalized data on citizens, It has also been claimed that this data allows political parties to deliver highly individualized messaging tailored to activate changes in citizen behavior—whether that is persuading them to vote for one party over another, mobilizing them to participate in campaigns, or discouraging them from turning out and voting. In your experience, how well does this perception match the reality of the party-based campaigns you have worked on?

Specifically, we asked Professor Richard Webber, the originator of the geodemographic classification systems Acorn and Mosaic, managing director at Experian Marketing (1985–2005), and co-founder of Webber Philips, to reflect on the insights he has gathered over his career. We also asked the information and privacy commissioner for British Columbia, Michael McEvoy, who oversaw an investigation into *Political Parties, Campaign Data, and Voter Consent* (2019).

Professor Richard Webber, Originator of the Geodemographic Classification Systems Acorn and Mosaic, Managing Director at Experian (1985–2005), co-founder of Webber Philips

The explosion of "big data" has transformed the way in which parties campaign for votes in elections and has brought to organizers a wealth of data on the demographics and preferences of individual electors.

Since the 1979 election, parties (in the UK) have supplemented historic canvass return with small-area classifications such as Mosaic and Acorn as predictors of likely voter preferences. Since 2009, social media data has proved invaluable not just for locating potential supporters, but for the customization of communications so that they match the aspirations and anxieties of individual voters. And yet, while new forms of data enable targeting to be more precise, area-level data continues to play an important role (Webber & Burrows 2018).

Notwithstanding their desire to access ever more granular data, most campaign organizers appreciate that engagement and partisanship continues to be driven by social and historical influences, not just personal characteristics. Such influences are relevant for deciding which electoral seats or districts have long-term potential, helping to guide decisions about where resources should be targeted.

The use of data to drive such decisions is particularly relevant where an area's demographics are changing. To take a UK example, the Labour Party was able to use such information to identify Worthing East and Shoreham as a winnable seat, while the Liberal Democrats identified Chesham and Amersham as a plausible by-election target because it was rich in the types of voters disaffected by the Conservatives' focus on the aspirations of "Red Wall" electors.

To give an idea of the way that geographic social and historical data can be used to identify and segment voters, it is useful to consider some of the segments I was involved in developing throughout my career in the United Kingdom. Within the Mosaic system, for example, a former category "Co-op, Club, and Colliery" identified the ex-mining community which so conspicuously deserted Labour in 2017 and 2019. Of the seats gained by the Conservatives between 2017 and 2019, all but a handful had at one time had a coal mine.

Conversely, the category "Town Gown Transition" indicates the type of community which, though not as exclusively student-centered as "University Challenge," provided Labour with almost all of its gains during this period. These are seats characterized by large numbers of senior academics, post-graduate students, and younger graduates working in the knowledge sector.

In earlier years, high proportions of people recorded by the census as walking to work have indicated a potentially fertile area for the Liberal/Liberal Democrat style of community politics, places (often falling within the category "Ties of Community") with a denser network of community contacts and social influences than the new estates clustered around motorway junctions from which workers drive in multiple directions to work in large-scale operations. Likewise, the Liberal Democrats have been a more effective challenger than Labour in "Upland Hill Farms" than in the prairie farmland of Eastern England characterized by "Agribusiness."

This form of area-based segmentation is used internationally to identify groups of likely supporters or opponents and involves the integration of different, but often publicly available data points. The precise data used continually evolves, and in an era of identity politics the demographics of the workplace could well become an increasingly relevant predictor in the future.

In the jargon of statistics, these multilevel models of voting behavior will continue to outperform targeting systems based exclusively on person-level data so long as people continue to discuss voting with friends, colleagues, and neighbors.

Michael McEvoy, Information and Privacy Commissioner for British Columbia, Canada

Electoral campaigning has always involved gathering personal information about voters, and in turn using this information to craft communications to the electorate. What's so different compared to 30 years ago are two things: advanced technology now allows for the storage and use of voter information on a previously unimaginable scale, and the internet provides a two-way technology that facilitates this collection of personal information at scale while allowing for the more precise targeting of messages to voters.

Gaining insight into this opaque process is not easy, but here in British Columbia we have a unique vantage point. British Columbia is alone in Canada in having a privacy law that applies to political parties. This means that political parties need to follow the same rules that apply to all organizations and are subject to the same oversight by my office.

And we have used that oversight authority. We launched an investigation into how parties collect and process personal information after receiving complaints about how they handle data, as well as over concerns about legislative changes that made more voter information available to parties and candidates.

That investigation revealed that the parties collect and analyze significant amounts of personal data. This data came from many sources, from traditional door-to-door and phone canvassing to the use of data brokers and social media. The information collected was used to sort and target voters. It was also used to infer additional information about them, such as their ethnicity and likely voting intentions and party support.

We found that some methods of collection and use did not comply with the law, particularly those hidden from voters, such as scraping their social media accounts.

As observed earlier, political parties have long sought to identify and mobilize their supporters. But the voter profiles and analytics we uncovered are more detailed than in the past. And the ability of the parties to perform predictive analytics adds a decided level of sophistication previously unseen.

We know that in the era of data-driven campaigns, parties are able to target individuals and groups of voters with specific messages and advertising. One example is the parties' use of a Facebook tool called a "look-alike" audience. Parties upload lists of individual supporter emails to Facebook, not just for direct advertising, but also to allow the social media company to analyze the attributes of those supporters and then serve ads to others like them. All of this was done without the consent of those supporters. Whether these techniques work was a matter beyond the scope of our investigation; however, it seems highly unlikely that parties would collectively devote resources to these efforts if they were not efficacious.

The good news was that our investigation did not uncover the kinds of corrosive efforts, such as attempts at psychological profiling or voter suppression, that have raised serious concerns elsewhere. The use of personal information for these activities would very likely be prohibited under our privacy law, as organizations can only process personal data for purposes that a reasonable person would consider appropriate in the circumstances.

While it is clear that political parties have a continuing appetite for more data, it is equally clear that citizens have a right to exert some control over their personal information. It is for this reason that the activities of political parties and other organizations should be subject to clear rules, enforced through independent oversight.

4
Analytics

The way data is analyzed and then employed as part of the campaigns that political parties conduct remains an under-researched area in the scholarship. Like many other areas of campaigning, there is a good reason for this. Parties are secretive about their processes and there is often anxiety at allowing "outsiders" to see why decisions are made (Dommett & Power 2021). The lack of empirical knowledge of data analytics is as problematic as the lack of information on what data parties have and the sources of this data. Both scholars and policymakers require a more complete understanding of these practices, including what statistical or computational processes are being employed, how sophisticated they are, and their uniformity across advanced democracies. As with the preceding chapter on data, it is therefore essential that some baseline questions are addressed about the types of analytics practices employed and how they are used.

Analytics, as one component of DDC, can be understood as the output produced by the sorting and scrutinizing of data—generally with the goal of creating insights that help decision-makers to decide how to use their limited capital and labor resources. In contrast, data can be understood as a key input, with technology and personnel the medium through which DDC is realized. The way an individual party chooses to undertake DDC can vary based on a range of factors, but the idea that some form of analytics occurs is a defining element of this type of campaigning (Baldwin-Philippi 2017; Römmele & Gibson 2020). It is therefore vital in this chapter to clarify exactly what types of analysis occurs, and how parties in different contexts utilize these techniques.

This chapter will proceed as follows. Beginning by highlighting limitations and insights within the existing academic literature on analytics, we catalog the different types of analytical processes that can be employed in campaigns. Then, in the second half of the chapter, we return to our empirical data, showing variation in the type of analytics conducted. This descriptive exploration provides the foundations for further investigations of the drivers of these variations in Chapter 7, our explanatory chapter.

Analytics: The State of the Field

While analytics is relatively new in electoral politics, it builds off preexisting tendencies in commercial marketing which have sought to use resources efficiently and to draw on the emergence of "big data" to make decisions which are perceived to be better informed. Elgendy and Elragal (2014, 219) describe how "data analytics is the process of applying algorithms in order to analyze sets of data and extract useful and unknown patterns, relationships and information." However, debate and confusion remain about the different analytics processes that parties can utilize, and the distinguishing traits between them.

Scholarship on the use of analytics by political parties is a small and rather undefined field. As with the chapter on data, there are very few fine-grained empirical studies that demystify the way political parties use analytics. Instead, scholars have tended to use terminology such as data mining, segmentation, testing, experimentation, or targeting without providing detailed discussions of what these terms mean, or how they interrelate. It is therefore often difficult to determine exactly what forms of analytics parties engage in when they conduct DDC, and whether the same analytical processes are utilized in different ways or for different purposes dependent on context.

While observing ambiguities within existing accounts of data analytics, there are a small number of accounts—originating largely from the United States and Australia—that provide useful insights for an attempt to demystify the kind of analytical processes employed in data-driven campaigns (Nickerson & Rogers 2014; Hersh 2015; Kefford 2021). In particular, scholars have focused on two types of processes—targeting and testing—as indicative of data-driven analytics. Seeking to move beyond mass messages to differentiated audiences, scholars have highlighted how data (at the individual and aggregate level) can be used to identify particular target groups with shared characteristics. Accounts therefore describe parties engaging in micro-targeting by "using data to craft and deliver strategic messages to subsets of the electorate (historically across many different media)" (Kreiss 2017, 3–4). Others similarly reflect that "[t]argeting voters is about (a) collecting data and dividing voters into segments based on characteristics such as personality traits, interests, background or previous voting behaviour; (b) designing personalized political content for each segment; and (c) using communication channels to reach the targeted voter segment with these tailor-made messages" (IDEA 2018, 10).

Similar trends are evident in literature on testing. Baldwin-Philippi (2016, 28–29) argues that testing is one of the key features of the new era of DDC. Describing a "culture of analytics" that goes beyond targeting, she argues that "tests on particular messages may tell campaigns a lot about which message or tactic works in a particular moment," but they can also "build knowledge throughout the lifecycle of a campaign." Although other scholars have spoken extensively about various forms of A/B testing or split testing (Chester & Montgomery 2017; Nadler et al. 2018), once again what processes underpin testing and when these processes are undertaken remain a "black box."

A key limitation of existing work is the excessive focus on analytics being used for subversive campaign practices. This narrative ignores the potential suite of practices for which parties use analytics. Understanding analytics as useful for less nefarious purposes allows scholars to better grasp the effect on organizations such as political parties and the potential challenges for liberal democracy. Indeed, if we move away from thinking about sensationalized accounts of analytics in US presidential contests, a more complex picture emerges. For example, there is an expanding scholarship which shows that political parties are interested in using analytics to experimentally determine the effects of campaign messaging (Pons 2016; Pons 2018; Jungherr et al. 2020). Hence, the utility of analytics is not simply to develop models to engage in manipulative practices (Gorton 2016), but, as some have started to suggest, is part of a broader move toward evidence-based and scientific approaches to decision-making that have the potential to advance democratic goals such as citizen engagement and literacy (Römmele & Gibson 2020).

As in the previous chapter, we also seek to emphasize that many of the analytical processes we observe are not new. While digital technology may have facilitated new forms of data analytics, and campaigns may have emphasized their significance (Issenberg 2012a, 2012b; Kreiss 2012), parties in advanced democracies have utilized various analytical techniques since at least the 1970s (Panebianco 1988; Negrine & Papathanassopoulos 1996; Norris 2000; Gibson & Römmele 2001; Farrell 2006; Negrine 2007; Vaccari 2013;). The role of analytics in campaign organization therefore needs to be understood as evolution more than revolution (Kreiss 2016; Epstein 2018).

Analytics: Processes and Functions

As described in the literature above, analytics is often discussed in abstract terms, with considerable conflation and confusion about the various terms used and opacity about the process that each form of analysis actually takes. To demystify this topic, we build on existing academic analyses about targeting and testing but we have added a third analytics technique—segmentation—which is often conflated or collapsed into discussions of targeting. We suggest that despite the obvious connections, segmentation reflects a different set of processes which can be employed independently of targeting.

Segmentation, targeting, and testing are long-standing components of campaigning in advanced democracies, utilized to maximize the efficiency and effectiveness of campaign goals and to inform strategic decision-making. Differentiating between the three components, we see segmentation as referring to the practice of dividing a given population into groups or individuals; targeting as enacting a given campaign action to a specific rather than a generic audience; and testing as scrutinizing and evaluating the efficacy of a given intervention. A party can therefore use segmentation to identify key seats or persuadable audiences, without triggering targeted communication. Furthermore, we recognize that each type of activity can be used to inform internal or external campaign activity (for example, analysis of data derived from a party's membership or the wider electorate) and can be deployed to advance different campaign goals (for example, fundraising, mobilization, or persuasion).

Examples of different analytics processes can be found in Table 4.1, where we seek to show how each type of activity can vary in terms of complexity. Conceptualized here as a spectrum, we focus our attention on the simplest and most complex analytics practices but recognize a range of activity between these points. Below we first introduce the points of differentiation between our categories, then in the latter part of this chapter we return to our cases to show variation in the types of analytics techniques observed.

Beginning with segmentation, we suggest not only that this activity is distinct from targeting and testing, but also that it can be done with varying degrees of sophistication. In its simplest forms, this activity involves the sorting of a range of simple and easily accessible data. Such sorting can often be based on "gut instinct" rather than scientific insight, or it can involve some basic sorting and filtering. To give an example, data from the electoral roll in

Table 4.1 Examples of Different Analytics Practices

	Segmentation	Targeting	Testing
Simple	Segmenting voter lists by demographic or geographic characteristics	Targeting large groups of voters with little differentiation in messaging	Testing campaign messaging or policies on focus groups or without any A/B testing or randomization or controls
Highly complex	Creating turnout, supporter, or persuadability scores for citizens based on statistical or computational techniques which draw on diverse data points	Targeting small groups of voters with highly differentiated messaging	Randomized controlled trials which measure the effect of campaign interventions such as GOTV canvassing on Election Day

the United Kingdom can be used for simple segmentation analysis to identify first-time voters by filtering according to electors' date of maturation information (i.e., the date they become eligible to vote). Segmentation is, however, not always this simplistic. What differentiates these more complex activities is the use of statistical techniques, the combining of multiple data points, and/or the use of modeling techniques.

In particular, work undertaken by external organizations such as Experian is indicative of highly complex segmentation practices. This process often involves combining multiple forms of data to infer insights about a particular group. As one interviewee from Experian described, they use geographic data alongside "lifestyle factors, so age, household composition, life stage, ethnicity" to build up a multifaceted picture of a particular group. This data can be used to identify geographic areas where individuals with certain attributes are likely to reside—for example, in the United Kingdom, areas likely to be populated by "students" or "pensioners" were extrapolated from party files (Webber 2006; Anstead 2017). It can also be used to develop voter types and personas that characterize multiple points of data. More complex segmentation techniques can also rely on statistical techniques such as regression that are used to identify particular demographic characteristics which may be perceived as significant correlates of support for a particular party or how persuadable a citizen may be to party platform or messaging.

Complex segmentation can also involve predictive modeling, and especially the use of computational techniques to analyze data. This often involves combining data to generate a score indicating how likely a citizen is to turn out, or to vote for one party over another, or how persuadable they are likely to be (Castleman 2016). What is common to these different kinds of modeling is the combination of multiple forms of data to attempt to highlight previously unseen patterns (Tufekci 2014). One specific form of modeling increasingly employed is multilevel regression and poststratification (MRP), a statistical technique used to understand and to develop predictions about sub-populations of the electorate (Hanretty 2020). This can enhance insights from data and analytics, as many advanced democracies contain regional, cultural, or social variations which traditional research operations may be unable to understand at a level of sufficient granularity. MRP is now used in a number of advanced democracies, by polling organizations such as YouGov (Wong 2019), academics trying to understand public opinion (Ghitza & Gelman 2013; Gelman et al. 2018), and increasingly by political parties to improve their modeling and analytics processes (Waters 2019).

As mentioned above, targeting activity is informed by segmentation as a chosen audience is identified to receive a particular message. At any level of sophistication, targeting involves delivering campaign messages, online or offline, to groups of voters of varying sizes. These groups may be based on age, geography, ethnicity (although use of this specific category of data is banned in certain jurisdictions), or any number of other factors, drawing on the different types of data outlined in the previous chapter. Targeting can be undertaken for many reasons including attempts to engage and deliver particular messages to specific groups of voters, and efforts to target resources (especially when spending limits are in place). When classifying targeting techniques in terms of sophistication, we see simple practices to include broad-based appeals to large segments of the population based on generic demographic or geographic characteristics such as gender or region.

At the other end of the spectrum, highly complex targeting is still focused on groups; however, the size of these groups is likely to be smaller, and targeting will rely on multiple characteristics, usually as a result of inferences derived from various datasets. An example of this is when parties identify multiple target groups in a single area and deliver different messages that reflect the attributes and/or interests of those in different parts of the area. One house may therefore receive a piece of direct mail about the environment, while their neighbor receives a letter about school provision, depending on who lives at each address. When highly complex targeting activity is undertaken, we tend to witness targeted messaging aimed at small groups of citizens, and see multiple variants of different, differentiated messages. This is particularly associated with digital communication methods, but as the above example shows, can also occur offline.

Finally, turning to our third analytical technique, testing, we differentiate this analytical process by its focus on scrutinizing and evaluating the efficacy of a given intervention. Testing can be used for a range of different purposes, including testing campaign messages, website functionality, or to evaluate the success of different calls to action. Differentiating forms of testing in terms of sophistication, we categorize simple testing to involve practices such as collecting data on engagement online or informally asking citizens their responses to messaging. These simple techniques involve minimal use of scientific methods to test given interventions. In contrast, highly complex testing involves more complex scientific techniques This can include the use of A/B testing to evaluate how different segmentations respond to different campaign interventions, placements, target groups, and delivery-optimization strategies. Alternatively, it could involve the use of techniques such as randomized controlled trials (RCTs) that aim to understand the effect of campaign interventions on particular sub-populations. RCTs are often considered the most effective way to test campaign interventions as they rely on scientific methods that enable campaigns to delineate the effects of interventions without relying on inferences or proxies for the effects.

The Different Use of Data Analytics across Our Five Advanced Democracies

Having outlined these points of differentiation, in what follows we provide an overview of parties' analytics practices in action. Drawing on this typology, we reveal the varied ways in which these different analytical techniques are utilized. Once again, our aim is not to describe all practices, but rather to use illustrative examples from each context to highlight commonalities and differences in country- and party-level practices.

Segmentation

Interviewees in each of our countries, and from across the party spectrum, described sorting information—often within their voter databases—to produce a "selection" of electors or members with specific attributes. In essence, this involves organizing collected information to reveal specific attributes about a population that shares certain traits (Davidson & Binstock 2011; Mattinson 2011). The segmentation processes we witnessed covered the full spectrum of complexity, ranging from those completely devoid of scientific methods—often based on "gut feel" or local knowledge about booths or areas in the electorate—to those relying on machine learning models or employing MRP. Across our five cases, the only case that was significantly different was Germany. Parties in Germany were the least likely to employ highly complex segmentation processes, which appears to be a product of the regulatory environment. Comparing party practices, we found a general trend of major parties exhibiting more highly complex forms of segmentation, with minor parties often appearing to struggle to invest in such techniques. Yet, interestingly, we also found varied practices within the same party, observing party grassroots using simple segmentation techniques, while central offices used both simple and highly complex techniques.

A major source of variation across our cases was the difference in techniques used by minor and major parties. In Australia, for example, we found that minor parties such as the Greens often relied on basic segmentation processes. As one interviewee disclosed:

> When we are competitive in House races, we are commonly drawing on very basic analyses like, well our vote is very strong in this area of the electorate based on the reported booth results and it's weak at that end. How do we want to structure our campaign, do we start at the strong or the weak end. We also rely on some basic analyses on what the field campaign tells us. So if our volunteers consistently provide information that suggests certain cohorts are persuadable, we take that into account, but I don't think we really even do that in any sort of meaningful way yet.

The Greens' ability to utilize more complex techniques was severely curtailed by the resources at their disposal, although there was an attempt to increase the sophistication of the practices they were employing, and supporter scores were increasingly being developed, as was common in the major parties. However, the major parties still used a wider range of segmentation processes, which were, in the main, more sophisticated.

The means by which these segmentations were secured did, however, differ. The Liberal Party, which has extremely close ties to C|T Group, relies very heavily on the qualitative and quantitative insights from external providers and has leveraged these ties to undertake segmentation work for them. In particular, C|T often provided lifestyle segments not dissimilar to that produced by organizations such as Experian. As one example, an interviewee from the Liberal Party digital team spoke about using these consumer segments to inform targeting strategy, explaining: "It was based on market research from CrosbyTextor, which was as broad as, 'We've got to target ute men.' Well, what do ute men look like? Well, you know, guys who like cars." In addition to using these broad, group-based segments, we found evidence that the Liberal Party is attempting to increase the sophistication of their segmentation processes by commissioning external actors to conduct predictive modelling.

In contrast, the Australian Labor Party has over the course of a decade developed a set of internal practices and processes that enable party personnel to often—though not always—engage in highly sophisticated segmentation processes. The party has a predictive model operation developed by both internal and external data scientists which includes developing supporter and persuadability scores (Kefford 2021). Since the 2019 federal election, Labor has also been using MRP. One interviewee explained its use in the following way:

> MRP is basically a model-based approach to seat-by-seat polling. We did that for the first time ever in 2019. The point of it was to really build out our predictive models of vote intention to incorporate more different variables, looking at things like attitudes towards different issues.

As shown below, these differences between minor and major parties were widely found, but in Australia we saw these analytics techniques being used for particular purposes that reflect the systematic dynamics of the country. The nature of the electoral system and the use of compulsory voting saw parties of all sizes use segmentation techniques to identify groups for persuasion strategies rather than mobilization (a strategy which contrasted to the use of segmentation for mobilization and persuasion in our other countries).

In the United Kingdom, segmentation was commonly used to identify target seats and groups, reflecting the single-plurality electoral system. Parties accordingly focused on supporter mobilization and, to a certain degree, persuasion in key marginal districts as a strategy for securing electoral success. As one interviewee from the Liberal Democrats described, segmentation was used for a range of activities, with parties undertaking "segmentation in terms of whether people are likely to vote, whether people are likely to be swing voters . . . whether they're likely to be donors . . . whether they're likely to be Remain or Leave."

Within the United Kingdom, all parties use simple processes to some degree. Especially among local activists, we saw simple segmentation focused on identifying supporters or non-voters in efforts to effectively focus campaign resources on mobilizing electorally significant voters. More highly complex practices were also commonly encountered, but these were evident largely within the major parties and were the preserve of party staff or external consultants. Interviewees from the Labour Party therefore described using multiple data points and statistical techniques to segment voters using disclosed and inferred data points. One explained:

> We have the marked register; we often append extra data to that. Then on top of that we can do large-scale modeling of the entire UK population. Once you've got a lot of recent data of who is voting Labour and then you've got some kind of socioeconomic benchmark that you can use as your constant, and in our case it was Experian's Mosaic, you could turn round and say, O61s, which are Experian's socioeconomic profile. It used to be young people at university living in university towns or in student accommodation and therefore that was their Experian's socioeconomic profile. And that would often say things like they're more likely to be social media users, less likely to have a car, more likely to read these websites, less likely to read these things. But once we've canvassed so many O61s and we know that this percentage of O61s are voting Labour, we can make a fairly accurate prediction that if there are uncontacted O61s there is a very high chance they're voting Labour. . . . And during the course of an election, it's obviously not unusual that you would have a tracker poll so that you could update your target groups as you went. If at the beginning of a campaign you thought this was your target universe, but then you start seeing shifts, it makes it much easier to be responsive to what's happening. That very much did happen in 2017 when we saw Tory vote collapsing in some groups. It

was very clear we needed to put some pressure on those voters to either not vote or not vote Tory and a growing swell of support for Labour meant it increased the size of our universe.

Another described how ahead of a general election they would routinely "produce predictive work using MRP modeling to estimate what we think was likely to happen." Parties often worked with external companies or academics on this process, but Labour developed internal capacity in 2019 to conduct this form of analysis. In both the Labour Party and the Conservative Party, we also heard accounts of companies such as Experian using numerous data points to "build models to score out an individual household or street's attitude to certain policies"; these scores focused on "the political hot buttons if you like, whether it be Brexit, or whether it be attitudes to unemployment, or local issues, national issues, regional issues, all sorts of things like that." The precise models and segments used by each UK party did vary, but the essential techniques were relatively consistent, as was the goal of identifying supporters and geographically important "swing voters." Parties' ability to deploy these techniques did, however, vary, with the Liberal Democrats reliant on a single MRP poll (Kearns & Alexander 2020).

In Canada, the same approaches were utilized. At the most basic level, widespread use of simple segmentation processes was evident. Often used by grassroots campaigners, or relied on by minor parties, we heard examples of simple segmentation used to inform GOTV activity. One interviewee from the NDP therefore outlined how "we definitely want to touch our supporters first and that's kind of how I build my data. . . . I don't know how anybody else does it, but it's pretty informal, I've talked to a lot of people. I use that map, I look at the ridings [and work out] where do we have the most supporters." As in the United Kingdom, segmentation was also used to identify geographically significant areas in which to focus campaign activity. One interviewee therefore explained how "if you're a riding that we know we can win, you're a Tier A. If you're a riding we're worried about, you're a Tier B." Such simple classifications were used, as in the United Kingdom, to inform investment of campaigning effort and resources.

Within the major Canadian parties, we more commonly heard about more highly complex practices that reflected the same principles. One interviewee in the Liberal Party explained:

> Effectively, what we're trying to do is find a faster way to identify our supporters, right? An election campaign in Canada lasts 36 days to 50 days, that's the law. Generally speaking they last about 40ish days. So you can imagine trying to canvass the entire country in that period is quite difficult. That being said, we do canvass between elections and so on and so forth. So what we're actually trying to do is just create efficiencies of where are our supporters and how quickly can we find them? What is the quickest route to identifying and finding them? And how does it represent itself? It's a list that we provide to local ridings saying, "Call these people, they're more likely to be Liberal than they are to be anybody else. . . . oftentimes it's just the basis of their previous support. A bit of the census data that's overlaid on it. . . . But overall it's primarily driven off of our previous identification of those individuals.

Liberal interviewees specifically spoke of the use of modeling to identity supporters, explaining that this work was done by central party staff, but they were more reticent about the utility of persuadability scores. As one interviewee noted:

> The likeliness of being a supporter is a list we generate for the local riding. Our technology allows us to make it plug and play, they don't need to do too much of their own work on that. Leave the analysis to us and you guys execute the work, because we can do it for the entire country. And the persuadability stuff, I haven't seen a ton of really successful persuadability stuff. Again, it comes back to having enough data inputs to know that this person is truly persuadable. And I don't know the political culture of other countries that well, but in Canada, people will tell you they're a supporter or they're not your supporter. And then, trying to get that fine tooth of who actually is persuadable that's a little bit more nuanced.

According to interviewees, much of this work for the Liberal Party was undertaken by Data Sciences Inc., thereby reinforcing what we see in most of our other cases, namely, that the type of sophisticated segmentation and modeling work is often facilitated by external expertise.

The United States—especially presidential contests—exhibits simple and highly complex segmentation techniques used by a range of different actors. In terms of rather basic segmentation techniques, US campaigns create their own and/or purchase simple segmentation groups from external providers that divide voters into different groups (e.g., Tunnl n.d.). Another standard approach is simply to model turnout in comparable past elections (as recorded in voter files) to make inferences about who is most likely to turn out in the next election (Castleman 2016; Jungherr et al. 2020). However, US campaigns also partition voters into increasingly specialized and specific segments or complex characteristics, such as a voter's persuadability, subjective beliefs, psychometrics, or similar categories that can describe the voter with increasing specificity. For this, models may use multiple questions in aggregate or may estimate treatment effects from randomized experimental tests (Castleman 2016; Hersh 2015; Issenberg 2012b; Nickerson & Rogers 2014). US campaigns append the resulting "scores" to the voter file for targeting since they represent estimated probabilities (of supporting a candidate or turning out to vote, for example). As described by David Shor (2021), reflecting on the Democratic campaign in 2020, "the basic idea is that we do all the surveys, we join all the data, we fit it to the model, and we score the file."

Dan Castleman (2016), co-founder at Clarity Campaign Labs—a consultancy firm offering data analytics services to campaigners—has spoken of how these approaches are extending beyond the high-profile contests:

> We have been working on enhancing our methods for providing accurate and useful models for not just presidential and statewide campaigns but for smaller campaigns as well (such as those for state legislature or local offices). To help these down-ballot campaigns in 2016, the Democratic National Committee has put together a suite of "off the shelf" models available to all their campaigns nationwide, and we at Clarity have been working on finding ways for multiple smaller campaigns to pool their resources and develop customized models that wouldn't otherwise be affordable or feasible.

An established network of data analytics firms and expertise is therefore evident in the United States and is increasingly leveraged by down-ballot campaigns.

In Germany, the use of a mixed electoral system influences the segmentation (and targeting) process—in contrast to the United Kingdom and Canada, and similar to Australia—and means that parties need to combine nationwide engagement with a more focused approach in electorally significant districts in order to increase their overall vote share beyond the districts in which they tend to be strong. This results in parties focusing on probability scores for the party-mobilization potential of voters living in geographical regions, such as constituencies or streets. Further, due to Germany's multi-party system and the potential for coalition formation after the election, parties need to factor in second-order effects, such as the preferences of voters for other parties.

Comparing the segmentation approaches evident in our other cases with Germany, sophisticated techniques appear to be less prominent as a product of the regulatory constraints on parties. As one SPD strategist clarified:

> There is a framework called data protection law, and it lays down certain rules within which you can and should and must and want to act. And thus the basic rule is always segmentation instead of individualization. So I work in segments, but I don't know which data or which personal data are in which segments. In addition, I never collect profiles about any people or build up any profiles, which means I never know that Ernie Müller drives a specific car and uses the toothpaste at Meyerstrasse 33, but I only know that there are people with certain characteristics in certain areas who may be more likely to respond to my messages than other people. In other words, the basic rule is segmentation and, ultimately, transparency—in other words, adhering to data protection in such a way that someone who asks for their data can get it at any time. And someone who signs a petition with us or signs the newsletter must also be clearly informed about what happens to the things we then do.

Likewise, a campaign strategist of the German Christian Democrats pointed out:

> It is not to say that parties in Germany do not try to analyze voter data at all. But their approach consists of historical-geographical election analyses and rough socio-demographic assessments, such as women over 60 in catholic areas are x percent likely to vote CDU. So we rely on classic target group analyses based on sinus milieus, i.e., typification of people according to social situation and basic orientation combined with expanded voter potentials.

Thus, while there are some similar institutional drivers in Germany as in our other cases, we see different manifestations of analytics.

Noting the influence of regulatory constraints, it is worth highlighting parties' ability to utilize sophisticated segmentation techniques—as well as targeting and testing practices—via social networking platforms. In particular, parties in all five of our countries were able to draw on Facebook and its algorithmic advertising ecosystem which compiles and analyzes hundreds of data points gathered from its users (for example, profile information, interaction histories, reactions of other users, features of content) to identify suitable recipients for political advertisers' paid media messages (Andreou et al. 2019; Kruschinski & Bene 2022). This segmentation capacity currently lies outside of European and national legislation (Harker 2020). This means that legally restricted European parties can "circumvent" existing regulations by "outsourcing" prohibited marketing practices to Facebook.

Targeting

Targeting, especially micro-targeting, is valorized and demonized in equal parts in popular commentary about political communication. The reality is often far less interesting or influential than is often claimed. Nonetheless, it remains a key dimension of analytics and DDC more generally and is ubiquitously used across our cases. For the most part, it was striking how widely evident simple targeting practices were, with parties focused on identifying certain broad groups of people with valuable characteristics and engaging in limited message differentiation. Indeed, reflecting on talking to other campaign professionals in other countries about targeting, one interviewee noted that they had "been often astonished at how similar the basic fundamentals really are," noting that "what many political campaigners found is that actually their target audiences were wider than they had imagined them to be." We did, however, observe variation, and found some examples of parties attempting to target citizens on a more personalized basis, and using differentiated messaging.

In Australia, in line with the previous discussion on segmentation, targeting practices ranged from the simple to highly complex. Doorknocking operations, in the main, did not involve targeting for any of the parties, while phone-banking was more targeted. This did, however, vary by party, with the major parties drawing on greater resources to use predictive modeling to maximize efficiencies. Digital campaigns for all the parties drew on the Facebook advertising system, and then most parties engaged external consultants to work on targeting and to manage ad buys in different channels such as YouTube and Google. Targeting online was often moderately sophisticated, with targets usually identified by broad demographic or attitudinal characteristics or based on personas from market research; however, as with segmentation, offline there was more differentiation. Here is where Labor's superiority in the predictive modeling space was most evident, with voters targeted at the individual level based on perceptions of their preferences and persuadability to campaign messaging (Kefford 2021). Interviewees from the Liberal Party suggested there were several reasons why they were not engaged in fine-grained targeting like Labor and the extent of resources was frequently noted, as was skepticism about whether it provided the necessary value-add given the institutional dynamics in Australia.

In the United Kingdom, targeting strategies varied across different parties. In many instances we saw parties employ wide-ranging messages delivered to large target groups. These strategies did not necessarily reflect the kind of resource constraints that affected segmentation processes, but often reflected strategic decisions. At the 2019 General Election, for example, the Conservatives eschewed highly individualized messaging in favor of broad appeals on digital advertising. Similarly, an interviewee in the Labour Party reflected that "in reality, a lot of the targeting that I think is the most effective is probably actually a lot more straightforward" and focused on broad demographic groups.

This approach was not, however, uniform, and we did find examples of narrower targeting and more differentiated messaging. In the Labour Party, for example, one interviewee described how they:

> had a tool to, basically, an algorithm that would then determine whether certain streets or certain individuals in certain streets would be targeted on certain campaign activities, depending on where you were in the campaign cycle, depending on when you last visited those individuals in that street, depending on things like the Labour propensity and turnout propensity and things like that.... They would click on an area that was high priority in this tool, for instance, then they would be able to target the individuals that we have identified as ideal targets, depending on where we were in the campaign.

Such insights were used to send targeted mail, online advertising, or to guide phone or doorstep canvassing activities. In particular, social media was widely used, with interviewees from large and small parties describing how they used tools on Facebook to identify targets by uploading lists, using Facebook's "look-alike audiences" function and by filtering according to Facebook targeting parameters.

Within the United Kingdom, while targeting was often evident in more sophisticated forms, we rarely observed the most highly complex applications where individual-level data was used to produce numerous personalized messages. Instead, as one interviewee in the Liberal Democrat Party reflected: "It's definitely still essentially about group-based targeting, so even though you generate some individual-level scores. But you'd still basically be like, 'Right, well these voters will get this message, and these will get that message,' it didn't get sophisticated down to the individual level, not for the Liberal Democrats, no." Similarly, Labour interviewees spoke about using:

> very traditional targeting groups. It would be things like Lib Dem squeeze. These are Lib Dems that we think we can get to vote for us tactically by going, "Only a vote for Labour can stop the Tories." Very traditional squeeze message. The difference is that we could run that audience for seats where we knew the Lib Dems had enough of a vote that it could be important, where it could make the difference and identify people who are either Lib Dem in the database or modeled to the "very likely think about voting Lib Dem."

Explaining this trend, interviewees mentioned the logistical and resource challenges of creating multiple messages for multiple small audiences. One interviewee reflected that "the complexity of that kind of targeting and campaigning is just hugely labor intensive in a world and universe where ... as well-resourced as Labour is in comparison to some other organizations, it's not like we had a whole team of people building ads for us, who could do these things." Interviewees also highlighted risks associated with sophisticated targeting activity (concerns that were also articulated in Australia). As one Conservative interviewee in the United Kingdom pointed out, "one big thing that I've learned and definitely carried forward is that there is such a thing as too targeted, too segmented." While another in the Labour Party recounted:

> We had instances in not the last general election but the one before in 2010, where we were really, really good at micro-targeting and we sent out a

mail shot to people about cancer care services. I'm sure you may have seen some.... Some people got the wrong end of the stick and thought we had access to data because a lady who unfortunately had cancer thought that we were targeting her because we knew and we had access to her medical records. She was furious about it. Of course, it was nonsense. We had no idea who had cancer... we just targeted a particular segment of the population who was likely to be affected by this. It was a big problem for us. The Tories immediately said, "Oh, Labour were abusing this data that they've got by nefarious means," which was completely untrue.

Such examples revealed a caution about the backfire effects of targeting (Hersh & Schaffner 2013), but they also reveal a faith in the power of basic data points. As one interviewee pointed out:

these basic core components of the basic demographics, again, voting pattern behavior, are probably the most important data you could look at. And those are fairly broad demographic categories, are typically very useful and very effective at everything you need to do. So why would you go further?

In practice, these attitudes meant we observed few examples of this form of fine-grained targeting in action in the United Kingdom.

In Canada, as in our other cases, targeting ranged from the simple to the highly complex. In terms of simple practices, we often saw parties focusing on broad messages targeted at large groups of voters. One interviewee in the NDP therefore described how they conducted a day of action focused on stopping the privatization of healthcare and targeted their activities to previously contacted individuals who "have signed any petition that has to do with healthcare and those are the people you're going to focus on." Similarly, one interviewee from the Liberal Party said that for their Facebook targeting:

we'd have to look at how many supporters we have versus how many supporters we don't in each area and then kind of gauge it from there.... Basically we gathered data from the last election and anybody that was a two; we gathered that data and then we focused on Facebook. We had your name and... we used your postal code and we focused ads targeting your postal code based on what your support level was. That's kind of what we would use the data for.

Highlighting the complexities that federalism brings to understanding DDC, one interviewee from the NDP also said that there were often multiple targeting strategies employed simultaneously and these were not often that well-coordinated. Local campaigns are often layering messaging on top of provincial, regional, or national campaigns. To what degree this happens depends on a range of factors, including what level of priority the area is given and the resources the organization has. According to an NDP interviewee: "[f]or our riding, we're a target riding, so we have the resources that staff could analyze that. But there may be a smaller riding that just relies on volunteers for that. So it's probably a mix."

In the United States, the situation is also mixed. While it is true that presidential campaigns since 2008 have often invested heavily in personnel and data to engage in targeted messaging, the messaging is often targeted at broad groups. Dan Castleman (2016, 3f.), for example, has noted:

> When targeting voters who are highly likely to turn out and support their candidate ("base supporters"), campaigns will seek financial contributions and recruit volunteers. Those with high support but uncertain likelihood of voting become targets for "get-out-the-vote" efforts to increase their turnout. And those with uncertain support will be targeted for persuasion. For the remaining voters—those highly likely to support the opponent—a campaign's limited resources are best spent elsewhere, as these voters are not very likely to respond to the campaign's efforts.

It therefore appears that strategic decisions are being made by well-financed campaigns to focus on broad groups, but it should be noted that other down-ballot races appear to adopt the same strategy (of broad targeting approaches) due to a lack of resources that prevents them from contemplating more fine-grained, targeted approaches (Baldwin-Philippi 2017).

The granularity of targeting in the United States also depends on the channels used, such as direct mailing, telephone, and door-to-door canvassing, or TV and social media advertising. For door-to-door canvassing, studies show that the issues, party positions, or candidate competencies covered in conversations can vary by election, voter, and constituency (Green & Gerber 2019; Nielsen 2012). For example, Green & Gerber (2019, 27), Nielsen (2012, 71), and Hersh (2015, 26) provide insight into how speech scripts or short questionnaires with different conversation openers and "talking points" on issues or candidates are used by US campaigns for different voter segments, resulting in different targeted conversations. There is also evidence of different target groups being given messages on particular issues of known interest, such as COVID-19 vaccinations or abortion rights (Tunnl n.d.).

While there has been significant media coverage of US campaigns running extremely granular targeting, there is some reason to question such depictions. In 2019 the Trump digital campaign is widely depicted to have run 218,000 ads on Facebook which were made up of "1,840 distinct versions of ad copy, of which the campaign ran anywhere from one to more than 3,000 versions" (Wong 2020, n.p.). But even in this example, the evidence points to the fact that the Trump campaign drew on Facebook's so-called dynamic ads, in which the selection and delivery of ad versions is based entirely on the platform's algorithmic automation and not on human labor (Ali et al. 2021; Crain & Nadler 2019). Indeed, Andrew Bosworth, the former Facebook executive in charge of the advertising platform, suggested in a private memo that Trump's 2016 election victory and his approach to Facebook after that "weren't microtargeting or saying different things to different people. They just used the tools we had to show the right creative to each person" (quoted in *New York Times* 2020, n.p.). Targeting is therefore evident in many different forms in the United States, but is not always, or indeed often, conducted in its most sophisticated forms.

In Germany, targeting practices differed between parties but are generally situated between simple or rather complex approaches. With regard to the canvassing operations of the bigger parties, they use argumentation cards or talking points which are less adapted to the attitudes, interests, or behavior of individual voters visited, but primarily cover the day-to-day problems or core issues of the parties and candidates in the canvassed constituencies. Thus, German canvassing campaigns mostly draw on geographic analyses to calculate the most promising constituencies for door-knocking without knowing anything specific about individual voters behind the doors. This is explained by a German strategist of the CDU:

> Our targeting in canvassing is highly coarse. In terms of data-protection law, the information about the voters may only be done on the size of a so-called microcell. It is not about the individual person or the individual household. Rather, a microcell consists of an average of 6.6 households. If you think for a moment about which people live in the six households in your immediate neighborhood, you can imagine how precise our targeting is.

For targeting online, we could witness that all parties draw on Facebook advertising. However, the targeting strategies were not uniform, and we found examples of narrower and more differentiated voter targeting. The SPD used Facebook ads in the 2017 federal election to target geographic regions and demographic groups with overarching messages but some individual adjustments. As one interviewee explained: "at the beginning we had an assumption of what the target group might look like later on, but because you can also control everything very nicely via the manager, we actually made it very individualized and very different from case to case. But our resources are very restricted so that we cannot create multiple fine-grained messages for all our voters." The CDU made a digital advertising campaign for each constituency in the 2017 federal election. Here, the CDU constructed audiences of mobilizable and persuadable voters for specific topics and campaign times by drawing on Facebook's core targeting options (age, gender, income, geography, work, behavior, and interests). The parties' perceptions of these voters on Facebook are based on voter analysis from milieu studies, polling, and audience analytics. Splitting voters into conservatives, mainstream, performer, and undecided, voters were targeted with distinct ads on Facebook and Instagram. However, only the platform's basic targeting techniques were used without uploading voter data for building "custom audiences" due to data-protection concerns. As one interviewee from CDU noted:

> So we haven't done custom audiences. I would like to do it, but we are not allowed to. There is a judgment from Bavaria, that it is quasi-illegal in Germany. I haven't created look-alikes yet either, because at some point I didn't see the point of completely exhausting everything. What we used was pure geo-targeting. But as a result, the two big campaigns where 60,000 euros flowed in, we used pure geo-targeting. So we simply selected the zip code, people who live there and speak German. Nothing more.

The smaller parties of the Greens and Liberals also made heavy use of Facebook targeting but were restricted by their budget and personnel, which led to not only a mix of very basic messaging to coarse audiences, but also ads with more tailored content. The Greens described their approach in the 2018 Hessian State election as follows:

> We wanted to provide content for all different target groups and are proud to say for the first time in our party's history, that we use the Facebook

targeting system excessively. For each motif, for each poster, or ad we have used up to 17 different audiences to which we wanted to play this out. Here, we not only wanted to reach our core voters or supporters but also people who are not on the line with our policies. In the end of the day we wanted all the people who are either directly affected in some way by our policies to see us, what we have up our sleeve for them. That's maybe good to illustrate with ads for people who are stuck in traffic jams or are pure meat eater. Our goal was that all of the target groups should see our message at minimum three times in the end.

However, smaller parties, such as the Left, described the problems of implementing fine-grained targeting, due to limited resources which restricted their ability to make use of it even on Facebook.

Testing

If we understand analytics as consisting of segmenting, targeting, and testing, the evidence points toward testing as the least ubiquitous and sophisticated across our advanced democracies. There are potentially a range of reasons for this: the domination in online communication of the technology companies, including the functionality and personnel they can provide to evaluate engagement campaign interventions; and the challenges of rigorously testing in the offline communication environment. Nonetheless, the evidence about testing—or lack thereof—paints a very different picture of DDC than the one we are often presented in popular commentary.

In Australia, testing could at best be described as uneven and routinely unsophisticated. While the major parties engage in unsophisticated message testing via qualitative research such as focus groups, and moderately sophisticated A/B testing on digital campaigns, sophisticated testing is rarer. However, there was some evidence this was changing, and again Labor was leading the way in this regard. In addition to their use of MRP for the first time in the 2019 federal election, the party started to take the use of RCTs more seriously. Labor interviewees spoke of an increased emphasis on conducting experiments when the contexts and conditions were right to generate new insights for campaign interventions.

One of these experiments happened in 2015 when an election was held for the House of Representatives seat of Canning in Western Australia. Working with an associated trade union, Labor designed a turnout experiment to take place on Election Day. As one Labor data operative explained:

> We decided to run an experiment in the most densely populated, most Labor part of the electorate. Our volunteers knocked on doors on Election Day and said, "Hey, there's a [sic] election on. Go out and vote." And they only did it to people who were likely to be Labor voters.... So we drew up a universe, half of them got a door-knock on the day from United Voice, half of them got nothing, and then after the election we checked the turnout— the list of people that turned out to see what effect that had and we thought, "Look, it's compulsory voting, right? People are going to turn out regardless." Among households that we attempted to door-knock—so this includes people who were not home and we had no effect on—the turnout was 4.5 percent higher for those households than the half we didn't try to contact.

The scope and scale of this experiment, however, are not representative of most testing undertaken in Australia by political parties, with the overwhelming majority being quite simple.

The situation in the United Kingdom was largely similar. Describing processes of "user research," one UK interviewee explained that they conducted "a lot of testing to make sure that what we're providing is useful and interesting to the target audience," but much of this testing was relatively simple. It was common to hear about the use of focus groups to test "slogans and issues." There were, however, some moderately complex methods evident. Interviewees described utilizing A/B testing whereby a control group was used to test the effects of a given intervention. One Labour Party interviewee described:

> spending hundreds upon thousands of pounds getting people to the website. So actually using data to better improve, A, the number of people who signed up and gave us their emails was very important, but then optimizing the next step of the journey, which was asking them for money. A very simple test we ran was things like what color button do we make the "ask"? Which had a surprising increase in the uplift of donations. Or, how did we stack the different donation amounts? Are we better to go 1, 5, and 15, or was it 3, 5, and 10?

A/B testing affordances on social media platforms were also widely utilized, with one interviewee describing how:

> if individuals were in segments, we'd target them through Facebook and then we'd assess with a kind of quasi-experimental kind of A/B testing, whether they respond to certain messages and then that would feed back to the digital team.

We did not observe examples of UK parties themselves conducting the most highly complex testing practices, such as RCTs. In part this was explained by a lack of resources, but it was also due to logistical constraints, with one interviewee noting that it was "much, much harder to do [this kind of] research in the UK (compared to the United States)" because of a need for a large control group. For this reason, parties drew on academic and external expertise—such as that offered by the US-based Analyst Institute—to learn about the outcomes of RCTs conducted elsewhere. Even in parties such as Labour where we saw most evidence of testing, interviewees reflected that "in terms of message testing, actually, that was something that's alarmingly in its infancy and it's something that I've found a bit concerning at times." This practice was therefore by no means commonplace or routine within UK campaigns.

In Canada, evidence suggests that developments are close to the United Kingdom and Australia, but behind in terms of the sophisticated testing that occurs. In explaining this, one interviewee from the Liberal Party suggested:

> Fundraising-wise, again, there's not just enough. People have done A/B tests on subject lines, but it's hard to get a large enough sample group to truly get some results. We pay attention to open rates, because those metrics say a lot about did you have a good subject line? Is the sender a person or someone we would want to open an email from? Then there's click through rates, which are extremely valuable for us to find; to see whether someone actually takes an action so you can adjust the body and the ask. And then they go to your website and whether they actually take an action there, what the ratio is there. You can adjust your landing page. So, that's probably the most valuable testing.

It is thus unsurprising that interviewees spoke more about the role that simple testing played. This included the use of focus groups to test out language and images for target groups, the testing available to them via the technology companies, and small-scale testing around new innovations. For example, an interviewee from the NDP spoke about a new peer-to-peer texting tool the party had been using, and when asked about the testing they were doing around mobilizing supporters, they acknowledged that the testing was "not that sophisticated yet and that's the big goal, is to really make it more robust."

Turning to the United States, the 2012 Obama campaign was especially significant in establishing the idea that testing should be a routine element of campaigning in order to optimize messaging and measure persuadability. However, as Sides and Vavreck (2014, n.p.) note, the idea that the Obama campaign was "testing everything . . . was far from the truth." As they went on to suggest: "Although the Obama campaign was willing to conduct small-scale experiments with fund-raising emails, neither they nor the Romney campaign was conducting large-scale experiments with campaign messages or campaign advertising."

Nonetheless, it is true that in 2012 the Obama campaign did experiment with fundraising emails, and different scripts for volunteers which did lead to some interesting findings, especially around mobilizing donations from supporters (Sides & Vavreck 2014, n.p.). But the most important testing and experimentation was around persuasion-based campaign messaging. As Sides and Vavreck (2014) have noted:

> the Obama campaign randomly assigned a sample of registered voters regardless of party registration to a control group or a treatment group. It then invested a massive amount of volunteer effort—approximately 300,000 phone calls—to reach the treatment group with a message designed to persuade them to vote for Obama. Two days later, the campaign was able to poll about 20,000 of these voters and ask how they planned to vote.

In the years since, evidence suggests there is debate about how ingrained sophisticated testing is, even in these highly resourced campaigns (Baldwin-Philippi 2016; Hutchinson 2020). This is particularly the case for down-ballot races and those less well-resourced campaigns which more closely resemble developments in other advanced democracies. However, out of our five cases, the United States undoubtedly exhibits the highest levels of testing, with multiple elements of campaigns subject to A/B and experimental testing, conducted either in-house or through external platform affordances (Scarvalone 2016; Voigt 2018).

In Germany, evidence suggests that the disconnect between the idealized version of DDC in popular commentary and the reality of testing is pronounced. While there was significant evidence pointing to the role that technology companies play in assisting and administering testing by allowing campaigns to choose budgets dynamically, beyond this, sophisticated testing was far less evident. German parties test several motifs in split target groups, mostly on Facebook or to a lesser extent on their election posters or email newsletters, to see which motif runs better. However, most importantly for testing, German campaigns use focus group approaches, described by one SPD strategist in the following way:

> In the beginning of the campaign, we did a lot of focus groups to see which campaigns and motifs and pictures work well and what people react positively to, what they might be interested in, about what they want to learn more about. And then, of course, campaigns, especially on Facebook, were adjusted to the results.

The reasons for this are mainly due to a lack of resources. One strategist of the Left Party suggested, "We didn't test our campaign material due to time management reasons. Of course, it would be interesting to try that out, but it takes time and personnel to do these kinds of analyses which we don't have." However, another reason which is decisive in limiting the role that testing has in German campaigns is the limited know-how about testing. A strategist from the Green party provided insight into this, noting: "So I would say now quite honestly, so that, how we exactly tested, was not in our area of responsibility. But, I am now personally simply over-questioned about how and if testing worked in our campaign." What is rather done in Germany is an overall campaign evaluation after the campaign, which is more or less extensive depending on how the campaign went. In that regard, a campaign strategist of the SPD explained the usefulness of data for that process:

> Since data always provides the opportunity for evaluation, I think it is now part of the process to get very much into such a mechanism: testing, testing, drawing conclusions, testing again, gaining new insights, in order to ultimately become better and better. And that simply takes time and also a campaign before the campaign, so to speak, and that's why I think it will somehow be a matter of using this time until the next election phase from a campaign point of view. To continue to work on tools, on forms of

strategies, to expand the database and to simply continue in this direction and not to stop now.

Conclusion

In this chapter we have demonstrated the diversity of analytics processes evident across our case studies. In particular, we have developed conceptual understanding of this activity by differentiating between segmentation, targeting, and testing as discrete analytical processes. Through our descriptive case study analysis we have shown that each process can be conducted with different degrees of sophistication, and that it can be undertaken internally by party operatives or by external consultants and vendors. No matter who is undertaking these processes, our evidence suggests that when it comes to analytics, local context and conditions matter, even more so than we found for data.

Summarizing trends within each of our cases, we found that, as with data, the United States is indeed leading the way in terms of sophisticated analytics processes. We found that both major parties utilize complex forms of segmentation, targeting, and testing and that practice in this context is often more advanced than elsewhere. However, we found less evidence of highly segmented targeting than commonly reported, and that alongside more complex techniques, simple means of segmentation, targeting, and testing remain common.

Once again, our analyses of Australia, the United Kingdom, Canada, and Germany revealed not only many commonalities, but also differences, which make it important to focus on practice beyond the United States. In each of these countries our three analytical techniques are widely utilized, but we saw important variations in how they are deployed by different parties. In Australia, for example, segmentation is widely used, but to advance subtly different campaign goals than those pursued in our other cases, and to different degrees of complexity depending on party—with Labor more advanced than others. This narrative was replicated in the United Kingdom and Canada, where we saw clear party divisions in the complexity of segmentation, with minor parties using simpler techniques.

Common across our other four cases was less sophisticated forms of targeting and testing than in the United States. We routinely found that broad messages were utilized by parties of all sizes in these contexts and that there was limited personalized messaging. We did find some evidence of varied testing practices, but it was notable that parties outside the United States were rarely able to conduct RCTs. Where testing was evident, it was again conducted most extensively by major parties, who utilized tools such as focus groups or A/B testing more extensively than minor parties.

Recognizing this variety of practices and the prevalence of (to different extents) both simple and highly complex forms of analytics in our five countries, our analysis points to the significance of systemic, regulatory, and party-level constraints. Frequently our interviewees cited a lack of resources, but we also found electoral dynamics to disincentivize individual-level targeting and regulatory challenges that made more complex forms of analytics challenging to employ. Ultimately, analytics can therefore be enacted in a variety of different ways, showing DDC to be a multifaceted activity.

Practitioner Perspectives on Analytics

The previous chapter has suggested that three forms of analytics are integral to data-driven campaigning: segmentation, targeting, and testing. Varying in degree of sophistication, we have suggested that analytics practices are widely utilized, are not inherently problematic, and primarily are used by campaigns to improve campaign efficiency. To test the resonance of this argument, we asked two practitioners to reflect on the current state of data analytics. Our practitioners are, first, Matthew McGregor, previous director at Blue State Digital,[1] an experienced staffer on campaigns for Barack Obama in the United States, the Labor Party in Australia, and UK Labour. Matthew is also the current CEO of 38 degrees.[2] The second is Campbell White, head of Public Affairs and Polling Asia-Pacific, for YouGov.

We asked them to respond to the following provocation:

A number of media commentators have written about parties' use of data to create models about voters that are able to profile and manipulate voters. In your experience, why do parties produce models, and what objectives do they seek to advance?

Matthew McGregor, Previous Director at Blue State Digital, and Digital Campaign Staffer in the United States, Australia, and the United Kingdom

Over the past 10 years, it is fair to say that the analytics processes used by campaigns are much more sophisticated. Even in the past five years, parties' ability to develop complex demographic models that enable them to make big decisions about messaging, narrative, and also target seats has improved, but the realities of campaign practice are plagued by a number of myths that just don't reflect actual practice.

When it comes to manipulation, the claims are just nonsense. You can think of it like this: Do we have the tools to target voters with more sophisticated communications than we could 10 years ago? Yes. Do we have access to tools that give us a better sense of what messages push people's buttons, in a general sense, than 10 years ago? Yes. Is that information, are those tools, at a level of sophistication that will allow us to manipulate individuals based on things we know about individuals? No, not even close.

The only way to understand the claims around manipulation is to think about what people mean by the word "manipulate." For some people, it is manipulative to use polling or focus groups to find out that people of a certain age are agitated about a particular issue, to hone an effective message, and to deploy those insights to try to solicit a favorable response. But for me, data is used to prioritize, optimize, and improve the salience of particular views. Those methods are used to advance simple campaign goals, such as mobilizing your base, moving low-propensity voters, or trying to win new support—not manipulation.

Another myth I've encountered is around micro-targeting. Across the many campaigns I've worked on, I've seen little evidence that parties can slice and dice and micro-target voters. Although the technical capacity does of course exist, when you look at the practice of campaigns, there isn't fine-grained micro-targeting. The best case of targeting I've even seen was in the 2017 General Election when Jon Cruddas was fighting a far-right candidate in Dagenham. Because of a lack of good data provided by the Labour Party, his campaign used HOPE not Hate data to break his constituency into 27 different segments, and based on the polling, those people got different messaging in their direct mail. So, Labour "Leave" voters all got messaging around law and order, and how strongly Jon felt about law and order. This kind of group-based targeting is as sophisticated as it gets. Parties don't do things like engaging in very, very tailored and targeted Facebook messaging or targeted phone canvassing. The idea that parties have micro-targeted Gary at Number 11, because we've been tracking him; we know he phoned a therapist last Thursday and went to the dentist the day after, all that stuff is horse shit. The reason being, that parties just don't have the resources—in terms of money and staff—to develop such highly differentiated campaigns.

Where I would say there is less hype is around testing. Testing is widely used, it's getting easier, and people are getting better at it. Campaigns of all types routinely put materials in front of focus groups to get people's actual feedback, and tools like A/B testing on Facebook have made a focus on optimization easier than ever before. In my experience there is, however, a substantial difference between what is happening in the United States and elsewhere. Because of the sheer amount of money in US politics, when I was working on the Obama campaign we were able to watch, on a live stream, people viewing our first big hit on Romney and gather real-time data about how people responded. A/B testing was also routine to test our own communications (i.e., email), but also to assess different versions of an ad, live, in Facebook's back end. We also explored salience testing. This involves polling on an issue in an area to get an understanding of where people sit on that topic, selecting one target area, and one control area, and then deluging the target area with messaging on a particular topic to see if it has an effect on attitudes. We were able to spend millions of dollars on TV and digital wraparounds to do this kind of testing, devoting resources that just aren't open to campaigns elsewhere.

Campbell White, Head of Public Affairs and Polling Asia-Pacific, YouGov

It is a cliché to say that there has been a complete revolution in the way polling is used by political campaigns since the turn of the millennium. Twenty years ago, we could generally access much less data about an individual, but arguably the principles of reaching a more representative cross section of the population were better understood and easier to implement—easier to implement, because response rates have declined for traditional survey methods like phone polls, better understood in that samples that are not inherently representative need to be scaled—or modeled—in more innovative ways.

Partially as a result of this, campaigns—and polls—have transitioned from mostly offline settings to predominantly online. A lot of the so-called polling failures we have seen over the past decade—which are not confined solely to public polls, by the way—result from challenges arising from this transition. Put simply, it takes time and a process of trial and error to get new methodologies to perform as well as established ones.

There's another factor related to this, which is probably less understood. The transition to living our lives online is that we have much more choice about our sources of information, and whom we choose to associate with. Thirty years ago, most people consumed news and formed their worldview through fairly consistent sources within their locations. In many Australian towns and cities there was a single print outlet and a limited number of TV networks. Our interactions with other people were largely limited to people who lived near us, who worked with us, or who were related to us.

Unfortunately, we flatter ourselves and our times if we think this diversity has necessarily made us more cosmopolitan or open-minded. On the contrary, the internet has meant that we can be more selective in terms of whom we spend time with, if we choose to do so—and many of us do. If we are very progressive and liberal, we can choose to limit our consumption of media to those that represent our views, and to socialize only with those who share our values. If we're conservative, the same is true. This may seem fairly innocuous, but the end result is that we are becoming more tribal, and the things that delineate our tribes are less about geography but instead more concerned with complex interactions between demographics and beliefs.

Conventional polling and campaigning have relied on fairly simple definitions of voters and their characteristics. Often electorates were treated as though they were internally homogenous rather than containing varying proportions of different tribes. Concepts like a "swing voter" have become less and less useful. Although this is intuitively recognized by campaigns and commentators, settling on something that strikes the balance between being useful, as well as meaningful and replicable, is harder. Frankly, there's a lot more spin out there than substance.

MRP is one approach which is being embraced by more innovative public pollsters and campaign teams; including by the 2022 Australian Labor federal campaign (the MRP for which was run by my team at YouGov). For both, it deals with the problem of having lots of data about individuals but not enough about individual constituencies—certainly not enough to reliably represent those constituencies through conventional methods of analysis. The assumption underlying the technique is that voters who share certain characteristics will make voting choices in similar ways despite living in different electorates.

To the extent that MRP is well known, it is commonly associated with projections of voting intention. I think the real utility of MRP, however, is in helping campaigns understand the tribal composition of the electorates they need to win. Understanding this accurately helps campaigns identify their target audiences, where they are, and how to reach them. Labor's majority in the 2022 election—despite a very challenging environment for major parties—is a testament to the value of techniques like MRP to help campaigns win where it counts.

5
Technology

What makes the data-driven campaign happen? While significant attention has been paid to the sources of data and the analytics techniques used by parties, less has been placed on the infrastructure that facilitates this activity. The technology of DDC can come in many forms. Whether thinking about databases, tools to simplify data collection and inputting, systems for data analysis, or platforms for online communication, technology permeates every aspect of the data-driven campaign. Yet in thinking about these various technological affordances, we lack a framework for thinking about what technology is utilized, and how different tools vary. Within this chapter we explore the ways that technology enables political parties' organizational management and voter communication processes when engaged in DDC. We highlight the potential for technologies to possess low or high functionality (see Figure 5.1), examine the origins and characteristics of these technologies for campaign organization and communication, and demonstrate the potential for parties to exploit their functionality to different degrees.

This chapter will first classify the different technologies that can be used to drive the organization or communication of DDC. We then engage in depth with examples of technology from each category and compare their usage by drawing on our empirical data from each of our fives country cases. We ultimately show that while some parties in some countries use cutting-edge digital tools and employ a range of highly functional technologies, parties rely on "ordinary" or "mundane technologies" with low functionality (Nielsen 2011; Baldwin-Philippi 2017). The reasons for these variations will be explored in the explanatory Chapter 7.

Existing Accounts of the Use of Technology for Campaign Organization and Communication

From the very beginning of empirical research on political party organization and campaign communication, the use of technologies, tools, or services has been a central object of interest. Researchers have investigated, for example, how technologies affect parties' day-to-day activity, and how they develop and invest in technological infrastructure (for example, Kreiss 2016; Epstein 2018; McKelvey & Piebiak 2018; Gerbaudo 2019; Gibson 2020; Barberà et al. 2021). Some scholars see the development and usage of technologies as the reason for the disempowerment of traditional political intermediaries—such as parties, interest groups, or nongovernmental organizations (NGOs)—in favor of "political organizing without organizations" (Margetts et al. 2015; Shirky 2008). However, other scholars suggest that a disempowerment of traditional political intermediaries is less common. Instead, they argue that what we are witnessing are gradual changes in political organizations through the use of emerging tools (for example, Bimber 1998; Gerbaudo 2019; Gibson 2020; Jungherr et al. 2020). According to Jungherr et al. (2020, 168) this might take "the form of organizational hybrids in which established structures, practices, and goals coexist with the realization of affordances brought by new technology and a pluralism of different types of political organizations." This book connects to the latter strand of research, which emphasizes the use of technologies in the pursuit of specific political functions or goals. In this regard, we distinguish two main political goals.

First, technology can be used for campaign organization. Various studies have shown that technology has a central impact on the organizational structures of campaigns and their daily work routines (Farrell & Schmitt-Beck 2003; Gibson 2015). Seen to have become integral to organizational business, often "mundane" technologies, such as emails, have been shown to be essential to parties' everyday intra-organizational working practices (Nielsen 2011). Indeed, previous studies have shown technology to be essential for fundraising (Hindman 2005; Kreiss 2012; Stromer-Galley 2019), volunteer mobilization and coordination (Nielsen 2011; Kreiss 2012, 2016), and data collection (Nickerson & Rogers 2014; Hersh 2015; Kreiss 2016). This significance has led various scholars to diagnose what is occurring as the professionalization of campaigns, seeing specialists in the use and development of digital technologies as increasingly central to campaigns' organizational structure (Kreiss 2016; Dommett 2019). These specialists can be found within parties, but also externally, with a digital consulting industry in the United States (Sheingate 2016; Chester & Montgomery 2019) and elsewhere (Farrell 1998; Newman 1999), which provides parties with access to technological expertise.

Second, technology can be used for campaign communication or gaining visibility in the information space. Scholars have documented in detail whether and which technologies are used by parties and campaigns to communicate with voters, tracing, for example, the use of email, websites, and social media (Magin et al. 2017; Epstein 2018; Römmele & Gibson 2020). These studies have revealed the evolution of campaign technology, demonstrating how parties adopt, deploy, and revise their use of different campaign technologies in response to new media and perceived best practice. Often diagnosed as "eras" of communication or campaigning, technology and particularly different media have transformed campaigns' message management and communication practices (Norris 2000; Kreiss et al. 2018; Römmele & Gibson 2020).

While this work demonstrates the importance of technology to party organization and behavior, it is often left unstated exactly how parties use technologies to organize and communicate in data-driven campaigns. In essence, we have little understanding of the technologies that enable a data-driven campaign to operate and communicate.

The Use of Organizational and Communication Technologies

In moving to classify the different types of organizational and communication technologies for DDC, we suggest that technologies can be imbued with low or high levels of functionality that campaigns can leverage to different degrees (see Figure 5.1). Recognizing that technologies do not come in single forms but can exhibit attributes that vary in terms of sophistication, it is useful to differentiate between the functional characteristics of the technology that parties utilize. To these ends, we suggest that technology exhibiting low functionality is characterized by few customizable options, low usability, weak collaboration possibilities, low connectivity of services, low automatization, or weak data security.

In contrast, technologies with high functionality can possess highly customizable options, high usability, peak collaboration possibilities, managed as a service, high connectivity of services, high automatization, or high data security. Operationalizing this differentiation, we suggest that an email system, for example, can possess low functionality if it only allows a single user to distribute content via a standardized template to a limited

	Organizational Technologies/Tools	Communication Technologies/Tools
High Functionality	highly customizable options, high usability, peak collaboration possibilities, managed as a service, high connectivity of services, high automatization, or high data security	
⇅	**Databases/CRM Software** **Campaigning Apps** e.g., messaging apps, campaign platforms and tools, online forums	**Websites** **Social Networking Platforms** e.g., telephone marketing, direct mailing, e-mail, digital website advertising
Low Functionality	few customizable options, low usability, weak collaboration possibilities, low connectivity of services, low automatization, or weak data security	

Figure 5.1. The functionality of organizational and communication tools.

list of contacts. Whereas an email system with high functionality may allow collaboration on the design of the email, it may allow high degrees of customization, gather metrics data on open rates and click-throughs, and allow unlimited email addresses to be contacted. Similarly, a database with low functionality can allow users to manually input data and provide simple filtering categories for data sorting, while a high functionality database can allow the automatic integration of different datasets, can provide sophisticated tools for analytics and hierarchical data access controls, and more.

In drawing these distinctions, as suggested above, we recognize the potential for the same system to be used in different ways. Two campaigns may therefore have access to the same system capable of high functionality, but one party may use that system in a way that only exploits low functionalities—example, by sending a standardized email—whereas another may use the same system to engage in A/B testing designed to optimize donation rates. We therefore argue that single technologies do not necessarily possess a single template of usage but can be utilized in a range of different ways depending on the broader context.

Organizational Technologies and Tools

While a range of organizational technologies or tools can be found within parties, we focus our attention on two that are particularly significant for data-driven campaigns. These are, first, databases and customer relationship management (CRM) software and, second, campaigning applications. Each technology is introduced below, highlighting the possible variations that exist in relation to functionality.

Databases and Customer Relationship Management Software

Party databases are the bedrock of much DDC activity. It is here that the vast array of publicly available data, disclosed data, monitoring data, and inferential data outlined in Chapter 2 is gathered, stored, and analyzed. The technology used to warehouse data ranges from basic software such as spreadsheets, to bespoke data-management systems. In addition to databases, many parties also possess CRM software. CRMs allow parties to manage the internal and external flow of communications, money, and other associated interactions. In many parties CRMs exist as a separate system to party databases with, for example, a party having a CRM to manage membership data, and a database for voter data. In other parties there is a single CRM which includes a database, while others again use one CRM with a central database at the national level and different CRMs and databases at subnational or local levels. Hence, there is complexity in the application and use of both CRMs and databases across our advanced democracies. Recognizing these possibilities, we examine these technologies together.

Both databases and CRMs can vary widely in their level of functionality. Those with lower levels of functionality offer little more than the capacity to store and sort information, often being used to filter lists that can be exported to enable communication via other channels such as email or doorknocking; they offer little integration or synchronization and can require manual labeling and additions. Those with higher levels of functionality are highly connective, synchronized, and customizable, having the capacity to automate workflows such as messaging across different social media channels to improve consistency. They can accordingly contain in-built segmentation tools, modeling and targeting functionality, and a centralized system to track key campaign metrics such as engagement, donations, or click-through rates from social media or email. Interestingly, some companies provide technology to parties in different countries, often adapting a common core system to reflect the specificities of the country. Others are bespoke and are built solely for one political party or national context.

Campaigning Apps

Campaigning apps are used by campaigns to improve the organization of party members and supporters, be that for data collection via a canvassing application, or activist mobilization. Accessible for download on a range of devices, apps provide a flexible and easily accessible means for parties to organize their activity and incentivize engagement. Apps exhibit low functionality when they provide simple organizational functions such as maps or campaign instructions. High functionality, in contrast, sees applications provide more interactive functions or could involve, for example, gamification—whereby users receive rewards for their activity and are often ranked in a league table to incentivize further engagement. Moreover, high functionality campaign apps are likely to exhibit more complex mechanisms for feedback and evaluation which can be used to optimize campaign activity.

The two types of organizational technology examined here, whether capable of low or high functionality (or used in these different ways), are also an important source of monitoring data, as they can be used to trace the number of campaign interventions (i.e., contact rate, number of activists canvassing), the response to campaign messages (i.e., email open rates), and the effectiveness of different organizational strategies (i.e., which "asks" result in activism). However, they are all also vulnerable to different security threats that reflect the particular way in which personal data is stored and accessed.

Communication Technologies/Tools

Turning from organizational tools to focus on the technology used to facilitate party communication, we concentrate on party websites and social networking platforms (SNPs).

Party Websites

While commonly viewed as static or outward-facing forms of technology, party websites play a critical role in DDC. While many studies about party websites show that their functions vary from informational to educational purposes and change over the years (e.g., Bimber & Davis 2003; Jungherr & Schoen 2013), they are also a key node in DDC as data-harvesting networks of political parties. The underlying technology used to develop party websites and to host the website can vary, and many parties draw on basic website design systems such as those from WordPress, while others use the tools available to them via the CRM systems they employ. Party websites can also vary significantly in terms of functionality. Those exhibiting low functionality tend to focus on information provision and have limited opportunities for interactivity. They may include basic extensions to allow donations or email sign-up, but are often stand-alone systems that are not connected to other party technology, and that gather limited monitoring data.

Party websites exhibiting higher functionality tend to facilitate higher degrees of interactivity and integration across different party systems. They can often be used as a platform to access phone-banking tools or to access member-discussion forums. More functional websites also tend to embed forms of "surveillance technology" to collect and track the digital traces of voters online (Zuboff 2019). These tracking technologies are a key source of monitoring data (see Chapter 2) to serve political online advertisements on other homepages or platforms based on actions users have taken on the party's websites.

Social Networking Platforms

As information intermediaries, SNPs filter, sort, and personalize information with the help of algorithms, evaluating hundreds of data points (e.g., user information, interaction histories, reactions of other users) to curate individual users' news feeds (Jürgens & Stark 2022). SNPs can be used to facilitate two forms of external communication by campaigns (Kruschinski & Bene 2022).[1] On the one hand, organic media content is not paid for (unless payment is made to 'boost' content (Meta n.d.), and can be placed with unlimited frequency. This content is primarily disseminated to an "owned" audience or, in other words, to individuals to whom the source already has a relationship or connection. On the other hand, campaigns can publish paid media content which needs to be paid for and can be targeted at selected users based on algorithmized ad-delivery processes.[2] Paid media content is scalable in price and can be used with a variety of targeting options.

Using SNPs with low functionality allows campaigners to post simple forms of organic content (such as basic text or pictures), to employ limited targeting parameters for paid content (such as location, age, or gender), and to employ basic testing and analytics. In contrast, using SNPs with high functionality enables parties to employ multimedia communication strategies for coordinated organic posting with, for example, certain systems allowing multiple users to post organic content simultaneously to maximize their impact.

In terms of paid media, platforms can allow campaigns to exercise high levels of control over the message, aims, and targets of advertising through highly customizable options. Political actors can choose from objectives (awareness, consideration, conversion), define individual targets based on contact information (e.g., emails, names), create new audiences with customer similarity based on estimations of users' shared qualities (e.g., users who like a specific page or profile, or users who visited a website) and fine-tune the performance of ads by testing. This allows parties to target content with specific campaign functions, selected issues, and tonality to fine-grained audiences and individuals during specific times in the campaign (so-called political micro-targeting (Bodó & Helberger 2017; Papakyriakopoulos et al. 2018)).

Variations in the Use of Technologies across Our Five Advanced Democracies

In what follows, we show that parties often use the same system in different ways. Looking ahead to our explanatory chapter (Chapter 7), we demonstrate that some technologies are only available to certain parties and give insights about some possible reasons. Hence, this section will illustrate that despite the advanced state and rapid development of technologies, political campaigns are not "well-oiled machines" in which sophisticated tools such as databases, CRM software, and campaigning apps drive all campaign decisions. In fact, it appears that not all parties have transformed or are transforming into digital parties (Barberà et al. 2021; Bennett et al. 2018; Gerbaudo 2019).

Organizational Technologies/Tools

All our interviewees described the use of database/CRM technologies and campaigning apps for organizational purposes. However, we witnessed a variety of functionality in different countries and between major and minor parties. Both organizational technologies are used with high functionality in the United States by both the Democratic and Republican parties, although the technological advantage of one or the other party alternates in different election cycles (Kreiss 2012, 2016). In the other countries, larger parties tend to draw on higher functionality in their use of technological organization, due to their higher monetary resources and know-how. In contrast, minor parties often encounter barriers to investing in such techniques.

Databases/CRM Software

In Australia, the use of databases and CRM systems capable of high functionality is uneven. Labor is the only party that has invested in a bespoke CRM. Campaign Central, developed for the party in 2013 by Magenta Linux at a cost of over $1 million (AUD), provides a level of functionality unrivaled by the other parties. This includes the ability to access a web-based application of the system for field campaigning, segmentation of voter lists, and a centralized database of voter engagement (Kefford 2021). In addition to Campaign Central, Labor uses NationBuilder to augment their campaign activity, especially in the provision of party websites and in managing various channels of communication.

In contrast, the Liberal Party has not committed to developing a bespoke CRM or database. Instead, the party is divided across and within state divisions, with the party still relying on the antiquated Feedback system which has been used since the 1980s, although some state divisions have experimented with off-the-shelf CRM systems such as i360 from the United States. In contrast to Labor's system, Feedback offers none of the high-level functionality such as segmentation that can be implemented once analytics processes have occurred—outside the CRM. Feedback is, therefore, much more of a repository of information about constituents, with some additional features such as centralizing direct mail operations, but has limited usability, collaboration, or workflow opportunities. Recognizing the limitations of Feedback, the Liberal Party has since 2020 invested significant sums of money to upgrade the system; however, challenges remain, according to interviewees.

The Greens as a minor party use three databases/CRMs, which have varied functionality and the confederal organizational structure of the national organization means that centralizing systems and data can be challenging. Thus, they currently employ NationBuilder, CiviCRM, and gVIRS. According to Hayman (2021), NationBuilder and CiviCRM are used as supporter databases to capture monitoring data such as event attendance, training in field activities, and prior volunteering. Additionally, these databases collate information regarding supporters' interests, drawn from self-reported information or which online petitions they have signed. gVIRS, in contrast, is used to store information on direct voter contact (Hayman 2021). Interviews that Hayman conducted with the Greens suggested the mixture of systems caused problems for the Greens, with one interviewee suggesting "CiviCRM and NationBuilder, they're not integrated . . . you can do batch uploads where you set the record straight, you just run that every so often . . . but it won't catch everything. You might have a different number or email listed in CiviCRM compared to NationBuilder." Hence, in Australia the use and functionality of databases and CRM software are quite varied.

In the United Kingdom, the major political parties have invested significant resources in the curation of databases for the management of voter information, creating systems with high functionality that can be used to enable simple or more complex forms of analysis by different actors (Chapter 7). Both the Conservatives and Labour have a long-standing history of investment in databases but have both upgraded their systems in recent years. The Conservative Party originally utilized a database called Merlin which one interviewee described as "sort of . . . very backward, I suppose you could say," and functionality was low. Indeed, one interviewee recalled:

> As recent as 20 years ago . . . we had a contraption called a Disk Fax, so now the constituencies didn't have to mail a disk to us, they could fax a disk to us. The constituents had a little machine, they'd put their disk in, and they would dial us up, and then we would take a copy of the disk at the other end. Invariably it was corrupt by the time it got to us. But we could do stuff much faster.

In 2014, the party updated its system, purchasing the VoteSource database which had higher functionality, facilitating centralized data collection, data integration, geographic selection, and data analysis.

The Labour Party has similarly updated their database system, and "spent around £2 million developing Contact Creator, a canvassing tool, and a further £300,000 on an updated version—Campaign Creator and Phone Bank (Williamson et al. 2010, 10). Hosted by Experian, Contact Creator provides what one interviewee described as a "single server database" that holds various forms of voter information, membership data, and modeling data, allowing users—via hierarchically controlled access—to input and export data and conduct data analysis. Labour does, however, have a number of other systems, notably a separate CRM for activist organizations. Having used NationBuilder in 2010, the party developed its own platform, Organise, a "volunteer management and communications tool" and they retain a separate member center (Labour Party n.d.). These, once again, have high degrees of functionality, with one interviewee describing how "on Organise, you can see how many people have signed up in each area. This will be producing data about engagement activity."

Similar investment has been made by the Liberal Democrats in a higher functionality database. To create a unified data system, the party purchased Liberal Democrat Connect, a system based on the Voter Activation Network (VAN). One interviewee described how it "allows you to input all the canvassing results, mix it up with lots of other information you have on people either through purchasing or through sort of getting it through different means. And it allows you to contact them on the doorstep and through direct mail, and telephone." The party also uses technology from Salesforce and NationBuilder, with Connect providing a "campaigning database that provides local campaign teams with the tools they need to get in touch with voters and build their supporter base" (Liberal Democrats n.d.).

While the three more highly resourced UK parties invested in highly functional databases and CRMs, there is evidence that all three find their systems to be unreliable. Interviewees described, for example, how limited server capacity limited the Liberal Democrat's system, while Labour's system was reportedly not ready for the 2019 general election because of missing improvements, fixes, and new features.

The Green Party does not maintain a national database, but rather voter information is held by local parties, with off-the-shelf programs such as Excel used to input and analyze voter data. In terms of functionality, the systems used can enable high functionality, but the precise functions available are not tailored to the particular forms of analysis desired by parties, and data is not integrated or cannot be easily shared in a secure manner between party units. This differential was described by one interviewee as being "entirely down to resource," noting that "the trouble is that it's not just that you buy a bit of software and you're done, you've got maintenance, these things quickly become redundant, or need improvements and they're expensive. It's easier for us to raise money for a campaign manager . . . than it is to say, "Will you give us £100,000 to buy a bit of software?" The party does utilize a CRM—CiviCRM—an open-source piece of software that has high functionality, but it is not tailored to the specific needs of the party.

In Canada, all the main political parties have developed their own databases, "using off-the-shelf voter list management software, either for download to a desktop personal computer or laptop, or for access through the Internet" (Bennett & Bayley 2018, 12). The Conservatives' Constituent Information Management System (CIMS) is powered by the same version of Voter Vault used by Republican Party systems and contains a range of data, allowing the party not only to record voter preferences, but also to generate walk lists, phone lists, email lists, and lawn sign allocations. The current CIMS system is, however, reportedly not fit for its purpose, with coverage of a recent post-2021 election report recommending that the party scrap CIMS in favor of developing "modern data campaigning capabilities in-house" (Boutilier 2022).

The Liberals established Liberalist in 2009, entering into a contract with the American company NGP VAN to integrate their database, mailing, and web presence into one system (McKelvey 2015). This system has high levels of functionality, being able to develop micro-targeted and demographic-specific messaging (Bennett & Bayley 2018). In contrast to the two major parties, the NDP does not rely on US-based software solutions, but adopted the Populus system for its database, which appears to run on foreAction, a system developed for parties and nonprofits by NetFore Systems in Ottawa (Bennett & Bayley 2018). This system replaced the previous "outdated and ineffective" database, but as in the United Kingdom, the systems for all three of these parties are not entirely reliable, and staffing and resource limitations mean their functionality is not fully exploited (Bennett & Gordon 2021, 437).

In the United States, both the Republican and Democratic parties made considerable investments into databases and CRM software since 2000 (Hindman 2005; Kreiss 2012, 2016; Bimber 2014; Jungherr et al. 2020). This resulted in the ever-growing use of higher functionality databases and CRM software by both parties in recent election cycles. The Republicans have historically lagged behind the Democrats in terms of creating data systems with high functionality and usability (Kreiss 2016). The party developed the national voter database Voter Vault, centrally maintained by the RNC, that individual Republican campaigns can access (Kreiss & Howard 2010). Voter Vault developed into GOP Data Center, and the party now works closely with Data Trust—a hybrid, private company that in the 2020 election cycle received payments of $14 million from the RNC (Open Secrets, n.d.). These databases and systems can be used to facilitate complex segmentation, with data available on districts and households, as well as individual voters, but require high levels of investment to verify data and ensure functionality.

The Democrats developed a new database system centrally managed by the DNC in 2004. This database, called Vote Builder, cost the party over $6 million between 2005 and 2007 (Kreiss 2012) and provided a uniform interface so that it can be accessed from every state and also can be used as a CRM. For the Obama campaigns, the Democratic Party created an interlinked IT infrastructure with a combination of database and CRM software at its heart (Bimber 2014; McKenna & Han 2014; Kreiss 2012, 2016). All databases were connected through Narwhal, to link previously separate voter information repositories and make them available for all arms of the campaign on the state and local levels (Nielsen 2011; Kreiss 2012, 2016; Nielsen 2012; Hersh 2015). After the defeat of Hillary Clinton in 2016, the Democrats made crucial fixes to their database operation, by upgrading Vertica to Big Query and launching Blueprint (Higher Ground Labs 2021). This move allowed campaign staff more access to raw data to manipulate for their purposes at a local level. The Democratic Data Exchange (DDx), a DNC-affiliated entity that allows state parties, campaigns, and independent groups to share voter data within the constraints of election regulations, also gained traction in 41 states. Campaigns including the Biden presidential campaign used the data points in DDx, most of them contact information, to engage with voters, target messaging, and support GOTV efforts (Ryan-Mosley 2020). Though some took issue with the platform's late rollout, practitioners generally agreed that DDx filled a critical gap in the ecosystem. Notably compared to our other cases, in US parties we therefore see higher levels of data integration and sharing, and much larger teams of staff devoted to maintaining and developing highly functional systems.

In Germany, especially the bigger parties have invested money, time, and human resources in database and CRM technologies in the past two election cycles, resulting in higher functionality. The CDU has been working since 2005 with a CRM called Citizen Relationship Management from Microsoft. All voter requests via phone, letters, emails, homepages, apps, or Facebook are entered into the CRM, which is connected to the Central Membership File that holds data on party members. One CDU party strategist explained: "Since existence, 880,000 requests have reached the party through the CRM, which makes a decisive contribution to further improving the database for future campaigns as well as ensuring modern communication." The party has attempted to professionalize their data operations. According to one CDU campaign strategist, the party has spent approximately €1.6 million from 2014 to 2017 to fund the self-proclaimed first German data-driven mobilization operation, called "connect17." The main technology behind it was developed in collaboration with a digital consulting agency aligned to the party and enabled selected campaign staff to access the database through a front-end interface called "Kampagnencockpit" to get information about registered local campaigners and supporters. They could also enter and update data manually, and collect citizens' questions and pass them on to the CRM system. Functionality has therefore improved, but is not as sophisticated as in the United States.

The SPD started working with a CRM software from Microsoft in 2004 which held basic functionality for organizing membership data and voter requests and was adapted and professionalized in collaboration with a German software developer and consulting company into "MAVIS." This member-address management database is currently in use and allows for medium functionality, as described by one interviewee:

> MAVIS is a great idea to collect, organize, and analyze party members of party branches, as well as smaller groups according to various criteria, such as age, party fee, gender, profession, etc. However, it is not really user friendly, sometimes error-prone, and provides incomplete data. That's why we are working on "SPD-Organize" which should allow for better usability and functionality as it will enable us to make data requests from the MAVIS database and other data sources which also include interested non-members.

Like the CDU, the SPD started using databases for campaigning and voter data strategically in the run-up to the federal election 2005. Although the SPD hired the Messina Group as external consultants for the 2013 federal election campaign, the party didn't buy US software. Rather, it helped the SPD and its staff to develop their party-owned database infrastructure for organizing and running the party's door-to-door and digital campaign. This comprises a voter database which is connected to a canvassing app and an online interface which allows campaigns access to data to facilitate campaign activity and the addition of new data. These software solutions are programmed by a collaboration of in-house party staff and external experts, which has its up- and downsides according to one campaign strategist: "Of course, our approach allows for data sovereignty and adaptability to the needs of our party campaigners. However, the development to a well-functioning infrastructure took us very long and there is still need for optimization and more functionality."

Smaller German parties also use CRM and database technologies for organizational purposes. However, they draw on technologies developed by medium-size companies (for example, Sensix and Chudovo) which have lower levels of functionality. The Green Party, the Liberals, and the Left tried to create a comparable technological infrastructure, specifically investing in CRM systems to collect, process, and organize members' and activists' data mainly through a web interface (the Greens: Wurzelwerk/Das Grüne Netz/Wahlatlas; the Liberals: meine freiheit; the Left: linksaktiv). This infrastructure is accompanied by databases with varying degrees of functionality for accessing and collecting voter information which are by no means as advanced as those for the major parties or compared to practices in the United States.

A general observation from all interviews in Germany point to the fact that the federal party headquarters are the driving force for developing databank and CRM software solutions and offer access for their local party branches for a fee. However, the local party levels often use cheaper self-made solutions with lower functionalities or none, which results in a scattered database infrastructure for all German parties.

Campaigning Apps

Unlike some of our other cases, campaigning apps are not used in Australia by any of the political parties. The closest that any of the Australian parties come to campaigning apps is Labor's mobile version of their Campaign Central software discussed above. This application provides data to members and supporters online through the internet. The other parties in Australia still use paper printouts to conduct their field campaign activities and especially door-knocking operations. Thus, while Labor's mobile version of Campaign Central is far superior to other Australian parties, it provides limited functionality beyond presenting the information and being able to add notes on direct voter contact.

Within the United Kingdom, increased investment is being made in campaigning applications, but the scope of technology is mostly limited to doorstep canvassing apps. The Conservatives, Labour, and Liberal Democrats each have mobile canvassing applications for doorstep conversations that connect to their databases, essentially replacing paper and pen canvassing with digital data access and input. Of these three parties, Labour has most extensively explored mobile applications, with a membership services app and a phone canvassing application—Dialogue—with high levels of functionality, such as awarding badges for campaign activity in line with principles of gamification (Manthorpe 2019). In contrast, the Green Party does not have such bespoke technology. We did, however, find some evidence of party activists in the Greens and associated with Labour creating their own mobile apps.

In Canada, mobile applications are used by different parties with medium to high functionality. The Conservatives have been using an app called "CIMS to go" since 2015 (Watters 2015). The app is an offspring of the developer of the central Constituent Information Management System (CIMS) database and is directly connected to it. Besides seeing basic voter information from CIMS, party canvassers can input new voter data or update entries after each door-knock. Lastly, it shows walking routes and can track the GPS location of activists. The Liberals have been using a mobile app called MiniVAN since 2015. The tool connects with the Liberal database Liberalist so users can export canvassing lists to their mobile device, see voters' identification and demographics, and enter new or updated information. Further, the app enables issue-related inquiries, and the responses are synced with Liberalist. The NDP started using an app called Dandelion, which was developed in 2017 and customized for the 2019 and 2021 NDP campaign. Dandelion is designed for door-to-door campaigns and can be connected to NationBuilder for organizing canvassers and amassing the voter database at the doorsteps. Described by one campaign activist, it "certainly saved some time, reduced some paper and some wasted resources to spread political messages. However, it crashed when it was needed most and also came with a duty to ensure data is safe" (National Democratic Party 2021).

US parties have the longest history of using campaign apps (Stromer-Galley 2019), and both parties use mobile apps for organizing their campaign activities with high functionality but different approaches. Since its launch in 2010, Democrats widely draw on MiniVAN, which is the mobile outreach solution from NGP VAN. This app allows canvassing campaigns to be organized by accessing individual household or voter information, organizing walk routes, and applying scripts. It also allows collection of voter data which is synced with the Democrat NGP VAN database and helps to streamline the organization and preparation process for canvassers. The number of Democrats canvassing with this app increased 230% between 2012 and 2018 (Wired 2018). At the 2020 election the Democrats also used the "Vote Joe" app, which asks for access to users' contacts, GPS data, and Bluetooth data (CNBC 2020). Despite having high functionality, such as the ability to prompt users to contact friends and family to encourage them to vote, this app had major security flaws (Whittaker 2020).

In contrast, Republicans have used a variety of apps run by companies like Advantage and i360, and by the RNC. Although all of these apps comprise roughly the same functionality as the Democrat's software solutions, Republicans stated that they lacked both usability and functionality during the 2012 and 2014 cycle. As a result, new tools were developed. The Trump 2016 campaign used uCampaigns smartphone app America First, which combined a gamified outreach tool, news aggregator, media creator, and virtual events platform, with a maximalist approach to data collection (Heine 2016). One feature allowed the app to match the phone address book contacts of supporters to a voter universe. In the 2020 election, the Trump campaign developed a new app with similar, high-level functions (Halpern 2020),

In addition to these official party apps, the United States is distinguished by the prevalence of other election-related apps. Indeed, one study found 412 apps mentioning Donald Trump published between June 2015 and January 2018 (Gómez-García et al. 2019). These apps have a range of different goals and varying levels of functionality, that often reflect differing levels of expertise and resources.

In Germany, all parties developed their own campaigning apps for organizing canvassing campaigns and collecting voter data, except for the AfD. These were designed to make door-to-door campaigns more efficient and to collect voter information in accordance with the country's strict data-privacy policies. While the CDU, SPD, and the Left have had their apps in play since the 2017 elections, the Greens and the Free Democratic Party released their mobile applications in 2019 and in the run-up to the 2021 election. The apps of both bigger parties and the Greens are the ones with the highest functionality.

CDU's Connect App was developed by a party-close digital consulting agency specifically for the party's mobilization activities. It allows voter data to be entered with the consent of the canvassed voter and allows the organization of canvassing operations, surveys of citizens, and the sharing of campaign messages on SNPs. In-app gamification elements, such as ranking lists and reward systems, provide incentives for activists to use the app. The same software framework is also used by the election campaign apps of the CSU party (Die CSU App). However, in May 2021, the app was temporarily taken offline after a software developer discovered significant security vulnerabilities in the app which allowed data to be viewed publicly for more than 100,000 door visits and around 18,500 campaign workers (Groß 2021).

The SPD's app was developed by party staff and digital media experts specifically for the party's canvassing purposes. The app allows canvassers to collect voter data and also includes gamification elements in the form of a reward system for canvassed households and a ranking list of the best canvassers. The Greens developed their campaign app for organizing their door-to-door-campaign and the distribution of their election posters. Users can see information about the "Potenzialgebiete" and already visited households from their web interface "Wahlatlas" on an interactive map. Data can also be collected about the voters. In terms of gamification elements, users can collect points for any house visit or for hanging up election posters, which are listed in an activist ranking.

Both the Liberal and the Left parties developed a campaign app with rather basic functionalities for organizing different campaign activities. The Liberals give users access to their "Potenzialanalysen" on an interactive map and allow them to collect data about households where they handed out flyers/direct mailings. Further, they enable users to indicate places where they put up election posters and conducted other campaign activities. Last, they encourage users to share campaign messages on social media or to input contact data from friends for campaign contact. For all these activities, points can be collected for a campaign ranking. The Left party has an app for rather organizational activities such as solving specific tasks, chatting with other activists, or marking various campaign activities on a map. Despite having some common functionality, the specific tools contained within these apps do therefore vary.

In addition to these nationally produced apps by the federal party, state party chapters are also developing their own app solutions for organizing their canvassing activities or other campaign actions. Some of them are developed by digital campaign agencies and provide high functionality. Others are self-programmed apps and provide rather low functionality. The reason for parties' state chapters to use their own technological solutions is described by one SPD strategist: "On the one hand, we are not satisfied with the costs and solutions of the federal party. On the other hand, we want our autonomy and thus complete access to all the collected data for organizing future campaigns in our districts."

Last, all parties in Germany except for the AfD also have party information apps in play. They vary in the degrees of functionality, but mostly concentrate on information and internal communication features, such as news updates, important messages, member exchange, and social-sharing possibilities. However, some encourage participation by gamifying the experience.

Communication Technologies/Tools

In terms of communication technologies, we were also able to identify the use of websites and SNPs in all our parties by looking at homepage technologies in 2022, in addition to our interview material. As with the previous section, we find that US parties and well-resourced parties in our other countries utilize higher functionalities, such as highly customizable options, high connectivity, and high automation of services. These were not, however, evident in the practices of smaller, less resourced parties. In addition, we observed country differences in the use of tracking technologies on websites and the sophisticated capabilities of SNPs. In particular, in Germany some of these options are not used in a highly functional way due to regulatory concerns.

Party Websites

In Australia, party websites are generated using a mixture of tools made available via CRM systems such as NationBuilder or are designed for the parties by external providers using systems such as Drupal or WordPress. Both Labor and the Greens frequently use NationBuilder for website design, especially for candidate pages, while the Liberal Party uses Drupal for central pages and often uses WordPress for candidate pages. The webpages of the Australian parties have low levels of functionality and are primarily designed for informational purposes. However, one of the most important ways that parties collect data online is through their websites (Kefford 2021). According to interviewees, data collected in this way includes information such as how long those being tracked spent on certain sites, as well as what sites they visited. This replicates what most commercial organizations do when trying to understand their current customers (Tactical Tech 2019). As outlined in Chapter 3, each of the party webpages had tracking cookies from Google and Facebook, among many others. There was little variation across the Australian parties in terms of the technology they were using to collect digital trace data, and this was largely consistent with what was evident across the parties in our other cases such as the United States, the United Kingdom, and Canada.

Political parties' websites in the United Kingdom exhibit different levels of functionality. In addition to containing a raft of information about party positions, the Conservatives, Labour, Liberal Democrats, and Greens have facilities to make donations, to join or volunteer for the party. Comparing across websites, however, it is notable that the Liberal Democrat and Labour sites provide more interactive opportunities, allowing visitors to search for events—with maps and filters provided—or to sign up to attend party conferences. The Conservatives and Green Party websites, in contrast, are far less interactive, with simple sign-up forms to volunteer. These two websites are, however, vastly different; while the Conservative website contains a range of integrated graphics, easy navigation tools, and a shop, the Green Party site has simple navigation and few pages, reflecting apparent differences in available resources and expertise. While historically many parties relied on NationBuilder to produce websites, only the Liberal Democrats have retained this system.

In terms of website platforms, Labour and the Conservatives have focused on creating website platforms that can be used and adapted not only by the central party, but also by local parties. As one Conservative interviewee described:

> We also provided centralized, standardized platforms and tools, and I know the Labour Party does this as well, whereby you build a template website that everyone can use. You make it available at a subsidized price, so that means you've got some element, of not control, but some element where

you can shepherd them towards the sort of stuff they should have on their website.

Both these major parties also spoke about using tracking technology and testing to understand more about who was using websites, and to optimize web design—practices that were not raised by interviewees in other parties.

While the major parties appeared better able to invest in and utilize high functionality, it was notable that many interviewees drew a distinction between their externally facing website and internal party systems. One interviewee from the Labour Party therefore reflected in 2017 that "the members' area of the website is total garbage and looks like a banquet site from 1999," while in the Greens one interviewee described "some attempts through our members' website to broaden engagement, but the tools are really primitive and it just doesn't work." Such examples demonstrate that all aspects of parties' web presence do not exhibit the same traits in regard to functionality, with internally facing technologies often limited in this regard.

In Canada, party websites, as in our other cases, draw on various technologies to manage communication with voters and supporters. The Liberal and Conservative websites use WordPress and overlay this with tracking technology such as those from Google and Meta, while the NDP has a tailor-made webpage. For the most part, these websites are, as Giasson and Small (2017, 115) note, used as a platform to gather email addresses with which to conduct further campaigning. They are also used to solicit funds, convey information, and recruit volunteers, with all three parties having a relatively consistent set of pages. Notably, the Conservative site has a simpler design and fewer engagement opportunities, but does contain a shop. The Liberal site allows users to search for nearby events and purchase merchandise, and the NDP eschews a shop in favor of encouraging users to "add your name" to a range of petitions. The precise functionality on offer does therefore differ around this common core.

Both US Democrat and Republican parties have used homepages with high functionality since the early days of the internet. Both parties have developed internal teams, but also extensive support for a well-established consultancy industry that specializes in optimizing digital presence and engagement. Homepages allow posting information, asking for donations, and building their own online communities. The precise nature of these interactions is more sophisticated than in our other countries with tools, for example, on the Democrats' website that allow users to split their donation between different candidates, and an event-searching tool that allows users to search on a range of different filters. Similarly, the Republicans offer numerous ways of taking action, with opportunities to join GOP communities or conduct an internship. Each website is extensive and highly professionalized, with clear investment in engaging content. Notably, within the US context these party websites are accompanied by a range of candidate and local party websites that are similarly more extensive and advanced than is evident in our other cases.

In both parties, the homepages of these various websites are equipped with tracking and testing technologies, but whereas these are mainly only found on national party websites outside the United States, within the United States they are routinely used by candidates and local parties. Indeed, one study which explored this during the 2018 congressional elections found that on the candidate homepages, "[o]f the 981 websites assessed, 87% have one or more trackers on them" (Patel 2018, 3). Moreover, it found that "Google trackers appear on around 75% of all pages assessed, while Facebook and Twitter trackers were found on 53% and 30% of pages respectively" (Patel 2018, 4). It is also common in the United States for campaigns to A/B test different buttons and motives in order to find the most engaging versions to prompt users to donate money, sign up for newsletters, or to download the campaign app (Issenberg 2012). Although national parties in our other countries do use these techniques, elsewhere they are almost exclusively the preserve of national parties (and not routinely) and are rarely used by local campaigns.

In Germany, all parties use homepages with varying degrees of functionality for their federal, state, and local party chapters, and for most of their respective candidates. For the most part they are created internally on content management systems including WordPress, Drupal, or Netlify. As in the United Kingdom, federal parties provide standardized homepage templates and tools that everyone can use for a certain price. However, not all local party chapters and candidates use this service. With regard to functionality, most of the differences can be spotted not in comparison of different parties, but on the different organizational levels of the parties. So, in general, the party websites at the federal level exhibit the highest functionality, while parties' state, local, and candidate homepages have a rather medium to low functionality. This can be described along two main elements. First, interactivity elements on the homepages are mostly situated on the federal party homepages, while local and candidate websites are mainly for information purposes. Whether it is a member area, an invitation to join a member community, asking for donations, or calling for party participation, those elements can be found on every homepage of the parties' federal level and are often connected to the main CRM systems. Second, most tracking software is embedded on the homepages at the parties' federal level. Although some parties deploy a fair share of tracking technology on their websites, it is mostly Matamo, Google, and Facebook analytics which are used to track and screen website visitors. However, user privacy-invasive tools such as Facebook pixel are seldom used.

Social Networking Platforms

As in all our cases, SNPs and the affordances they offer to parties are used extensively by the Australian parties. All of the parties use Facebook and Google advertising systems, and this includes organic posts and paid advertising via custom and look-alike affordances. The major parties in Australia—Labor and the Liberal Party—use a combination of in-house and external consultants to develop and execute campaigns online, especially on social media. As one interviewee from the Liberal Party suggested: "If we know someone or a company are the experts on a particular platform or channel, we try to use them to deliver messages to the people we want to speak to." While the social media companies have engaged with the political parties in Australia as far back as 2007 on how to use the affordances they provide, the engagement with Australian parties on how best to execute ad buys, or ways to best draw on what the platform provides, is nothing like that evident in the United States (Kreiss & McGregor 2019). During the 2022 federal election, paid advertising spending on Meta platforms was reported as approximately $12.5 million (AUD). This includes a reported $5 million (AUD) from Labor, and $3.5 million (AUD) for the Liberal Party (Antrobus 2022).

SNPs, as in our other cases, were widely used by all political parties in the United Kingdom. Both organic content and paid advertising were utilized. Although widely taken up, financial returns show large differentials in the amounts being spent with platforms, with the Conservatives spending just over £1million, Labour £2.4 million, the Liberal Democrats £1.3 million, and the Greens £93,000 on Facebook at the 2019 general election (Dommett et al. 2022, 17).[3] Though both forms of campaigning tool were utilized on SNPs, parties varied in their use of each tactic and their levels of functionality. The

Green Party was heavily reliant on organic activity, and while spending some funds on advertising, rarely used higher functionality in terms of targeting or message testing and optimization. Other parties utilized these techniques to different extents in accordance with differing electoral strategies. Reflecting on the 2017 general election, for example, an interviewee within the Labour Party described how:

> our operation almost entirely needed to be organic. We required and relied on people deciding themselves that they wanted to share our content with their friends and family on Facebook and on email and Twitter and so on, whereas the Tories paid Facebook and Google and YouTube to put that content in front of specific people who consumed it, whether they wanted to or not, through paid advertising . . . our operation was totally geared around what would work and be successful organically.

In contrast, Conservative figures, interviewed in relation to the 2017 general election, spoke about the value of paid advertising and described how they had utilized high functionalities available on different platforms to test the response to content on different platforms—finding out that "tons of people are on Facebook, and that's the best place to advertise." Similarly, Labour spoke about the utility of SNPs, but outlined the utility of different platforms for reaching certain audiences. Reflecting evolution in the affordances of SNPs, parties' use of these tools is adaptive, but it appears that the major political parties and parties with greater levels of financial resource exploited higher levels of functionality in their engagement with these platforms.

In Canada, all parties used organic as well as paid media on SNP. One interviewee in the NDP described using SNPs because "wherever the people are, that's where we're going to go. That's the bread and butter of politics is talking to people and forming collectives of like-minded folk. And currently that's where people are, on Facebook, on TikTok, on Instagram." Using Facebook's Ad Library, we found that between July 31 and August 29, major political parties in Canada had spent nearly $2.5 million across Facebook, Instagram, and Messenger. The federal Liberal Party alone spent $1.5 million on 7,038 ads, far outpacing the combined spending by the other major federal parties. It has been suggested that the Liberals seem to do more targeting of their social media ads (Dubois & Owen 2019). In the 2019 election the Conservatives ran fewer ads but ran them in a "broadcast" style across the country, whereas the Liberals ran more ads but with lower spending per ad, targeting them more specifically at geographical areas and demographic groups (Dubois & Owen 2019). This follows a pattern from early twenty-first-century campaigns where the Conservatives targeted broad personas (Delacourt 2012). Social media was also used for generating data on voters to contact them outside of the SNP (a tactic we also saw used in our other cases). One interviewee explained that "most of our digital outreach, whoever was signing a petition or was engaging with our social media in any way, if we got their email, we sent them an invite to join and volunteer."

In the United States, both the Democrat and the Republican parties have a long history of using SNPs either with the help of agencies or with in-house teams, and practices that first emerged in this context have been taken up widely in our other cases. Unlike in our other countries, US-based campaigns have historically received far higher levels of support in how to optimize platforms for campaign goals (Kreiss & McGregor 2018), and spending in this context far outpaced practice in our other cases. In the 2018 US midterm elections, for example, political advertisers spent over $1.4 billion on ads between May 2018 and June 2020 (Ridout et al. 2021a). In the 2020 US presidential campaign, Joe Biden's campaign spent $213 million and Donald Trump's spent $276 million in the entire election circle (Ridout et al. 2021b).

US campaigns have mobilized extensive and far-reaching organic and advertising campaigns, not only through party accounts, but through candidate pages and via (super) PACs and other organizations (far outpacing practice in our other countries). Across these accounts, features such as custom audiences, look-alike audiences, and A/B testing are routinely used to test content, and are now an embedded feature of campaigns (Baldwin-Philippi 2017; Kreiss & McGregor 2018). Targeting via so-called dynamic ads—in which the selection and playout of ad versions is left entirely to Facebook—is also utilized, with campaigns uploading different images, videos, or text versions to Facebook so that personalized ad variations are played out based on predictive analytics, tailored to each viewer (Ali et al. 2019; Crain & Nadler 2019). Indeed, these techniques enabled the 2016 Trump campaign to play out Facebook ads in several thousand variations per day (Kreiss & McGregor 2018; Voigt 2018). Interestingly, within the US context there is evidence of engagement with a wider range of SNPs than in our other countries.

In Germany, all parties used SNPs for organic as well as paid media with medium to high functionality. All parties except for the Left and the AfD supplemented their organic posts with political advertisements. In the six weeks leading to the 2021 federal election, the seven main parties spent between €2.5 million and €4.2 million on Meta platforms (Righetti et al. 2022). Whereas the major parties leveraged high functionality, such as A/B testing, the smaller parties used lower functionalities, hardly targeting small-scale voter groups or using A/B tests. Rather, large amounts of money were spent on individual ads with singular content. This resembles communication strategies for traditional media, where messages are sent to a broad audience. However, the content used for the advertisements were less granular than is often assumed, with one interviewee from the CDU highlighting that "the personal resources were simply missing to create individual ads."

All parties in Germany made use of core and look-alike audiences to target voter groups. However, custom audiences are only used sporadically. This was explained by one SDP campaign strategist: "So we did draw conclusions about certain key interests on one channel or another, but we didn't do any data-matching between Facebook and our databases, which would have been quite possible, be it through a Facebook pixel or by matching e-mail addresses to distribution lists or to groups on Facebook or what many people call a custom audience; we didn't do that, quite deliberately, for data protection reasons."

Conclusion

In this chapter we have demonstrated that different technologies are used with differing functionality for organizational and communication purposes in each of our five countries. To understand these differences, we have introduced a new framework that distinguishes between high and low levels of functionality and have suggested that software can either be created with differing levels of functional capacity or can be used to exploit those functionalities to greater or lesser extents.

Briefly summarizing our findings, we found that the United States is, once again, the most advanced when it comes to the use of technology. We found a wide variety of software solutions, exhibiting high levels of functionality and continual investment in the integration and maximization of available insights. The Republicans and Democrats have made significant and ongoing investment in their database and CRM systems and have sought not only to integrate and verify data, but to facilitate and routinize complex analytics practices within these systems. There is also innovation around campaign applications, websites, and the use of SNPs, with new tools and affordances regularly appearing in the United States. Although at various points the Republicans or Democrats have lagged behind each other in a particular aspect of campaign technology, the technology "arms race" drives ongoing investment.

Beyond the United States we found that campaign technology is a central element of DDC, but its form and uptake vary considerably. Across our four other countries, we found that the major parties which had the most resources invested more extensively in campaign technology and accordingly cultivated and used higher functionalities. Although not as advanced as in the United States, major parties often purchase campaign database software from US companies and adapt it for their own purposes, and invest in campaign apps, websites, and paid SNP activity. Minor parties, in contrast, often had to develop their own systems or were reliant on open-source software which tended to exhibit lower levels of functionality. They also had fewer resources available for website creation and maintenance, for political advertising, or for the creation of SNP content.

Finance was not, however, the only source of variation. Systemic factors sometimes played a role, as we saw that German parties exhibit a larger number of regional apps than in other countries. We also saw practice in this country limited most extensively by regulatory constraints. Party structure and ideology were also influential in accounting for differences, with some parties, such as the UK Labour Party and Canadian Liberals, using their websites to try to drive more offline engagement than their conservative counterparts. In general, however, across Australia, the United Kingdom, Canada, and Germany we saw less routinized use of high functionality, with software either incapable of such process, or parties unable to invest in such activity.

What was notable from our findings was the way in which external companies, such as Meta and Google, provided important campaign infrastructure to facilitate higher functionalities. Small and large parties therefore routinely spoke about using Facebook's targeting options and A/B testing tools, with smaller parties revealing that they had allowed the party to engage in this kind of activity for the first time. External companies such as SNPs can therefore help to facilitate new campaign practices, but they can also allow parties to circumvent privacy and electoral restrictions by outsourcing the collection of data to a company not restricted by national data protection laws (such as in Germany).

Practitioner Perspectives on Technology

The previous chapter suggested that campaigns can utilize a range of technologies to facilitate their organizational and communication work. It also argued that campaigns can access and utilize technology with low or high levels of functionality, resulting in different DDC practices. What is presently unclear is whether the idea of campaigns as slick technology-intensive operations is accurate. To test this idea, we asked Jochen König, co-founder and CEO of Cosmonauts & Kings GmbH—a consultancy firm specializing in digital communication for politics in Germany, which has diverse German political parties as clients—and Katie Harbath, CEO of Anchor Change and former director of Public Policy, Global Elections at Facebook to respond to the following provocation:

Given the advanced state and rapid development of digital technology, conventional wisdom is that nowadays political campaigns are well-oiled machines in which sophisticated technological tools such as campaigning apps, databases, or voter management software drive all campaign decisions from messaging to fundraising to canvassing to organizing to targeting resources to key districts and media buys. In your experience: How well does this perception match the reality of the party-based campaigns you have worked on or with? Are all campaigns really "technology-intensive"? Do they work like well-oiled machines where one gear meshes with the other? Do technological tools really decide winning or losing? What explains disparities?

Jochen König, Co-Founder and Managing Director of Cosmonauts & Kings GmbH / Civical GmbH, Germany

Election campaigns in Germany in 2022 do not fully utilize technology or data, and are far from "well-oiled machines." Rather, parties and campaigns in Germany are in the midst of a transformation to digitize their organizational structures and expand their technological capabilities. While it is the case that data and technology are being used in particular areas of campaigning, for the most part they are not integrated into all sub-areas of an election campaign. This is why there can be no talk of well-oiled machines, let alone of parties in Germany as digital platforms.

With regard to the use of software solutions for voter management, targeting, canvassing, or media budget distribution in election campaigns, Germany, like Europe in general, is rather at the beginning. This is because the software solutions that exist specifically for political campaigns, with few exceptions, come from the United States. The American software providers often do not meet German and European data-protection standards. Therefore, they can only be used to a limited extent or not at all in Germany and Europe.

However, the trend in the European political tech market is toward SaaS[1] and CRM solutions for election campaigns and political campaigning, with the aim of enabling small election campaigns and local party organizations with little budget and digital skills to plan and organize campaigns digitally and to reach voters. Parties in Germany will use these software solutions, especially their digital campaign infrastructure, in the coming years to improve the coordination and management of election campaigns and communications at all levels, from local to national.

Even though DDC in the United States is much more advanced from a technological perspective than in Germany and Europe, they should only serve as a model to a very limited extent. The approach of using technology and capital to collect as many personal data points as possible about voters in real time is detrimental to the democratic opinion and will-forming process in an increasingly digital public sphere in the long run.

The future of DCC and digital political communication in Germany and Europe lies instead, in my opinion, in building digital political relationships between parties and voters. The basis of this digital political relationship must be the individual data sovereignty of voters, based on technological approaches such as self-sovereign identity. In the context of DCC, this means that every voter should be able to share his or her data with a party or political organization sovereignly and according to his or her own chosen level of anonymization. Parties are thus enabled to collect and use verified data from individual voters without processing personal data that allows conclusions to be drawn about an individual voter that they do not explicitly want.

In conclusion, my assessment is that technology and data do not determine victory or defeat in German election campaigns today. In the course of the upcoming and overdue regulation of digital political advertising, a growing political tech market for DDC in Europe, as well as the potentials arising from new technological approaches such as Self-Sovereign-Identity and Blockchain for the creation of individual data sovereignty, parties in Germany and Europe will be able to build sustainable digital political relationships with voters in the future. Under these conditions, DDC has the chance to make an important contribution to a digital democratic public sphere, on which the future viability of liberal democracies will also depend.

Katie Harbath, CEO Anchor Point and Former Director of Public Policy, Global Elections at Facebook, United States

Technology has historically been an important part of the narrative around campaign success. Whether thinking about radio, television, websites, or social media, successive campaigns in the United States and elsewhere have claimed that technology allows them to connect with voters in new ways and deliver data-driven messages. And yet, while it's no doubt that presidential and national party committees on both sides of the aisle do use technology to execute sophisticated operations, that does not necessarily translate down into gubernatorial, senate, or congressional races. It's rarer at the local level unless you are running for mayor of a major city. Instead, many of these campaigns rely on the easy-to-use tools made available by platforms such as Facebook, Google, and Twitter.

I saw all of this come to life from the very beginning of my career. My first job was at the Republican National Committee in 2004, where I helped run what was then known as the eCampaign operation. For the next six years, I led digital operations on campaigns at the congressional, senate, and presidential levels before I went to Facebook in early 2011, where I built the global teams that help campaigns use the platform to reach voters.

The first Facebook ads I bought were in 2010 when I was the chief digital strategist at the National Republican Senatorial Committee. At the time we were just excited to be able to target ads to specific locations with far more precision than television. The national parties around this time also set out to build out their data operations—both within the parties and through private enterprises. The goal was to make data sharing across campaigns and the party easy so that any campaign could have a data-driven campaign. However, while the data might have been available, there weren't enough trained campaign workers to know how to analyze and use this data to work across all campaigns, meaning the latest technological tools and data insights often couldn't be utilized.

Today, political and issue advertising through the platforms looks very different. Social media platforms have made it easier than ever before to be able to create targeted messages and connect with different audiences—enabling ordinary activists to engage in sophisticated campaigning. And yet, the providers of technology are constantly changing what they offer to campaigns in response to a range of external pressures. Most notably, following the 2016 election and the Cambridge Analytica scandal, companies came under intense pressure to reduce or even remove the ability for campaigns to micro-target ads. Some, like Twitter, decided to ban political ads altogether. Others, like Google and Facebook, reduced the number of targeting options and introduced ad transparency tools so anyone could see the ads that campaigns were running. While this might have made it less likely a campaign could get away with running ads with misleading messages, it also presented challenges—especially for those campaigns and organizations who don't have the resources to develop their own sophisticated data operations. According to digital strategist Beth Becker, many organizations on the progressive left have stopped running ads on Facebook as they don't perform as well as they used to. She said, "The added difficulty in doing the targeting to ensure you are reaching the right audience is a bar too high for many smaller organizations, many of whom don't have the capacity to spend the added time needed to figure this all out and thus just quit trying (Becker n.d.)."

The challenges created by campaigns' reliance on volatile and constantly changing external providers are often particularly felt by campaigns outside of the United States as well. While in some countries parties are able to develop and maintain their own databases and technological solutions to facilitate data-driven campaigning, in many places stricter privacy laws, less available data, and limited labor resources have created a reliance on platforms and the tools they offer for targeting. Changes in platform policy can be particularly difficult for these campaigns.

While the use of data and technology has undoubtedly changed how campaigns are run around the world, only the most well-funded have the resources to incorporate sophisticated tech tools into their arsenal. Instead, most rely on technology and platforms that provide tools that are easier to use and less time-intensive.

6
Personnel

Imagine the kind of individual involved in DDC and it is likely you will picture a stereotypical (often male) computer geek. As work by Baldwin-Philippi has meticulously shown, popular accounts of DDC have tended to offer a particular and often mythologized account of those involved in DDC, depicting the dominance of "geeks, hackers, nerds, and scientists" who are "uniquely qualified to access the truth" revealed through complex data analytics (2020, 2). Epitomized by the iconography of "the cave" within Barack Obama's data analytics team—whereby pictures showed a group of men hunched over their laptops in a small dark room—these types of individuals have come to be associated with DDC not only in the United States, but around the globe. Characterizations accordingly cite the importance of party staff or external consultants who have the "capacity to crunch the numbers, run experiments and predict outcomes," and who are likely to possess "more apolitical" characteristics due to a focus on data insights rather than political imperatives (Römmele & Gibson 2020, 603).

This depiction of DDC personnel, when viewed against the backdrop of previous research on party organization, is particularly notable for what it ignores. Existing scholarship has mapped the role played by a range of different individuals and groups within parties, but in prevailing accounts of DDC these actors are conspicuously absent. It is therefore far from clear how these "nerds" work alongside party members, staff, or elected representatives, and what exactly it is that they are doing. Indeed, we know very little about how very different organizations have adapted to DDC, making it unclear who the people involved in DDC are and why different groups are prominent in different contexts.

In this chapter we examine the variety of actors who can be involved in parties' DDC. Using examples from our five cases, we look back at the three elements of DDC reviewed in the previous chapters and consider who, in each of our cases, is involved in data collection, analytics, and the use of technology. We first review the existing literature to extract insights and highlight limitations, before providing a classification of the kinds of individuals who can be involved in data-driven campaigns. Finally, we illustrate variation in the type of actor involved in each component of DDC, showing that data-driven campaigns come in different personnel configurations. This descriptive exploration informs our subsequent explanatory analysis in the next chapter.

Existing Depictions of Party Personnel

The question of who is engaged in campaigning is a long-standing topic of interest among academics. There have been numerous studies looking at the people who make campaigns happen (Newman 1999; Nielsen 2011; McKenna & Han 2014), and yet when it comes to DDC there has been little work directly devoted to the question of *who* is engaged. What has instead emerged, embedded in wider accounts tracing the significance of data and analytics, are indications that experts both inside and outside party structures are pivotal.

Some scholarship has drawn attention to the data experts and highly trained staff who now exist *within* party organizations (Gibson 2020, 2). Römmele & Gibson (2020), for example, describe "an intensification and diversification in the type of specialist units that now manage the campaign with new database and analytics teams emerging alongside message testing units and teams set up to run experiments in mobilising voter turnout." Elsewhere, accounts in the United States have described campaigns' moves to hire "more than 50 data analysts . . . to predict the individual behavior of tens of millions of American voters" (Engage 2018, 2) as part of a wider organization devoted to digital and technology (Engage 2018). Obama's campaign in 2012 was particularly depicted in these terms, with reports highlighting how 30%–40% of staff hired by the campaign were devoted to data and technology and had significant data expertise. Such practices have been seen to inspire parties elsewhere to appoint data and analytics experts, creating an impression that DDC is the preserve of certain kinds of staff.

In addition to this narrative, a second strand of literature points to the role played by external actors. Scholars such as Hankey et al. (2018, 20), for example, have described the role played by data brokers, "companies that make tools for 'digital listening' and for tracking voters as they move across devices;

and political campaign strategists who advise political parties on when and where to spend their digital money in a campaign."

Parties' use of external vendors and consultants for DDC is not unique; indeed, such actors have long been used to provide, for example, "opinion polls and statistical techniques" (Kusche 2020, 4). When it comes to data, external actors are often seen to play a critical role in helping parties adapt to new data competencies and execute sophisticated data practices. Simon (2019), for example, has mapped an emerging industry of companies (originating largely from the US) that engage in political campaigns and initiatives (see also Richterich 2018). Elsewhere, Bartlett et al. have described how "[s]everal firms also offer assistance in mining and targeting voters, including so called 'marketing clouds' offered by, among others, Adobe, Oracle, Salesforce, Nielsen, and IBM" (2018, 27).

Other work has pointed to the role that digital advertising firms (Barrett 2022) or social media companies can play in supporting party activities (Kreiss & McGregor 2018). External actors are therefore often described as important sources of expertise and innovation that help parties enact the data-driven campaign.

Whether focusing on internal or external actors, the importance of specific personnel to DDC is underpinned by the fact that, as Kreiss and Howard (2010, 2) argue, "[d]ata alone is not valuable.... It needs to be made meaningful to campaigns in some way." Internal data experts or external actors are seen to be critical to this process. Such ideas align with the suggestion from Farrell et al. (2001) that "[n]ew technologies require new technicians." Hence, to work with data, "[p]arties must make a conscious commitment to integrate modern technology into their party operations and campaign strategies" by employing or hiring data specialists if they want to adopt these techniques (Hatch 2016, 197).

In focusing on these two groups of personnel, existing accounts of DDC have suggested that actors wield power and are responsible for how a data-driven campaign operates. Indeed, Römmele and Gibson (2020, 596–603) have argued, in their "scientific" conception of DDC, that there is "an increasing centralization within parties which has shifted to national staff and away from local operatives," and that leaders and political representatives have been "subsumed by data-driven decision making," leading decisions to be made in a "more 'rote' and machine-like" manner. From such a perspective, the personnel conducting DDC are highly influential, not only in determining what is done, but also for the organization of campaign activity. This perspective suggests that smaller, more professionalized organizations, staffed by expert professionals and contracting external expertise, are likely to be the norm.

And yet, as repeatedly articulated within this book, DDC is not a singular activity, but is a practice that can come in many different forms and can be enacted in a variety of different ways. This holds true for campaign personnel and party organization, making it important to understand who is involved in DDC and what role individuals play.

Party Personnel

Challenging the idea that DDC is the domain of a particular type of actor, we find that a range of different actors and groups can play a role. Inspired by preexisting scholarship (Katz & Mair 1993), we identify three different types of party actors that can play different roles in DDC.

First, we identify the party grassroots. While not all parties have grassroots actors (Mazzoleni & Voerman 2017), scholarship has routinely pointed to the presence and significance of party members, supporters, and activists who conduct campaigning activity, offer financial support, and who are "loyal voters" (Katz & Mair 1993, 597). Conceptualized in different ways (Duverger 1967; Scarrow 2015), grassroots actors can have alternative types of affiliation which vary in their strength and obligations. Some therefore pay a membership or affiliation fee, some have a stake in party decision-making, and others have only loose ties to party organizations. What is common is that grassroots actors create a *voluntary* affiliation with a party, meaning they do not receive material rewards (Lees-Marshment & Pettitt 2014). While members and supporters are by no means always active within parties, many volunteer their time and resources to advance party goals (Scarrow 2015; Webb et al. 2017). This can provide parties with an important, free source of expertise and labor which parties can manage in a variety of different ways, reflecting party structure and attitudes toward local autonomy and central control. When it comes to DDC, the grassroots actors can play a more or less prominent role vis-à-vis other actors, conducting different activities.

Second, we identify party officials. Once again operating as an umbrella term, officials can include elected representatives, elder statesmen (or retired politicians), or party staff who hold positions in the upper echelons of party hierarchy. Often working in centralized party headquarters, officials can also be found at local, regional, national, or international levels within parties and are distinguished by their role in coordinating party activity, setting strategy, and offering leadership. While a small proportion can hold these roles in a voluntary capacity, most are paid for their work, either by the party or state institutions (in the case of elected representatives). Not all staff are, however, hired on a permanent basis, and it is common to see short-term contracts and a general fluctuation in staffing numbers throughout the electoral calendar. As a category, party officials can often appear as a coherent group, but there can be different degrees of power-sharing, with individuals often seeking to advance competing strategies (Carty 2004; Bolleyer 2012; Kefford 2016). What defines this group is their role "at the apex of the party organization" (Katz & Mair 1993, 599), meaning they are responsible for shaping practice and coordinating party activity. When it comes to DDC, officials can often (but not always) play a pivotal role in designing and executing party strategy, using data not only to inform decisions, but also to manage the wider party organization.

Third, we identify external actors or, in other words, organizations and individuals who comprise a wider ecosystem that supports and informs party activity. Previous work has focused on party consultants, exploring the roles that specialist firms or individual experts perform for parties, particularly in election campaigns (Medvic 2003; Grossmann 2009). Dalton and Wattenberg (2000, 55) have therefore argued that "[e]lection campaigns are now highly professional affairs, involving public relations consultants and media specialists." Others have pointed to the presence of polling experts, market research professionals, data analysts, and strategic gurus in informing party activity (Farrell et al. 2001; Sparrow & Turner 2001). These actors are by no means homogeneous, as consultants can be ideologically aligned or unaligned to parties and differ in the degree to which they focus exclusively on political work (Farrell et al. 2001, 14). In addition, Dommett et al. (2020) introduce the acronym CLANS to highlight the role that companies; local volunteers and activists; academics and professional researchers; non-party campaigners and groups; and sister parties play in party activity. Their work suggests that a range of other actors can support party activity by providing strategic advice, specialist knowledge, capacity, and infrastructure (see Table 6.1).

Table 6.1 Actors Involved in Party Organization

Party Grassroots	Party Officials	External Actors
Party members	Elected representatives	Companies (including consultants and service providers)
Party supporters	Elder statespeople	Academics and professional researchers
	Party staff	Non-party campaigners and groups[a]
		Sister parties
		Affiliate organizations

[a] Examples include Progress in Australia, MoveOn in the United States (Karpf 2012), GetUp! in Australia (Vromen 2016), and Momentum in the United Kingdom (Dommett & Temple 2018).

The Different Personnel of Data-Driven Campaigns across Our Five Advanced Democracies

Having identified the potential role that grassroots actors, officials, and external actors can play (Table 6.1), we now present empirical evidence that shows the alternative configurations of data-driven campaigns. Reflecting back on our previous three chapters, we consider who is involved in data collection, analytics, and the use of technology, and show that much DDC is executed by "campaign assemblages" (Nielsen 2012, 103) that vary in form.

Data Collection

Reflecting back on the four types of data highlighted in Chapter 3, we first found widespread evidence that grassroots actors are often critical in collecting disclosed and inferred data via doorstep and phone canvassing, email surveys, petitions, and direct mail surveys. While there was some evidence of certain grassroots actors collecting monitoring data, disclosed data and inferred data were most commonly collected by this group. The degree to which different parties could rely on their grassroots actors for data collection, and the degree of autonomy they were afforded, varied considerably in line with party-level factors. Second, party officials play a significant role in gathering publicly available data and monitoring data, with party representatives more likely to play a role in collecting disclosed and inferred insights.

Variation was again evident, as available resources curtailed parties' ability to hire staff, and there were different degrees of centralization in how party officials worked. Finally, when it came to external actors, these groups contribute to all four types of data, but stark differences in parties' ability to hire external expertise or access external networks of support are evident. These differences are unpacked by country below.

In Australia, all three groups of actors played an important role in the collection of data. Australia has an embedded history of canvassing activity, and the parties covered here have an active if somewhat small membership base to deploy for data-collection activity (Davies 2020). Many parties have embraced fluid notions of membership and supporters to access additional grassroots resources (Gauja 2015; Kefford 2021). Unlike some of our other cases, the party grassroots actors have very little agency in determining what data is collected or in innovating. Australian parties are extraordinarily hierarchical, and the party grassroots are viewed primarily as a labor resource. The only partial exception to this is the Greens, who through their history of social activism and social movements (Gauja & Jackson 2016) provide the grassroots actors with slightly more agency over what data is collected, if any, and how (Hayman 2021).[1]

Mirroring a trend also observed in the United Kingdom, Canada, the United States, and Germany, candidates and party representatives worked alongside grassroots activists in the collection of disclosed and inferred data via canvassing activity. For the most part, party staff contributed to the collection of a different type of data, playing a critical role in accessing publicly available data insights in the form of the electoral roll, as well as augmenting data that was publicly available with data that they paid for, including, for example, phone numbers of voters. In each Australian party, it was therefore staff who collected data from the electoral commission and census and inputted this into party databases—providing the data which grassroots actors then used to gather further disclosed and inferred data.

These actors were also critical for gathering monitoring data, as they designed and implemented systems to track campaign activity and to trace the effectiveness of specific interventions, such as fundraising emails. While nearly every party conducted these kinds of data-collection activity in-house, there were some types of data that parties relied on external actors to collect. Companies were particularly important for the collection of disclosed and inferred data and were seen to provide services that party staff were not able to perform. The Liberals, for example, used C|T, or its subsidiaries, to collect data via robo-polls, as well as to do qualitative research.[2] Labor used YouGov to do polling work such as their daily tracking polls of marginal seats across the country during the campaign, and used companies such as UMR and Visibility for more qualitative insights. Likewise, the Greens have worked with Essential Media to collect inferred data. We also saw best practice being shared through sister parties, with a former digital staffer for Labor explaining how, following the 2015 UK election, operatives from the UK Labour Party came to Australia and advised them on email harvesting operations (Kefford 2021). In short, the collection of data in Australia brings together a wide array of actors to collect different data points.

In the United Kingdom, we saw many of the same trends. As with Australia, grassroots actors were almost uniformly seen as vital for data collection; indeed, one interviewee from the Liberal Democrat Party described how "the activists are vitally important for collecting data." There were, however, clear differences in the degree to which parties could rely on this group, as party membership was not uniform and parties have "opened up" to different degrees, with some developing supporters' networks to boost their grassroots resource, and others relying more exclusively on their membership (Gauja 2013). This means the Labour Party currently has more than twice as many activists as the next nearest party (Loft et al. 2019). There are also differences among the characteristics of each parties' grassroots actors. Research by Bale et al. (2019, 36) for example, has shown that the Conservatives possess an older and less active membership demographic than, for example, the Liberal Democrat Party. These party-level differences mean that grassroots actors played more or less pronounced roles in different parties.

Grassroots actors were predominantly focused on gathering disclosed information through canvassing activity, but we saw a few examples of local activists collecting monitoring data. This was evident primarily in target seats, with activists conducting fairly rudimentary campaign activity tracking by, for example, monitoring the number of contacts made. For the most part, such monitoring data was instead gathered by party officials. Party staff particularly, but not exclusively, in larger parties therefore monitored local campaign action, using the data collected to inform the strategic targeting of additional resources in line with the dynamics of the electoral system. Party staff also ensured that in electorally significant areas where there was a lack of grassroots resource (because of the uneven geographic distribution of party membership), additional resources (in the form of canvassers brought in from other areas, or party representatives) were deployed. In some parties, this led to local staff being hired to lead data collection, with the Labour Party and the Conservative Party both particularly investing in these roles. The focus on key seats often meant that in these places party officials exercised tighter control over the type of data collected, with one interviewee in the Labour Party explaining how, in these contexts, canvassing sessions were "more or less dictated kind of top-down." However, in less electorally significant areas, local activists often had more freedom to deviate from centralized data-collection scripts.

As in Australia, party staff also played a key role in securing and inputting publicly available data. Different parties were, however, able to devote different levels of staffing to data collection. While some parties developed in-house teams, others were reliant on external actors—and were often able to afford such services to different degrees. UK financial data, for example, shows that every UK party commissioned external polling (Dommett et al. 2022, 46), but the Conservatives and Labour were able to devote far higher levels of resources, while the smaller parties had limited ability to conduct polls or purchase other data insights. In some instances, ties to non-party campaign groups, such as Momentum (Rhodes 2019; Dennis 2020), or to other organizations—such as trade unions—were also leveraged to gather data, with these groups used to recruit participants to attend parties' canvassing activities. Parties' ability to access such ties was not, however, uniform, with left-leaning parties seen to have access to a wider array of cognate organizations than conservative parties. Regulation also played a role in curtailing the actions these groups could take on parties' behalf (HM Government 2022).

Canada, like other countries, has an established history of party membership, and local canvassing activity is perceived an important determinant of electoral success (Carty & Eagles 1999). One interviewee from the Liberal Party pointed to the significance of volunteers, noting "a database is fine to have, but you need the volunteers." Across left-leaning parties in particular, we found a sustained focus on up-skilling and integrating volunteers, viewing them as a vital resource. Indeed, one interviewee in the NDP described their aim of getting activists "more familiar and interested in data," explaining that:

> if our volunteers aren't on board, if our organizers and our activists aren't on board, then we really can't do the work because they need to be convinced

that if I provide my friend's phone number, I know that it is not being misused by the party.

Within many Canadian parties, grassroots actors have a high degree of autonomy. Canadian parties in general tend to operate as stratarchical organizations (Carty & Eagles 1999; Carty et al. 2000; Carty 2004), meaning that local associations are often left to their own devices in running campaigns, while the national party deals with federal parliament and the national campaign (Coletto et al. 2011). As with the United Kingdom, party membership differs significantly, providing parties with different levels of grassroots resource. As detailed by Cross (2015), membership data is patchy, but the Liberals and NDP historically have a higher membership than the Conservatives of Canadian Alliance.[3] For the 2015 federal election, the Liberals claimed to have 80,000 campaign volunteers and the NDP 40,000 (Radwanski 2015). The number of activists each party can deploy is therefore varied. Unlike in the United Kingdom, in Canada the collection of disclosed and inferred data was not conducted exclusively by volunteers, as electoral law allows parties to pay individuals to become "poll cats."

Party officials once again played a key role in gathering publicly available information and monitoring campaign interventions. While parties did possess a national headquarters, they tended to hire larger numbers of staff at regional levels (relative to parties in Australia and the United Kingdom) to organize elections in different federal areas (Coletto et al. 2011; Cross 2015). These arrangements reflected the dynamics of the political system, with party finance rules making resource sharing between provincial and federal wings largely impossible (McGrane 2019).

We also saw external actors play an important role. Though Canada does not have a culture of consultancy akin to that in the United States, we found some parties with long-standing relationships to certain companies. One example of this is the exclusive contract between analytics company Data Sciences Inc. and the Liberal Party (McGregor 2017). Moreover, the Liberal Party has used Pitney Bowes for things such as cultural name-matching services (Delacourt 2013). The Conservative Party in Canada has in the past used Politrain Consulting and Stack Data Strategy for undefined data work (Boutilier 2022) and is known to have worked with Spectrum Electoral Demographics for more specific insights on constituency-level demographics and with Environics for demographic data (Bennett & Lyon 2019). Likewise, the secondary literature points to the NDP having previously purchased data from Environics Analytics, as well as Viewpoints Research who provided demographic data on Canadian citizens (Delacourt 2013). As in the United Kingdom, non-party campaigners did not directly contribute data, as electoral legislation prevents coordinated campaigning.

In the United States, a different culture around personnel exists from that evident in other countries. As in other contexts, grassroots activity was a key component of data collection, and both the Republicans and Democrats have large-scale activist mobilization efforts in the run-up to elections, although as Nielsen (2012, 49) details, these differ in precise form. It is therefore common for US campaigns to call on neighborhood teams composed of "3–4 core team members, and half a dozen or more regular volunteers, while data, canvass, and phone bank captains were a constant presence across teams" (McKenna & Han 2014, 138). US parties, like those in Canada, also supplement their volunteer base by paying non-members to do canvassing work (Nielsen 2012). There has also been evidence of unusual practice, with Mike Bloomberg's presidential campaign in 2020 drawing on prison labor to make canvassing calls (Washington 2019).

Notably, in contrast to other countries, party officials and external actors play a far greater role. Party officials, elected representatives, and candidates are, akin to other countries, expected to engage in data collection, but in the United States, they are supported by far larger numbers of campaign staff. These staff gather publicly available, disclosed, monitored, and inferred data themselves, but local staff are also often hired in larger numbers than in other countries to lead the data-collection activity of grassroots actors (Hatch 2016). Party staff based in campaign headquarters also often work with external companies and, in contrast to our other countries, have an established infrastructure of external actors to draw upon. The 2022 US Campaigns and Elections Consultant Directory, for example, lists nearly 200 different companies that can support campaigns, and while not all are focused on data collection, many of these actors provide commercial data (either disclosed or inferred) or gather monitoring data. Often seen as the innovators of campaign practice, US campaigns are less reliant on insights from sister parties or non-party campaign organizations. The use of academic insights was also less prominent than in some other cases, with the commercial sector and the campaign staff dominant. This reliance on external, paid companies and consultants and the focus on hiring staff to support election campaigns means that US parties have relatively weak infrastructure for *ongoing* data-collection activity because, as Kreiss (2016) has demonstrated, after an election, campaign staff tend to disperse (Bureau of Labor Statistics 2020).

In Germany, party grassroots actors, officials, and external actors are all important for data collection (Niedermayer 2013; Rudzio 2015). Party grassroots actors are mentioned as the "centerpiece" or "heart" of every campaign by all German party strategists. German street and canvassing campaigns are organized on a national level but are executed locally on the ground by party members and volunteers, making activists crucial for the collection of disclosed data. Differences can, however, be witnessed between parties. German party membership differs significantly between the parties, creating an apparent advantage for the CDU and SPD, which both have around 400,000 party members, far more than the smaller parties (the Left has 60,000 and the AfD 30,000; Niedermayer 2020). However, as in the United Kingdom, party members are demographically different, so the membership of both the CDU and SPD is older than among the smaller parties. This has disadvantages for the collection of data with technology, as older members are often less adept at utilizing new tools for data collection, a dynamic that led the CDU in 2017 to task the youth wing of the party to organize and conduct most canvassing and data-collection work.

Elected representatives and candidates are often involved in the collection of disclosed data as they join grassroots actors for canvassing activities. One CDU interviewee explained this approach as quite effective since "often candidates acted as drivers for the canvassing actions and pulled local party members along who would otherwise refrain from going from door-to-door and collecting data." German party staff are critical for gathering other data sources. They download publicly available data from statistical offices of the state or the Federal Election Commissioner, or buy data from the register of residents or the population register. They conduct surveys via emails or direct mail to poll members or monitor member statistics or voter contact with the party organization. They also gather inferential data via analytics processes. Differences in the collection activities by campaign officials between different parties can be seen with regard to the size of the parties and their resources. Bigger parties have a wider personnel pool with knowledgeable staff and can create better financial incentives to hire staff with the right know-how to collect different data sources.

When it comes to external actors, German parties mainly rely on polling companies. The main traditional polling companies—Forschungsgruppe Wahlen, infratest dimap, and Institut für Demoskopie Allensbach—have close ties to the big parties. However, online polling companies such as YouGov or Civey are increasingly being hired. External actors are also often paid by German parties to collect data sources when the parties lack internal know-how, to collect monitoring or inferential data. Examples are the Deutsche Post Direkt, which sold data to the FDP for direct mailing and to the CDU for canvassing. In addition to commercial companies, interviewees cited the significance of academic ties. One interviewee described how "there's always an influx of people from academia that you talk to" in order to gather information. As in our other cases, financial resources often account for the differences in German parties hiring external actors for data collection. Yet party attitudes can also play a role. In recent campaigns, for example, the Greens and the Left have voiced reticence about the collection of some forms of personal voter data. A party strategist of the Greens during the 2016 state election in Rhineland-Palatinate, for example, said:

> We don't purchase any voter data from data brokers due to conflicting views in the party. Some party members view the collection and use of voter data as incompatible with our party policies. And we try to respect that and only draw on Facebook for targeting voters and marketing services for sending out direct mailings.

When it comes to data collection, we therefore found that an assemblage of actors played a role, but that parties differed in exactly who engaged in what type of data-collection activity.

Data Analysis

In terms of data analytics, we observed variations in the degree of analytical sophistication that the same type of actor was able to perform in different parties. Summarizing the broad trends: first, when it comes to segmentation, all three types of actors engage in this activity, but simple segmentation tended to be conducted by a small number of grassroots activists in organizational roles, while more highly complex practices were performed by party staff and external actors (almost exclusively companies or academics). Looking at party-level differences, not all parties were able to execute the most sophisticated forms of analysis, often because they lacked the resources to hire internal or external actors to perform such functions. Second, in terms of targeting, we primarily saw grassroots actors and party officials engaged in targeting activity (with differing degrees of sophistication), although some external groups facilitated this activity. Across all our parties, some form of targeted messaging occurred; however, parties' capacity for message differentiation was not uniform. Finally, in terms of testing, this activity was mainly the preserve of party staff, but we also saw external actors, particularly companies, consultancies, or research institutes, offering insights. This was particularly the case when it came to more sophisticated forms of testing, with a number of parties lacking internal testing capacity.

In Australia, we observed differentiation in the activities of different actors. For the most part in all of the parties observed, we found party staff and external actors to be dominant in regard to analytics. This does not, however, mean that grassroots actors were not involved. While most ordinary activists had little exposure to these processes, those volunteering to lead campaigns did engage in the segmentation of voters and in targeted messaging. Often deploying unsophisticated uses of these techniques, we heard interviewees speak about using targeted mail to deliver certain messages to specific voters, and about the importance of engaging different audiences on the issues that mattered to them. We also saw grassroots activists segmenting electorates out by booth results[4] to identify the desired geographic audience. These practices were evident in all the Australian parties and were also found in parties across our other four countries.

In terms of the more sophisticated analytics practices, in Australia (and in our other cases), these were performed by party staff and external companies. In the Liberal and Labor parties, for example, we saw staff hired to work on analytics or as data scientists. In parties with resources available to hire leading experts in data analytics,[5] such as Labor, we found staff responsible for constructing persuasion-based models, developing sophisticated targeting strategies, and engaging in complex message testing and even using experimental methods (Kefford 2021). In contrast, in less resourced parties, such as the Greens, there were fewer staff, who often had less specific expertise (due to the breadth of their role), leading them to focus on relatively unsophisticated or moderately sophisticated analytics processes. We also often saw Australian parties drawing on external companies for support with data analytics, and particularly segmentation and testing. This included Blue State Digital for Labor and IMGE for the Liberal Party, as well as a huge number of digital advertising companies who were often hired for their expertise on different channels. While companies were the predominant source of analytics work, a number of parties also utilized academics and external researchers to conduct analysis, with the Labor Party and the Greens using academics to gain advice on modeling and input on MRP work.

In the United Kingdom, many of the trends evident in Australia were replicated. For the most part, ordinary grassroots actors were largely uninvolved in analytics processes, with one interviewee from the Liberal Democrat Party describing segmentation and modeling "as far as activists and so on [are concerned] . . . kind of a black box." Once again, however, a small number of more senior activists engaged in simple forms of analytics. Facilitated by access to databases that included basic data-manipulation tools, activists in most parties were able to conduct segmentation and develop strategies for targeting, or to choose to apply target criteria developed by the national party to their local area. Within Labour's Contact Creator database, for example, activists can filter data to identify lists of undecided voters who have a phone number on the system. Access to these systems was not universal (as the Greens have no such system), and where available was curtailed, with one interviewee describing:

> there's quite a heavily complicated set of permissions that allow individuals to log in and only view the rights for the electorate within the specific area that they're looking in and that itself is quite a big thing. We have about 7,000 individual users that can log in to the front end and view, basically, local members that can view and access and run off reports and do things with the database.

In addition to providing tools for data analysis, in most parties we found staff encouraging activists, and particularly local campaign coordinators, to deploy basic targeting techniques. Whether encouraging targeting via direct mail by providing templates for different targeted letters or supporting activists to use tools like targeted Facebook advertising, there was an emphasis on focusing campaign activity on specific, electorally important groups. When it came to testing, we found limited evidence of this activity among grassroots activists, although a very small number of volunteers spoke about using A/B testing on Facebook.

Party staff were more directly engaged in data analytics. As in Australia, the Labour Party employs targeting analysts and a targeted content manager (Common Knowledge 2020), while the Conservative Party employs a data analyst. However, the number of staff devoted to this work varied by party. In the Green Party, we saw one individual holding a portfolio role around digital, which saw them responsible for a wide range of data curation and analysis as well as digital infrastructure and IT issues. The Conservatives and Labour had more dedicated staff, but these were not consistently employed, and numbers were limited.[6] In the major parties, staff spoke about conducting highly sophisticated analytics practices in-house, discussing their use of complex segmentation and testing in particular, but in minor parties, such as the Greens, such techniques were not deployed—largely due to a lack of expertise and capacity.

UK parties also relied to different degrees on external actors. The main parties drew extensively on support from companies. Interviewees from the Labour Party spoke about their relationship with Experian as being critical to their data operation, with the company providing data, modeling, and database functionality for a cost of over £1 million at the 2019 general election. Similarly, the Conservatives drew on insight and modeling produced by the company C|T, spending £1.7 million with the company at the 2019 election. Smaller parties reported being less able to hire external expertise. In certain cases, this led them to rely on academics as opposed to companies, with one individual hired by the Green Party recalling how post-election they used the publically available British Election Study (Chapter 3) to model:

> what they should expect from every seat according to the sociodemographics, etc. And then, compared that to what they actually did get, and then were able to produce like the 50 best overperforming Green seats and the 50 underperforming seats. And so then they could recalibrate from there.

Although major parties did sometimes call on academics for advice on MRPs, the Greens were reliant on this group because of the cost of alternative expertise.

In terms of third-party actors, we found that a number of advocacy organizations offered insights that helped parties to innovate. Staff in the Labour Party therefore spoke about using research from the Analyst Institute to gather intelligence on RCTs and field tests that they could not afford to conduct themselves. As one interviewee outlined:

> The Analyst Institute is a US organization for progressive campaigners who work in politics and data and campaigning. They had a lot of research around vote planning and how they'd done randomized control trials in the US around vote planning.... They've got randomized controlled trials going back to 2012. That would quite often be our place to go to get ideas about how to improve things we were doing.

As in the previous two countries, in Canada activists played only a limited role in data analytics and deployed simple techniques. Party staff and external companies were predominant. The Liberals and NDP both publicly hired data directors (National Post 2014), and while the Conservatives have released little information about their staffing strategy, previous research has suggested they had an in-house analytics team well before other Canadian parties (Patten 2017). Though larger parties, such as the Liberals, reported extensive expertise and investment (Ormiston 2015), smaller parties reported limited expertise. As described by one interviewee from the NDP:

> We have two really incredible data scientists that work for, basically every NDP branch. They're all over the place. They worked in the last election federally, are going to work in Ontario, are going to have worked in Alberta, they're getting shipped around the country. And because they're experts, they're very familiar with our systems, they're very familiar with our numbers, with everything and it really... there's just a need to build that institutional memory with other people. To train more people on it and that's hard to do. It's very difficult.

Interviewees reported that expertise was limited, with one from the Liberal Party reflecting that because they "don't operate on huge budgets, so you couldn't maintain these people in a four-year electoral cycle, not for the amount of people you need." This dynamic was not unique to Canada (and was evident in Australia, the United Kingdom, and Germany), but marked a point of contrast with the United States, where larger numbers of party staff possessed analytics expertise.

In Canada, we observed some differences from parties in other countries as, once again, the federated nature of the political system meant that while parties did have analytics expertise in headquarters, they also paid staff at a local level to conduct analysis. Interviewees in the NDP therefore explained that analysis was conducted by local paid organizers who focused on the "collection and the strategizing" of data, with little input on strategy from central party staff. This analysis was not always the most highly complex, but it was deployed with high degrees of autonomy.

In terms of external actors, once again, DataSciences were cited as significant to the Liberals' analytics operations (McGregor 2017), a company advertising their services as combining "sound data management, advanced analytics, machine learning and AI, and cutting-edge digital engagement strategies to better measure audience intent, communicate efficiently, and produce measurable results with the power to shift public perception" (Data Sciences n.d., n.p.). We also heard about the importance of relationships with sister parties, with an interviewee from the NDP describing how they:

> have relationships with UK Labour and Australian Labour and New Zealand Labour and the German, whatever they're called, the party that's just got into power. And so every once in a while they come to us and we go to them and we share experiences and how have you been dealing with campaigning.

Interviewees explained that external actors often allowed parties to access additional expertise and capacity. As one interviewee from the NDP described, "the reason you use a consultant is because you need a level of expertise for a short period of time that you couldn't afford to attract as a full-time position. That's why you go out and find someone who is an expert in something because you don't have the money to staff your organization with high-level experts." The ability to locate such expertise was, however, not easy, as the same interviewee went on to describe:

> there are some areas where there isn't that type of expertise in Canada, just because the market is so small. In the situations where we're dealing with market challenges in Canada, there's usually a number of options based in the States that do international work, or at least are pretty familiar with the Canadian landscape, just because it is really niche kind of expertise areas and there are not a lot of people that do them.

These dynamics often led parties to look to the United States, where the supply of consultants and the number of companies and other organizations devoted to campaigning are significantly higher than in other countries. And yet, the knowledge that these US-based experts possessed was not always appropriate for the Canadian context, limiting the perceived value of hiring such experts.

The main points of contrast between the US case and the others examined here are the number of party officials devoted to analytics, and the use of external actors capable of conducting sophisticated analytical processes. Similar to practice in the United Kingdom, we see (senior) local activists given autonomy to engage in segmentation and targeting activity, especially among the Democrats. These techniques were relatively unsophisticated and mirrored the approaches found in other countries. In contrast, when looking at the sophistication of the analytics practices conducted by party staff and external actors, more complex examples were evident. As previously mentioned, both major US campaigns from at least 2016 onward have possessed large numbers of staff who are devoted full-time to data analytics. The practices conducted by these teams tended to be much more sophisticated and resource intensive than in other parties. There was accordingly widespread testing of campaign messages and affordances, using experimental methods and RCTs (Issenberg 2012a). We also saw external actors, particularly consultants, commissioned to bring external expertise and to deliver the most sophisticated segmentation techniques. Despite this, US campaigns (and indeed, campaigns in our other cases) face what has been described as a "people gap" in data. According to Audra Grassia (2016), former deputy political director for the Democratic Governors Association:

> Managing, using, and understanding data takes [sic] technical training, and no matter how many people we put through data-training programs, the dearth of well-trained, skilled data scientists and analysts working in politics is not likely to change rapidly.

Finally, in Germany we saw trends more akin to Canada, with the federated nature of campaigns and curtailed resources (compared to the US) limiting parties' ability to contract personnel able to conduct the most sophisticated forms of data analysis. Grassroots activists were hardly involved in data analysis; instead, most of the analytics work was done by party staff who are empowered in many parties to engage in qualitative focus-group work and to conduct segmentation and targeting activities that vary in complexity. Again, party size and resources determined parties' ability to hire statisticians or analytical experts. The bigger parties drew on their internal party expertise and networks and hired experts for the election period. Situated in parties' headquarters in Berlin, one to four staff members were responsible for the whole data analytics operation of the individual parties and their campaigns. Some smaller parties such as the Left described how they were "more or less a one-man-show for digital campaigning who needs to do the data stuff, budget planning, advertising buying, and targeting. You get the sense how much time I can devote to each of these tasks." Although other parties were able to hire more staff, their ability to deploy more sophisticated forms of segmentation, targeting, and testing were limited. This had mostly to do with a limited understanding of data analytics, with one interviewee from the Left Party asking what "predictive modeling" was. This dynamic was also evident in Canada, where research by Munroe and Munroe shows uneven knowledge of data and analytics techniques among campaigning staff (Munroe & Munroe 2018, 16).

In terms of external actors, despite a willingness to learn from external actors, the lack of a domestic consultancy market limited available and relevant expertise. Although some domestic consultants and agencies were hired to support data analytics tasks, other consultants were brought over from other countries. In that regard, the specificity of German regulation terrain meant big obstacles for their analytical models and ideas. Indeed, one consultant we spoke to recalled how they:

> once did a presentation to the leader of a European social democratic party, about the digital campaign that we ran in Obama 2012. A senior staffer from the campaign gave a presentation about our campaign on the ground. He went first, and at the end of it, the leader of this party, ... a very, very serious, fairly humorless man, said to my colleague, "This was a very interesting presentation. Everything you have said is fascinating. I wrote down your recommendations; you have 11. Of the 11 recommendations, 7 of them are against the law in our country. Do you have any other recommendations for us?"

For this reason, German parties were often not able to replicate the use and type of analysis evident in the United States.

Technology

Finally, turning to consider technology, across our cases we found evidence that different groups of party personnel were responsible for creating and utilizing organizational and communications technologies. Summarizing our findings, we found that single technologies were often used by multiple actors within a single party, but that party officials and external actors exploited higher level functionalities. We found that many parties provided training to equip activists to use technology, but this was not universal or always successful in securing uptake. We also observed the significance of party officials in commissioning and maintaining technologies, but found a few instances where grassroots actors were responsible for building new technological tools or were able to capitalize on commercial tools. In terms of external actors, we found that these groups often helped to build technological capacity, but that outside of the United States the role of companies was curtailed by available resources and a desire to develop functions in-house.

In Australia, databases and CRM systems are utilized by each of our types of personnel, but in different ways. While grassroots actors in each party inputted data and exported canvassing sheets, they utilized limited functionality. In contrast, party officials used this technology to perform a range of different tasks, and specifically to generate analytics insights in terms of segmentation and testing.

More variation is evident in the types of personnel involved in communication technologies. When it comes to party websites, this was almost entirely the domain of party officials and external actors. The design and construction of central party websites tended to be done almost entirely by external providers who embedded complex functions, while candidate and elected representative pages were often created internally by party officials using relatively simple templates and digital packages. In terms of SNP use, this was more varied with each of the three different types of actors using SNPs across the three parties. Each party had digital campaign staff using targeting and segmentation functionality provided to them by the SNPs, either placing advertisements themselves or working with external vendors. Each of the parties also exhibited grassroots use of SNPs, but this was primarily focused on less complex organic media engagement and managing social media accounts.

In the United Kingdom, databases and CRMs (where available) were used by grassroots and party officials. Many parties provided training to facilitate grassroots access, but not all were able to do so. As one interviewee from the Green's described, "[w]ith Civi for example, there's all sorts of functionality then that those local parties don't know exist. And have never been trained to use, and . . . these systems are . . . never simple to use, so it does require training." In this party, grassroots actors were therefore often unable to use party systems or could only exploit limited functionality, but even in parties where training was provided, this focused on limited functionality, and many activists found party systems difficult to navigate. In contrast, UK party officials exploited higher functionalities and ensured that systems remained operational. These dynamics were also apparent in party-provided campaign applications. We did find some examples of grassroots activists in the Labour Party and the Green Party creating mobile applications, such as the My Nearest Marginal App created by the external campaign group Momentum (Pettitt 2020, 70) and the "plenty of reasons to vote Green" app. While these apps were simple and had limited functionality, they required significant expertise to maintain and update, showing that officials were not the only source of technological expertise. In Labour we also saw innovation through Campaign Lab, where volunteer activists with data skills aimed to build technological solutions, but such practice was not commonplace.

In terms of communication technology, party websites were routinely created either centrally using internal expertise or through external company support. These actors were instrumental in creating templates for local parties to use, resulting in considerable uniformity in digital presence (especially in target seats). However, we did find instances of local innovation, where local parties created their own web presences. These tended to contain less functionality than nationally directed sites and were maintained in a sporadic manner.

The rise of SNPs and tools for online advertising allowed grassroots activists in the United Kingdom to use technology as never before. This was particularly the case in the Labour Party and Liberal Democrats, where analysis of the Facebook advertising archive showed that local parties placed a significant number of advertisements at the 2019 general election—with 1,848 advertisements placed by local Labour parties and 1,361 by local Liberal Democrat parties, compared to the 350 advertisements placed by local Conservative parties (Dommett & Bakir 2020, 217). In these instances, technology facilitated higher-level functions that previously had been the preserve of officials and external experts, but which could now be used by local activists. Party officials and external actors remained key in creating websites and providing support for the use of SNPs, often facilitating grassroots activity. Indeed, we found party staff to be offering training in all parties, with the "Conservative Academy," launched in 2018, training activists in how to "employ Facebook, email and websites" (Morris 2018, n.p.). Within the Labour Party, there were also attempts to facilitate more complex grassroots use of technology, with the party providing a 100-page manual for activists about how to create and optimize Facebook advertising via its system Promote. In addition to supporting grassroots activity, party officials often worked to deliver large-scale advertising campaigns on SNPs, drawing on internal expertise and external support to design and deliver this activity.

In terms of databases and CRMs, as with Australia and the United Kingdom, Canadian party systems enable hierarchical access, allowing grassroots actors to access small amounts of local information and perform basic functions with the help of training. Oversight is retained by party officials, who are able to execute more complex functions and analytics that, in turn, are fed to local campaigns (Patten 2017). As in the United Kingdom and Australia, in many Canadian parties staff were devoted to the technological upkeep of databases. One interviewee in the NDP therefore described how their data staff focus on "maintaining the database, they're cleaning the database, they're fixing it when it breaks. They're importing data, they're exporting data." Similarly, in the Liberal Party we heard about the need for continual staffing investment, with one interviewee noting, "you do need dedicated people who all the time are watching the system to ensure that they're as secure as they can be." While party officials were therefore those deploying higher functions, they spent much of their time maintaining and preserving party technology.

In terms of communication technology, many of the same trends were apparent. Officials were responsible for building websites and embedding tracking technology, often drawing on support from external providers to gather specific expertise. They also deployed SNPs to communicate national messages, using complex techniques—often supported by external expertise and advice (from companies and sister parties). While there was evidence of grassroots use of tools for local communication on, for example, Facebook groups, there was less extensive evidence of the use of paid media locally.

Within the United States, technology is widely used by all actors to facilitate campaign activity. In particular, party officials play a crucial brokering role, as in our other cases, in facilitating grassroots use of databases, CRMs, and campaign apps for basic functions (for example, inputting, segmenting), maintaining system functionality, and commissioning and developing new capacities (Kreiss 2016, 117). Yet, to an extent unprecedented in our other cases, officials are also able to draw on the expertise and advice of a range of external actors who, either in concert with parties or independently, develop technological tools. One reason for this is described by former deputy political director for the Democratic Governors Association in 2014, Audra Grassia (2016) as follows:

> Innovation is often driven from the bottom rather than the top. People in leadership might be too far removed from the day-to-day of data management and analytics to really understand the added value of doing things differently. As leaders, it's important to empower people who are responsible for generating insights from data to find faster, cheaper, and better ways to answer the core questions of a campaign. . . . Facilitating a creative culture that listens to and entertains innovative solutions will help build a collaborative environment where everyone feels invested in the data infrastructure.

Technologies such as Act Blue, a small-donation fundraising system used by the Democrats (Rubenstein 2022), have therefore been developed by nonprofit organizations outside the party, but provided crucial infrastructure for donations in the 2020 and 2022 elections. The Republicans also explicitly use incubators such as Startup Caucus (Miller 2022), which was founded in 2019 to stimulate the development of new commercially produced campaign technology. Such dynamics are particular to the United States and reflect the viability of electoral businesses in this market because of the amounts expended by parties and associated campaigners.

In terms of communication technology, the vast array of external companies and consultants and the increased budget available in most races (compared to our other countries) means that local candidates and parties often have access to website designers who can embed high functionality features into designs (Kreiss 2012). The national parties draw on internal and external expertise to create highly functional websites, meaning that web presence in this country is more professionalized than in our other cases. In terms of SNP use, in the 2016 election, party officials worked closely with SNP staff (Kreiss & McGregor 2018) to maximize the effectiveness of advertising campaigns. Unlike in our other cases, non-party campaign groups play a significant role in the use of SNPs, with political action committees placing millions of dollars worth of digital advertising to promote specific candidates (Mie Kim et al. 2018), employing internal expertise to exploit the functionality of these platforms. These developments are shown by Barrett (2022) through network analysis of political groups registered with the Federal Election Committee in the United States. Her analysis reveals:

> that the number of political committees and companies have both dramatically increased since 2008 and that Facebook and Google have become the two most central members of the network. As influencers of the targeting and content of campaign messages, these companies should be considered consequential members of electoral party networks.

In Germany, party grassroots draw extensively on databases and CRMs for data-collection activity via campaign apps, but as party members in Germany are generally older, parties have to invest in training focused on promoting simple functions, and technological uptake is not always forthcoming. Party representatives, candidates, and campaign staff use this resource more extensively, often deploying these systems to organize grassroots and other local campaign activities. This is due to the fact that German parties often use candidates or locally deployed staff as middle-men and -women for connecting the federal with the local level in terms of organization and conduct of campaign activities.

Communication technologies such as homepages and Facebook advertising are often used by party staff in the parties' federal and local headquarters for their own homepages and political advertisements. But they are also used in an interplay between candidates and the party staff. Candidates can buy different communication possibilities from the federal party and can either manage the deployment and content themselves or leave it to the party staff. The German Christian Democrat Party, for example, developed "packages" designed to facilitate the use of digital targeting. As one interviewee from the Christian Democrats described:

> The question was: how can we make it possible for our candidates to be involved in social media advertising? And then we offered them entire advertising packages, i.e., for Google and for Facebook, where we said, We'll set it up for you, and for your constituencies, so that you can buy various packages and then we play out the ads for you.

External actors especially play a role in the use of communication technologies and digital advertisements. All parties hire lead agencies who work with party staff to create and deploy campaign material such as posters or digital advertisements. Furthermore, interviewees from many parties spoke about various companies pitching to them to provide infrastructure or service, with one interviewee from the CDU describing how they received pitches from "Facebook, Google and Jock (a medium-sized German company, here from Berlin ... that specializes in mobile advertising)" about using their platforms for campaigning.

Conclusion

In this chapter we have considered who is involved in DDC. While much attention has been paid to the role and significance of "geeks" or staff with specialized analytical and statistical expertise, in this chapter we have sought to reveal the vast array of actors who contribute to DDC. Exploring the contribution made by grassroots activists, party officials, and external actors to each of the other three components of DDC—data, analytics, and technology—we have shown that campaigns are unique assemblages that draw on different groups. It is therefore important not to think about DDC as the preserve of particular actors, or to envisage certain activities to be only conducted by one group.

Reprising our case study findings, we have shown that practice in the United States does indeed suggest that DDC is a highly professionalized affair that involves hiring numerous staff and external actors. In this context we see campaigns drawing on a wide range of specialized expertise for data collection, analytics, and technology, integrating commercial insights and support from other campaign organizations alongside grassroots activism and a large internal staff. If we look beyond this case, however, we see that practices in the United States are not replicated in the same configurations elsewhere. Indeed, in our other countries we found that it was rare for parties of any size to hire more than a few staff, and that only more highly resourced parties were able to draw routinely on paid external expertise. Instead, we found that parties constructed their own bespoke campaign assemblages, drawing to different extents on grassroots activists for different tasks, giving them varying degrees of autonomy and in some cases paying them. We also found that our parties hired staff at different levels of campaign organization, with, for example, more centralized operations in the United Kingdom and more decentralized staffing in Canada. Moreover, we found that external actors were available and integrated to different degrees, with some parties calling on academics for expertise, others on consultancy companies, and others on like-minded campaign groups. The precise configuration of personnel staffing data-driven campaigns was therefore varied.

These insights are significant for our understanding of DDC because they suggest that US practice is not widely replicated and that different factors can condition the precise nature of any campaign assemblage. In particular, our cases suggest that resources matter, but so too do systemic factors such as the electoral system, regulatory limitations such as those curtailing coordinated campaigning, and party-level factors such as attitudes toward campaigning or party structure. The people who conduct DDC can therefore vary significantly depending on the specific characteristics of a given context, making it important to attend to the contribution of a range of different personnel.

Practitioner Perspectives on Personnel

In the previous chapter, we argued that the people involved in data-driven campaigns can vary significantly. And yet, it's not clear whether practitioners working in this space share this assessment of the practice of data-driven campaigns. To consider this question, we asked two practitioners: Hannah O'Rourke, director of Labour Together[1] (a network for activists in the UK Labour Party), co-convenor of Campaign Lab[2] (a collective of Labour-supporting technologists building new election tools), and convenor of the commission that conducted Labour's 2019 general election review; and Dr. Amber Macintyre, project lead on data and politics at the civil society organization Tactical Tech,[3] to respond to the following provocation:

When people imagine the individuals responsible for party campaigns, and specifically data-driven campaigning, they often think of highly trained computer scientists or statisticians who are expert at producing complex data models. In your experience, who are the people running parties' campaign operations, and how much expertise do they have in data and analytics?

Hannah O'Rourke, Director of Labour Together, Co-Convenor of Campaign Lab, United Kingdom

The people using data in campaigns differ depending on the type of campaign, the level of the campaign, and the kind of data generated. Data is ultimately just information. It can be information gathered from canvassing or generated by interacting with an advertisement on Facebook.

At a central level, data is key, as it allows you to better understand the types of voters you need to win over, what they think, and where they are located. As voter loyalty declines and in the absence of a core vote, this kind of work becomes very important. Data at this level helps you to build

MRPs and try to predict electoral outcomes; it also allows you to start to learn, experiment, and innovate. With data from the marked register and on local activity, you can start to quantify and compare outcomes moving toward more evidenced-based campaigning.

The people working on this side of campaigns professionally are highly skilled, but there is an opportunity to harness the skills of a broader movement. On the left we have many supporters who have really valuable data science and development skills and are willing to donate their time and effort to help parties to win. One of the reasons we set up Campaign Lab was to mobilize these supporters and give them a way to contribute to the Labour Party's campaign through hack days. While internally data science work has to be delivered by paid employees, hack days with volunteers allow for more experimentation with new methods or techniques which (if they work) can be brought back and incorporated into the work of the party. Members of this volunteer-led experimental group can learn from each other, work on interesting political data challenges, and try out new things that might not be thought of in the busy heat of the day-to-day campaign environment. A priority for Labour—and other parties—is to explore how to manage a relationship with these volunteer communities, to develop more open ways of working, and to set up architecture like sandboxes, shared schema, anonymized or synthetic datasets, and integrations to facilitate this.

Yet alongside this central level, many of the day-to-day campaigning decisions are made by local organizers or volunteers on the ground where data literacy might be more limited. Labour is very much a people-powered movement, so a key priority for us needs to be empowering activists with the insights generated by data so they can be used. The volunteer organizer designing a local election leaflet should be able to access insights on what messages or language might work well in that area according to national polling and analysis. You might have the best data in the world, but what's important is how it's actually used. Are insights from analysis shared? Do other people on the ground understand those insights well enough for them to actually affect activity? This is why we need to make sure the tools and systems we build for activists distribute these insights in a way that's easy to understand. Technology used by our movement shouldn't come with a 30-page instruction manual; systems should be much more user friendly and intuitive. Some of the projects Campaign Lab has done in the past have aimed to make existing Labour tools and data more intelligible and more user focused. One of our best tools was something that took targeting data insights from central systems and visualized them as a graph, which made it easier for volunteers on the ground to understand which road groups to prioritize.

The data skills needed can also be different depending on the type of campaigning. Areas like relational campaigning involve different kinds of data and analysis. This is an important new area for parties to develop. Currently the questions we ask on the doorstep are quite extractive, as they are used to help model voter support, intention, and turnout. But what if we started asking broader questions on the doorstep to gather information about local issues in a more systematic way? This is already done in many places informally, but we are yet to develop the tools and processes to make use of this data. This form of campaigning is more about developing deeper kinds of community power. It still requires systems and data analysis, but it may look more like network mapping—it's a deeper approach that could help political parties rebuild support in communities in the longer term.

Dr. Amber Macintyre, Tactical Tech, Germany

As the lead of Tactical Tech's research on data and politics, I've worked with a wide range of individuals involved in implementing and monitoring political campaigns around the world. From the growth of new companies and consultancies devoted to selling data collection and analytics services to campaigns, to small, under-resourced teams of volunteers, the people involved in campaigns are diverse. My work has highlighted three things that often are absent within current debate about the people conducting data-driven campaigns.

First, we have repeatedly found in our research that technical experts, in the form of consultants, private companies, and data brokers, are working with political groups on data-driven campaigns. Work conducted by Tactical Tech has cataloged over 500 companies working with personal data to support political campaigns internationally. From large companies that work in multiple countries—such as uCampaign or C|T—to more specialized and country specific actors—such as Eskimi or Liegey Muller Pons—a range of companies are selling expertise in data collection, analytics, or optimization. Following the public outcry surrounding the alleged practices of Cambridge Analytica, there has been significant concern about the capacity for these actors to perform not only sophisticated, but democratically problematic forms of data gathering and analytics. And yet, the lack of transparency about who these actors are and what they actually do for campaigns means we have limited understanding of the range of different external actors supporting campaigns, the precise activities they perform—and the skill level they perform them with. There is a need for caution when characterizing the personnel of data-driven campaigns, as while external experts may play a role, it's not clear how extensively they are used, what precise expertise they offer, and whether their sales pitch matches the actual tasks they perform for parties.

It's not often recognized that rather than routinely working with, or permanently employing, experts with specific data skills, many political parties only intermittently work with external experts. Often due to a lack of resources, parties are frequently only able to work with consultants or companies for short periods of time, and often in reaction to a particular problem. This means that parties tend to rely on their own internal expertise. A staff member or activist with some experience with social media will therefore often end up being drafted to work on technology-driven communications. Alternatively, staff often have to train themselves for particular tasks, using articles online or contacts with other campaigners. The expertise evident within parties is therefore often far from embedded and often newly gained, revealing a complex and less stable relationship with expertise.

Finally, the prevailing focus on the idea of "expert" data professionals limits our understanding of the varied skills and capacities of those involved in campaigns. Not every single person working in political technologies is a highly trained computer scientist or technologist, and there can be a huge variation in skills or training among staff and activists. Some experts may therefore be hired for their expertise in Facebook advertising, but they may know little about how to exploit the full functionality of a CRM system such as Salesforce. Others may have expertise in data entry and analysis but know little about digital political communications. These different types of expertise are all vital for data-driven campaigning, hence it is misleading to focus only on the presence of expertise in statistics or modeling—parties need to draw on a wealth of diverse political and technical expertise and skills to conduct a data-driven campaign.

7
Explaining Variation in Data-Driven Campaigning

As detailed in the previous four chapters, the core components of DDC—data, analytics, technology, and personnel—are not manifest uniformly in different contexts. Across our five countries, and within the parties found in each of these contexts, we not only see different types of data, different methods of data analytics, different types of technology and personnel, we also see variation in the prominence and form of specific data-driven activities. These insights offer a vital corrective to singular depictions of DDC, showing that while some practices found in US presidential elections are evident elsewhere, there is little uniformity. These differences matter for our understanding of DDC as an international phenomenon. Yet they also, as we will discuss further in the next chapter, have implications for debates about the democratic impact of this activity, suggesting that any "problems" with DDC will not necessarily be consistent across country and party contexts.

In this chapter, we build on our party-based, multi-level framework of DDC (see Chapter 2), and the analysis in each of the previous four chapters, to explain why differences emerge. Applying our theoretical framework, we discuss how systemic, regulatory, and party-level variables affect the practice of DDC. Due to space constraints, we focus primarily on explaining country-level differences, but we do devote some attention to party-level variations, explaining how and why parties differ in their use of DDC.

System Level

We begin by interrogating the system-level variables that may affect DDC. As outlined in Chapter 2, we identify the potential significance of the electoral system, system of government, party system, and hybrid-media system for DDC. Empirical observations from our cases suggest that system-level variables are most influential in explaining the form of parties' analytical processes, while providing less explanatory power for the types of data collected, technology used, and personnel engaged in DDC. Taking each variable from our theoretical framework in turn, we reflect on how each affects the manifestation of DDC observed in our cases.

Electoral System

Beginning with the electoral system, as outlined in Chapter 2, we suggested that campaigns may be incentivized by different aspects of the electoral system to focus on particular groups of voters. Within our cases we did indeed find evidence that the electoral system can condition parties' use of DDC, particularly shaping data analytics and, to a lesser extent, data collection and technology. Across our cases, we encountered different electoral systems. While the United Kingdom, Canada, and the United States use single member plurality for elections in most instances,[1] Australia and Germany use different electoral systems. These variations induced parties to engage in different data-driven practices. In those countries which use the single member plurality system, and where voting is not compulsory, parties are incentivized to focus on identifying and turning out supporters, rather than focusing on persuasion and wide-ranging engagement. As one Canadian interviewee reflected:

> What we do and how we use data are as simple as we want to connect with voters who believe what we believe and we want to hear from voters who share our values. . . . It's a coalition-building exercise so that you can make electoral gains, so you can implement the things that all the people you've collected together believe in. It's that simple.

The precise dynamics of the electoral system did, however, affect where exactly parties sought to gather data and focus analytics efforts. In the United Kingdom, for example, one interviewee reflected that "[r]ightly or wrongly, the first-past-the-post system in the United Kingdom hands a lot of power to undecided voters in marginal seats," leading parties to focus their activity on specific geographic areas rather than nationwide. This dynamic was also evident in the United States and Canada. In these contexts, we observed that while major parties were often able to maintain some minimal campaign activity in most areas, smaller parties had to choose where to place their resources—resulting in less extensive campaign activity. The electoral system also had an impact on analytics activity, with a focus on certain forms of segmentation and targeting techniques in different systems, as well as different degrees and types of testing. In Canada and the United Kingdom, emphasis was placed on identifying supporters and focusing on mobilization activity.

In other electoral systems, different dynamics were observed. Australia, for example, uses a mixed electoral system, consisting of alternative vote for the House of Representatives and single transferable vote for the Senate. This means that political parties in Australia are required to think carefully about the best way to attempt to persuade voters to preference them first on their ballots, but also to secure as many second preferences as possible from voters.[2] Similarly, the German electoral system combines candidate and party-based elements in a personalized proportional system which includes principles of majority voting as well as proportional representation. Thus, each voter may cast one vote for a candidate in one of 299 constituencies, and one vote for one party's list of candidates in a particular state, which determines the percentage each political party gets in the Bundestag (The Federal Returning Officer 2022). Parties accordingly need to combine nationwide engagement with a more focused approach in electorally significant districts to increase their overall vote share beyond the districts in which they tend to be strong. These systemic differences lead parties in our different countries to identify alternative groups of voters as electorally significant, leading to competing targeting strategies and alternative goals for message testing and GOTV activity (for example, persuasion or mobilization, and broad or narrow appeals).

The rules related to voting can also be significant. Australia's use of compulsory voting means that parties, as in many of our other cases, focus on segmenting voters based on their partisan leanings, but they also attempt to maximize their share of the "undecided" vote, and to harvest as many second preferences from voters who give their first preference to a minor party or Independent. Apparent in the Labor Party, for example, interviewees reflected that, in developing their campaign for the 2019 federal election, they attempted to segment voters from Australia's populist radical right party, One Nation, into two buckets: "Red One Nation" and "Blue One Nation." "Blue One Nation" were viewed as socially and economically conservative, more likely to preference the Liberal National Party[3] above Labor, and therefore were viewed as unpersuadable. In contrast, "Red One Nation" were perceived to be persuadable, as they opposed privatization of government services and supported increasing investment in local services, including health and education. Seeking to identify voters in this way, Labor engaged in segmentation practices and message testing to develop effective campaign messages that could be targeted to different groups as a response to electoral system effects.

In regard to technology and personnel, we found less evidence that the electoral system was significant. We did, however, observe that within our cases, parties needed to be able to access technology that was specific to their own electoral system and context. For many parties, commercially available technology was not suited to their needs because it had not been developed in similar electoral contexts. Reflecting on their experience, one interviewee in the UK Labour Party said:

> NationBuilder is one of the platforms that we've currently got and we use. It has its place, but my view of it has always been it's not quite what we need. Because there's enough off the shelf products, designed for an American market, . . . but things like British electoral geography are far more complicated than American electoral geography.

In this way the electoral system exerts an influence on the suitability of different technologies, often prompting parties (especially major parties) to develop their own technological solutions—something we also witnessed in Germany and Australia.

System of Government

Turning to the system of government, within Chapter 2 we suggested the configuration of political institutions could affect DDC, specifically pointing to the differences between unitary and federal systems, and to the different dynamics of presidential or parliamentary systems. Within our cases, we found evidence of both of these being significant. First, in terms of unitary and federal differences, most of our countries—Australia, the United States, Germany, and Canada—are federated systems, while the United Kingdom is unitary (or more technically, an asymmetrically decentralized unitary state due to devolution to Scotland and Wales). This difference was evident in data collection and sharing practices. In Australia, for example, state-based Green parties did not always share all their data with other state Greens parties, meaning that analytics processes were often conducted at the state level. Similarly, in Canada, parties such as the NDP often did not share data between ridings, and different publicly available data was available in different areas (something we also saw in the United States). These federated dynamics differed from what was apparent in the United Kingdom. Although in this country there were specific branches of national parties in Scotland and Wales, in this context data was more consistent, and hierarchical party structures were commonplace, resulting in more consistent approaches.[4]

We also found that a country's presidential or parliamentary system affected the type of data collected, the analytics processes used, and personnel employed. In presidential systems, the heightened focus on a single candidate often leads campaign teams to be constructed around particular individuals for particular time periods (Kreiss 2016). In the United States, we often saw polling and data collection activity focused on the presidential candidate, especially in the Trump campaign. In this instance we saw a heavy reliance on consultants and external actors brought in to collect data, conduct analytics, and provide technological solutions and expertise. This dynamic was not, however, always evident. Whilst historically, both national parties in the United States have had little enduring infrastructure (Crotty 2009)—leading to a focus on the need to contract external personnel—in more recent years the Democratic National Committee has made more ongoing investment in data and organizational infrastructure. This made some current practice, in data collection and technology specifically, more reminiscent of that found in parliamentary systems with stronger party organizations. We also observed that other elections occurring within presidential systems—i.e., for Congress or Gubernatorial elections—could not finance the same degree of external expertise, resulting in subtly different DDC practices dependent on the particular election under consideration.

In our parliamentary systems, political parties were more stable organizations and we routinely saw members and party staff to be central to data collection activity. While external actors and consultants were often still utilized, these ties tended to last over multiple campaigns and be between the national party and external actors, rather than being associated with a particular candidate. We therefore saw close links between, for example, Labo(u)r parties in Australia and the United Kingdom and the company BlueStateDigital. There were, however, some exceptions to these systemic differences. We found, for example, evidence in Canada of a strong relationship between Justin

Trudeau and Data Sciences that reflected a more presidential style of consultancy engagement. Similarly, in the United Kingdom, a personal relationship between Boris Johnson and Lynton Crosby (of C|T Group) led to a similarly close tie. In general, however, we found that parties in parliamentary systems tended to have more enduring and less personalized relationships with external actors than in presidential systems.

In parliamentary systems, we also saw that electoral fortunes are not focused on one candidate, but are constituted by the collective success of multiple party candidates. When it comes to data collection and analytics, this led to segmentation, targeting, and testing techniques designed to maximize support across multiple levels, providing both national and local insights simultaneously. As one interviewee from the Canadian NDP reflected:

> in order to elect [our candidate] for prime minister, we would need to elect a majority of our candidates. And so that translates a little bit differently because these are all smaller elections that are happening across the country and all of them need to go well.

In parliamentary systems, therefore, analytics is often focused on providing geographically granular insights, seeking to understand not only how party leaders are affecting the vote in different areas, but also individual candidate and party performance in these areas. This is a key reason MRP is increasingly used in parliamentary democracies, such as Australia and the United Kingdom.

Party System

Our third systemic variable, the party system, specifically draws attention to the number of "relevant" parties and the degree of competition and/or cooperation between parties. Our empirical data demonstrates that this has implications for data collection and analytics, with differences emerging between systems dominated by two parties and multi-party systems. In the United Kingdom, for example, the major parties could focus on securing a majority by seeking to mobilize supporters in electorally significant areas. As one Conservative interviewee reflected of the 2017 general election:

Our job was to reinforce the positives about Theresa May. And frame the election in a way that Jeremy Corbyn could not possibly win it. And make sure that our voters that turned out were this new coalition of slightly more Brexit-y voters . . . and Labour voters didn't. Because they didn't like this Corbyn guy.

In some countries, we saw this focus on two-party politics lead to the use of DDC to optimize attack ads and negative campaigning. Indeed, in the United States and Australia, where there is an established history of more negative and confrontational politics (Fridkin et al. 2004; Iyengar & Ansolabehere 2010), we saw analytics used to develop and refine attack ads.

In contrast, in Germany, parties need to engage in coalition formation after the election. This consideration affects the data collected by parties and the analytics performed because, rather than being able to focus on securing a simple majority, parties need to factor in second-order effects, such as the preferences of voters for other parties. Parties therefore often gather data on wider electoral dynamics, and engage in a more granular form of analytics that examines the various permutations that may affect a party's fortunes, using these insights to develop messages and campaign strategies. These dynamics also mean we did not see the same focus on attack optimization, with, for example, German parties focusing more on coalition building.

Hybrid Media System

Finally, turning to the hybrid media system, we highlighted the importance of the wider media environment in which political parties exist. We suggested that parties in different countries exist in different media contexts in which different amounts of traditional and digital media providers are present, and where parties find media more or less accessible due to partisan biases.

Across all our five countries we found parties engaging with a range of different media providers. In addition to traditional broadcast outlets in each country, parties placed content on a range of traditional and digital outlets to disseminate their message. The starkest trend to emerge from across our cases was the importance of new media platforms for parties in all our countries, not only as a platform for deploying targeted messages, but also as a means of accessing data about citizens, and conducting simple analytics processes (such as segmenting, targeting, and testing). Despite variations in internet penetration across our countries (Reuters 2022), all our parties were reliant on digital platforms such as Facebook and Google. While across our five cases access to the affordances of these platforms was relatively consistent, in the United States, it was notable that a close relationship between platform companies and presidential campaign teams allowed parties to receive more detailed guidance on how to maximize the effectiveness of audience segmentation, targeting, and message-testing capacities (Kreiss & McGregor 2018). Interestingly, in terms of party-level differences, minor parties' ability to access these types of data analytics services was seen to level the playing field for parties unable to develop or finance their own analytics services.

There were, however, differences evident in our cases in the precise dynamics of the hybrid media environment that affected the way campaigns behaved. In Australia, for example, the predominance of private media interests with particular (right-wing) ideological proclivities caused many progressive parties to seek alternative media channels. The Labor Party, for example, in recognizing the challenges and opposition within dominant media conglomerates, has attempted to focus their attention on social media or ground campaign activity to connect with target audiences. We also saw parties in the United States eschewing engagement with certain media channels in preference for more favorable media sources or direct engagement (such as through peer-to-peer text operations). In these contexts there was a concerted investment in new technology to facilitate such contact. Whilst engagement with social media was observed in the United Kingdom, Canada and Germany, unfavorable partisan news media appeared to be less of an incentive in these contexts.

Summary

Reviewing the explanatory power of the systemic factors within our theoretical framework, we find these variables help to account for variation in DDC. In the main relating to data analytics, and to a lesser degree data collection, personnel, and technology, these factors play an important role in explaining the variation in practice we observe between countries.

Regulatory Level

Turning to the regulatory level, our theoretical framework highlighted the significance of party regulation, campaign regulation, data and privacy regulation, and media regulation. In explaining variation in DDC, these variables were most significant in accounting for variation in the data collected, the technology used, and the personnel engaged, but were less influential for analytics.

Party Regulation

Our first variable, party regulation, focuses on the potential for the regulation of party finance and organization to affect DDC. Across our cases, we found extensive evidence of the impact of financial regulation. Parties in Canada, Germany, and the United Kingdom are subject to stricter donation rules than found in Australia or the United States (Van Biezen 2004). In Canada, for example, recent rule changes mean that corporations and unions are no longer able to give donations to Canadian parties,[5] and donation limits are capped (Elections Canada 2022), creating what one interviewee described as "stringent campaign laws." In Germany and the United Kingdom, there are no limits on donations, but there are disclosure requirements (also evident in Canada). For example, in Germany donations above €10,000 must be published in each party's annual report, and above €50,000 must be reported to the president of the Bundestag, who then publishes the information on the parliament's website (German Party Law 2021). Parties are therefore subject to different rules that affect their ability to raise funds and solicit donations.

Donations alone, however, do not account entirely for the differing capacities of parties. We also saw variations related to state funding. In the United States, parties do not receive state funding, but in Australia, Germany, Canada, and the United Kingdom, funds are available to differing degrees (Van Biezen & Kopecký 2007, 242). In the United Kingdom, parties can access limited state support in the form of policy-development grants and short money (Fisher 2002; Electoral Commission n.d.).[6] The amounts available to parties are, however, not consistent (see, for example, Institute for Government 2022). In Australia there is a set formula for party spending based on the votes that parties receive in each federal election.

Party regulations therefore exert a significant influence on the financial resources available outside elections, with parties in each of our countries having to navigate the constraints and opportunities present in their particular system. These rules were routinely cited as important for DDC by our interviewees. While parties in the United States were therefore relatively unconstrained in their ability to gather donations, parties across most of our other cases expressed frustration at the limits placed on their ability to generate funds—especially where state subsidies were lower. Indeed, one official from Canada said that available finance was "probably the biggest explanatory factor." Thus, the implications for the amount that could be spent on each aspect of DDC limited the extent or complexity of data, analytics, technology, and personnel employed.

Interestingly, when it came to organizational rules, our analysis provided less evidence of constraints on party behavior. While some mention was made of restrictions to coordinated activity between trade unions and political parties in Canada and the United Kingdom, for the most part our interviewees did not suggest that organizational constraints affected their ability to collect or analyze data or invest in technology. While some regulatory constraints may therefore exist around which external actors (and in what capacity) can play a role in party operations outside campaigns, we found this type of regulation to play a less extensive role in explaining campaign variations.

Campaign Regulation

Turning to campaign regulation, this variable focused on the rules and procedures governing election campaigning. In particular, we concentrated on campaign finance and media access, noting constraints on DDC. Within our cases, we found that financial regulations impacted parties' ability to invest in data, technology, and personnel, while varied rules around media access during campaign periods—and particularly television advertising—resulted in different forms of analytics and technology being used in different ways.

Focusing first on campaign finance, in many countries there are specific rules governing campaign finance (Van Biezen 2004, 714). Notably, in Germany, there is no distinction between campaign funds and political party funds (Bundestag 1994), meaning there are no specific regulations devoted just to this period. In contrast, in our other cases there are a range of requirements that vary from being more (UK and Canada) to less (Australia and US) stringent. Canada, for example, has expenditure limits for federal elections that apply to spending between June 30 of an election year and the beginning of the official campaign period, or what is now termed "the preelection period" (Pal 2021). At the 2021 federal election, this was approximately $30 million (Canadian) for the three major parties—the Liberal Party, the NDP, and the Conservatives (Elections Canada 2022). Similarly, in the United Kingdom, spending in the election period is limited by national campaign spending limits of £30,000 per contested constituency and local candidate spending limits of on average about £15,000 during the campaign within a regulated period (Dommett & Power 2019). Such restrictions are not found in the United States or Australia. As outlined in the previous section, this has significant consequences for the resources available for parties, affecting the ability of parties in more regulated contexts to invest in data, analytics, technology, and personnel, and particularly more costly variants of these activities. Reflecting on this point, one interviewee noted that "America is by far and away a big outlier, and that is 100%, down to two things: money, and the legal framework. You need money, and you need the legal freedom."

In regard to media access in the campaign, we also found specific regulatory provisions that affected parties' ability in different countries to utilize media. In Germany and the United Kingdom during election periods, public service broadcasters are obliged to allocate airtime free of charge for all parties, but beyond these allocations, commercial television advertising is not allowed. As a result, parties in these countries did not exhibit differentiated targeted messaging on television but developed a message for this medium to have broad appeal (using more or less sophisticated forms of message testing dependent on the resources that specific parties had available). In contrast, in the United States, such restrictions do not apply, and it was possible to observe parties and candidates placing targeted advertisements on different television platforms at high volumes (Fowler et al. 2021). Interestingly, across our cases, campaign (and media) regulation was less extensive in regard to online media, with few state restrictions on, for example, online political advertising. As a result, online media was widely used for campaign communications in all our countries, often resulting in different practices being evident in offline and online media.

Data and Privacy Regulation

Our third variable, data and privacy regulation, is perhaps the most well-established regulatory influence on parties' DDC activity. Across our cases, Australia[7] and the United States have the two weakest legislative and regulatory regimes regarding data and privacy. Indeed, Australian parties are completely exempt from privacy legislation (Privacy Act 1988). The lack of regulation has a number of consequences. In both cases, parties have comparatively easy access to substantial amounts of information and can purchase data from external sources. It is therefore possible for parties in these contexts to buy insights such as data about magazine subscriptions or credit history with relative ease. As one interviewee reflected of the United States, "they're able to match data to other things [in a way] that is not legal in any other country or context in the world."

Canadian federal parties are also exempt from privacy laws, but there are several other mechanisms in place to limit how Canadian parties use citizen data (Bayley & Bennett 2012). The two main pieces of legislation in Canada are the Privacy Act and the Personal Information Protection and Electronic Documents Act (PIPEDA). The Privacy Act applies only to federal government agencies and institutions. PIPEDA is the legislation that governs the use of data by private organizations. These pieces of legislation specify that Canadian parties cannot purchase the same level of commercial information on voters as is possible in the United States (Patten 2017), and that they must create their own databases using publicly available information or information they collect themselves. This means, as Patten (2017) has argued, that most of the data available to Canadian political parties is either publicly available or self-generated through direct voter contact methods, with regulation, as one of our interviewees put it, "undoubtedly shap[ing] what you can and can't do."

In contrast, the United Kingdom and Germany are subject to extensive regulation under the General Data Protection Regulation (GDPR). This specifies that data must, among other things, be "processed lawfully, fairly, and in a transparent manner in relation to the data subject," "collected for specified, explicit, and legitimate purposes," "be accurate, and, where necessary, kept up to date," and be "processed in a manner that ensures appropriate security of the personal data" (Hankey et al. 2018, 11). When introduced, this legislation curtailed campaigning practice. In the United Kingdom, for example, interviewees explained that they were no longer "allowed to hold individual level ethnicity data. . . . So, the party [was] never able to target electors based on their ethnicity." Another noted:

> I used to speak to my US counterparts all the time and they'd tell me about incredibly targeted and clever things they were doing which we could absolutely replicate, but the law just wouldn't allow us. I think GDPR is the kind of biggest restraint on what people do and probably for a very, very good reason.

The precise impact of GDPR did, however, vary in accordance with country-level differences. Within the United Kingdom, parties are able to claim an exemption to GDPR requirements for direct consent for data collection and analysis under an exemption in Section 8(1)(e) of the Data Protection Act 2018.[8] This allows political parties and consultancies to conduct activities including "communicating with electors, campaigning activities, supporting candidates and elected representatives, casework, surveys and opinion gathering, and fundraising to support any of those activities" without needing to engage with the data subject (Hankey et al. 2018, 20–21). This does not mean that parties are exempt from data protection law, but it does mean that parties can collect and analyze data without express citizen consent.[9]

The significance of these local exemptions is apparent when looking at Germany, which imposes more national-level regulations limiting the amount of available data that parties can access, or process (Kruschinski & Haller 2017; Weitbrecht 2019; § 50 Abs. 1 of the Federal Act of Registration). Indeed, German law forbids candidates from the collection, combination, and long-time storage of personal data on voters without their consent (Hessian Commissioner for Data Protection and Freedom 2023). In that regard, only the processing of anonymized data which cannot be traced back to a specific or identifiable natural person is allowed. This means that, as detailed in Chapter 3 and 4, data can only be analyzed if it does not lead to the de-anonymization of a specific or identifiable natural person. Put simply, this makes the use of inferential or relational analysis almost impossible because it would threaten to de-anonymize the individual identity of voters. Thus, marketers and parties have started to analyze data from so-called microcells, which contain an average of 6.6 households. Such country-specific restrictions mean that even when operating under the same general framework (GDPR), campaign practice is not uniform because of different national manifestations of data and privacy regulation.

Looking at practice across our cases, data and privacy regulation can have significant implications for data collection and analytics, but it also has implications for technology and personnel. In terms of the former, such regulations create alternative requirements for parties' data systems. In Canada, one interviewee reflected, "The big pieces of our infrastructure are custom made. . . . And part of that, again, is because of the regulatory structure, like we can't just open the box on a fundraising CRM that XYZ charity could use because it doesn't do the things that we need to do to be compliant with the laws." We also saw similar implications for personnel, with parties in more stringent regimes often having to hire permanent staff devoted to ensuring compliance with data-protection law, and being less able to share data with external providers.

One important point to emerge across our cases was the capacity for parties to circumvent national data-protection laws by using the segmentation, targeting, and testing tools offered by Meta and Google (Andreou et al. 2019). Currently, international and national legislation is not well equipped to address and regulate algorithmic social networking platforms and their opaque advertising ecosystems (e.g., Harker 2020; Dommett & Zhu 2022). We saw parties in countries with strict national legislation utilizing these platforms to circumvent national restrictions on parties use and storage of data, often using social media platforms' advertising infrastructure to gain access to particular audiences of interest (Dachwitz 2017; Kruschinski & Bene 2022).

Media Regulation

Finally, within our theoretical framework we also drew attention to the potential for media regulation to affect DDC. As outlined above, the media market within each of our countries is not identical, and national broadcasters dominate to different degrees. In part, these differences reflect alternative regulations around media competition. In the United Kingdom, for example, the Enterprise Act 2020 requires that all media mergers be reviewed to ensure that they do not lead to a substantial lessening of competition (Seely 2017)—thus a diversity of media outlets is available to parties (for use in compliance with campaign and other media regulations). In contrast,

Australia has one of the most concentrated media landscapes of any democracy. Over the last two decades, three or four major media conglomerates have owned close to 90% of the non-digital media landscape, with one company, News Ltd., completely dominant. Reforms to the Broadcasting Services Act in 2006 further entrenched the powers of media conglomerates, opening the way to "increased ownership across media platforms" (Lidberg 2019, 13). Parties in different contexts do not, therefore, have access to the same diversity of media channels, affecting when and how they field campaign communications.

In terms of media restrictions, interviewees often spoke about platforms' efforts to self-regulate, implementing policy changes that affected what was possible on digital platforms. As one interviewee noted, digital companies frequently made changes that had a large impact on campaign action:

> There [are] already changes iOS have rolled out around how Facebook's pixel works, how Apple records email opens. And I think as the kind of privacy and what's often called surveillance capitalism aspect of advertising becomes more in the forefront of the public's mind, you will see that kind of extremely targeted, data-driven stuff become more complicated.

In response to such developments, parties have needed to adapt their campaign activity to what was possible on different platforms, resulting in not only different data-collection and analytics strategies, but also different uses of technology and personnel.

Our cases also showed campaigners subject to different platform-imposed regulations dependent on their location, a point particularly evident in relation to political advertising. Many interviewees spoke about the restrictions imposed by platforms themselves on data analytics and targeting capacities. In the United States, for example, a decision by Facebook to ban political advertising one week ahead of the 2020 presidential election fundamentally curtailed the form of analytics that campaigns could undertake. Similarly, we heard from one interview in Canada about how "Google has opted out of advertising during political campaigns," making it impossible for Canadian parties to use technology available to parties elsewhere. Despite being large multinational companies, these restrictions were not enforced uniformly, resulting in country-level differences in how these tools could be utilized.

Summary

In summary, regulatory-level factors offer important explanations for the variation seen between countries in terms of DDC. In particular, financial constraints imposed within or outside election periods and data and privacy regulation exerted a significant impact on parties' ability to collect data and employ particular forms of data analytics.

Party Level

At the final level, our theoretical framework highlights the significance of resource, structure, ideology, and attitudes to campaigning. These variables are particularly adept at accounting for differences *between* parties, showing why parties in the same context behave differently, and why those with similar organizational traits in different contexts may behave the same. We found party-level factors to have explanatory power for each of our four aspects of DDC.

Party Resources

Our first party-level variable, resources, exerted considerable power in accounting for the variations we found between parties. Financial and labor variations were particularly influential, affecting parties' ability to conduct data collection, analytics, technology, and personnel. Comparative financial data is challenging to gather (Poguntke, Scarrow, & Webb 2020), but we saw examples of parties in the same country having access to very different levels of resources. We also witnessed large differences in parties' ability to generate funds. While in the United States there is an established culture of party donations and fundraising, in our other country case studies, interviewees told us about the difficulty of raising party funds. These financial differences were cited as significant for all aspects of DDC, because, as one Canadian interviewee noted, many campaign decisions (in terms of purchasing data or investing in staffing) "goes back to money."

In terms of analytics, parties with fewer resources found certain forms of analytics out of reach. In the UK Liberal Democrats, one interviewee described how they didn't "think the party ever has the resources to run that [more sophisticated form of] analysis," while an interviewee from the UK Green Party similarly reflected that a lack of resources meant they were only "slowly getting to a position where we can segment as well, and actually send out targeted emails." Such practices contrasted notably to better resourced parties where a lack of funds did not tend to prevent certain activities, although we did find that outside of the United States, even well-resourced parties were limited in the sophistication of their activity—with limits, for example, on parties' capacities to employ multiple MRPs.

We also saw that available financial resources cause variation in parties' ability to invest in technological systems. Focusing particularly on databases, many interviewees spoke about the need for, as one Canadian interviewee put it, "upfront investment" to facilitate activities such as segmentation, targeting, and donation soliciting. In Germany, for example, one strategist from the Christian Democratic Party described how:

> In comparison to the other parties, we used our resources and time over the last years to develop connect17 to be the first German campaign which draws on data analytics and a mobile application for door-to-door and social media voter mobilization.... Until then, there was no comparable campaign infrastructure in Germany since the other parties didn't have the resources and know-how at their disposal during that time.

Parties' ability to invest in infrastructure was, however, not equal, and small parties, such as the UK Greens, did not always possess data systems. We also heard of instances where major parties' capacity to invest was limited, with one interviewee in the well-resourced Canadian Liberal Party noting that "we, again, don't have as much money, so we don't really have a unified CRM." These differences suggest that outside the United States, parties can be frustrated to different degrees by limited resources.

Financial resources were also influential in accounting for who was involved in DDC. While in the United States limitations were not as apparent, in our other countries parties routinely explained that resource constraints affected their ability to hire internal staff. In nearly all of our non-US parties, minimal investment was made in staffing outside the electoral calendar, and even in election periods staff numbers were small. In Germany, for example, many parties "struggled with staff, time, expertise, money and strict data protection regulations to establish a high-tech driven hunt for individual voters" (Kruschinski & Haller 2017, 4). Parties' use of external actors was also affected by financial resources, with even well-resourced parties often unable to retain external companies. One interviewee in the Canadian Liberal Party said that in Canada, the parties "don't operate on huge budgets, so you couldn't maintain these people in a four-year electoral cycle, not for the amount of people you need." Similarly, the less-resourced NDP party reflected that "the reality is that we can't staff as robustly as the Republican Party. We can't staff as robustly as the Conservative Party. We can't hire every consultant firm under the sun to help us win elections." As such, the use of external consultants was often curtailed by budget, meaning that parties were often not able to invest in personnel as extensively as desired.

Beyond financial resources, we also observed parties to have access to different forms of labor. As outlined in Chapter 6 on personnel, parties have different numbers of grassroots activists, with membership figures and supporter numbers varying dramatically by party and across country (Kölln 2014). Such differences mean that parties have access to different amounts of voluntary labor, particularly for data collection. In addition, our interviews showed parties to be able to access different sources of external personnel. Many interviewees spoke about the importance of sister parties in providing expertise and advice on DDC practice, but not all parties had access to such networks (a point linked to ideology) or had connections to similar organizations such as trade unions or commercial groups, resulting in further inequalities that particularly affected data-collection activity.

Party Structure

In terms of party structure, we highlighted the potential for two possible influences on DDC: first, the distribution of power within a party; and second, the organizational configuration.

Our parties differed in how centralized power was in consequential ways. Some parties were highly centralized and saw power concentrated in the hands of elites. In the United Kingdom, for example, the Conservative and Labour parties are highly centralized, and operate a model of what Stromer-Galley (2019) describes as "controlled-interactivity." This was manifest in central guidance and systems for the collection of data, and centrally provided technologies. In contrast, in other parties central control was less extensive. Indeed, in Canada one interviewee from the NDP noted:

when it comes to our ridings, it's really that the top-down will not work for the NDP.... Because our on the ground activists are very vocal, they're very engaged, they're very... they're a part of every decision.... We have regional organizers that support them and a central outreach team that supports our on the ground candidates as well.... But it really is about providing them with the tools necessary for them to be as successful as possible.

These differences were often connected to alternative party structures. For example, the Green Party has a more decentralized structure and power lies primarily with the grassroots rather than elites. Indeed, one interviewee explained that "the Green Party is a bottom-up thing and local parties are autonomous, regional parties and federations and local parties and so on." In contrast, in Germany, whilst party organization was often decentralized, it was overlayed by what was described as a "snowflake model," with the Christian Democratic party's mobilization program "Connect" (McKenna & Han 2014, Figure 7.1) in which party officials were hired at the federal level to lead the overarching strategy, data gathering, analysis, and training. These federal actors shared authority with units at the state level, seeing power distributed between state and national parts of the party. Across our countries formal structure and systems of control therefore intersected in important ways.

Noting this intersection, we observed that, in terms of data collection, centralized parties tended to exhibit more uniform and standardized practices. Evident in the Labor Party and Liberal Party in Australia, the Liberal Party and NDP in Canada, and in the Labour, Conservative, and Liberal Democrat parties in the United Kingdom, we found party elites providing canvassing scripts that were taken up by the grassroots actors across the country. This resulted in less variation in collected data and facilitated more reliable segmentation of electors. Not all parties, however, adopted standardized scripts, and we saw evidence of more decentralized and autonomous local parties adapting scripts to reflect local priorities. The Greens in Australia are one such example. Organized along confederal lines, the state-based parties often differ not only ideologically, but also in how they approach campaigning. This allows grassroots actors to sometimes drive changes in messaging or process.

Similar patterns were evident for data analytics. In centralized parties, resources tended to be concentrated within the national headquarters and focused on the national campaign. In Australia, for example, a former campaign director for the Liberal Party at the sub-national level reflected that while the party used sophisticated analytical techniques for federal elections, at a state level, "in terms of data modeling or anything like that, there's none of that in place for any of the campaigns I've worked on."[10] Similarly, in Germany analytics practices were not uniform at all levels of the party, with an interviewee from the German Social Democrats describing how the national party had struggled to transfer the logics and know-how of data analytics to the local level for the 2017 federal election, noting:

> The federal level completely failed to deliver a clear strategy for using data analytics in the federal election 2017. Therefore, we started to build our own data-driven campaign, including our own app, in collaboration with a consulting company.

While some parties did aim to facilitate local innovation and analysis, across the parties we examined there were no substantive attempts to enable local activists to utilize the form of sophisticated tools available centrally.

Variations were also evident in terms of technology. Highly centralized parties often developed or purchased technology through a central office and disseminated this throughout the wider party. One interviewee in the German Christian Democratic Party, for example, described the introduction of the new canvassing app, noting that:

> the party had to invest a lot of staff, money, and time to introduce the app to all state and local party chapters in the run-up to the election to convince them to use this technology for canvassing so that the campaign HQ could actually see how many doors were knocked on. Still many party activists didn't use the app.

Similarly in Canada, one interviewee from the Liberal Party described how among local parties "it's like, two-thirds, maybe; I don't know, probably 80% use whatever the dominant party is using" and a far smaller proportion "who are experimenting and doing their own thing." The degree of central control therefore affected how technology was introduced and rolled out, with more decentralized parties exhibiting more local innovation and variation in the technological tools utilized.

On a slightly different note related to party structure, we observed that while many parties have local presences across the country, with local branches in each electoral district, this is not always the case. Indeed, even many more established parties can lack a local presence in all parts of the country. As one interviewee from the Canadian NDP described, in some ridings, they have:

> a good volunteer program, that works really well for them because they can maintain their relationship with volunteers. But in other places, that's not the case. The riding association might not exist between elections, it might not be as strong, it may not have capacity to run events between elections or have volunteer opportunities.

Parties can therefore often lack a comprehensive local structure, making it challenging to engage in universal data-collection activities. These different structures—intentional or otherwise—mean that parties have to engage in particular strategies in regard to data collection and staffing, considering where resources need to be deployed to gather additional data.

Party Ideology

In terms of party ideology, we highlighted the potential for parties' ideological agendas to affect perceptions of acceptable campaigning practices and to inform parties' ties to other actors and sources of expertise. Within our analysis we found some evidence for these ideas, which were particularly important for explaining differences in data analytics and personnel.

For the vast majority of the parties we examined, the use of data was not a point of ideological concern. We did, however, find some parties exhibiting hesitancy. In Canada, for example, the Green Party explicitly states in its privacy policy that it does not use personal data for micro-targeting as it does not agree with these practices. In Germany, factions of the Social Democrats, the Greens, and the Left Party oppose the use of personal data for targeting voters. Other parties were less concerned about data collection and analytics and saw these techniques as important tools for connecting with citizens. These differences translated into alternative analytics practices, with some parties open to the use of targeting, and others more reticent.

When it came to external ties, we found ideology commonly played a role in shaping relationships with external actors such as sister parties, affiliate bodies, or consultancy companies. While conservative, social democratic, and liberal parties often spoke about long-standing links with other parties elsewhere around the globe, or with trade unions or affiliate bodies with shared ideological objectives, the networks of actors that parties from different ideological perspectives could access were not consistent. Newer parties, for example, spoke of the challenges of engaging with like-minded international parties, with one interviewee in Canada citing the difficulty of establishing relationships because of preexisting ties they have to other longer-standing Canadian actors. Elsewhere, Green parties reflected on the lack of established structures for sharing data-related expertise internationally, especially when compared with conservative or social democratic parties.

We also heard about the significance of being able to find an external provider with similar ideological values. One interviewee from a company used by the UK Conservative Party observed, "I don't think you can come in from a completely different point of view, or a totally different angle, and be able to do that job." The need for ideological alignment was seen to be important because it shifted relations from, what one Canadian interviewee described as, being a vendor to being a partner. While vendors were often easily available, it was seen to be critical—and yet often challenging—to find a partner who could be willing to "take your call at midnight during the middle of the campaign to help you solve a problem." This was particularly the case outside the United States where the consultancy market is much smaller. Ideology can therefore exert an influence on the choices made by parties, particularly in relation to analytics, and can constrain the personnel available to facilitate different aspects of DDC.

Attitudes to Campaigning

Turning to our last variable, attitudes to campaigning, we suggested these attitudes may have an influence on DDC, noting the potential for different views among elites and grassroots actors to exert an impact on campaigns. First, interrogating the effect of elite attitudes, we found that in many parties there were elites who advocated for investment in data and analytics. As outlined in Chapter 6, most parties tended to invest in at least some minimal staffing expertise or infrastructure around data analysis, but the critical mass of support and understanding was not always evident. While often connected to resources, we found that some parties (or those responsible for campaigning strategy) did not see DDC as a priority for investment. Data was not always seen to be reliable, and some party officials were skeptical of its value, especially when compared to local knowledge and expertise.

Interestingly, many parties reported a shift in attitudes toward campaigning. Speaking about their experience in the UK Labour Party, one interviewee noted a recent shift in strategy, outlining how "in the past we were executing tactics which were informed by the politics and not informed by the data and that's a big difference this time around" as there was a shift away from "the preferences of politicians" toward data insights as a driver of party activity. And yet, some interviewees reported little change. It was therefore possible to observe parties in which data was not seen as integral to campaigning, and there was limited weight placed on the importance of building this infrastructure and investing in data-related expertise. As a party strategist of Germany's the Left Party described in 2016:

> I barely passed my statistics course. [. . .] You do not need such skills when you are working in a party. No matter what anyone tells you, it is not true.

We found few traits that predicted the presence of these attitudes, finding them to exist within very different parties.

In terms of grassroots attitudes, we found very different attitudes toward data that conditioned different behavior. In many parties, and especially those with established mechanisms for providing local campaigning tools and guidance, activists tended to be willing to engage in expected data-collection activity and often demonstrated little evidence of questioning the value of specific data-collection tasks. There were, however, some exceptions. In Australia, we saw evidence of rouge campaigning, with local activists departing from centrally derived strategies. One example of this came in the 2013 Australian federal election, when key party officials at the sub-national level in the state of Victoria decided to largely ignore the strategy from the central campaign and leader's office to develop a field campaigning operation. In other parties, such as the Greens and Labour in the United Kingdom, we saw those with particularly positive attitudes toward data developing innovations and leading best practice—as evident in the creation of the activist group Campaign Lab to develop data insights for the Labour Party.

Summary

Reviewing this discussion, party-level factors are particularly important in explaining between-party variations. While our systemic and regulatory factors spotlighted differences between countries, these factors show

how parties with similar attributes in different places can exhibit similar tendencies in their use of DDC.

Conclusion

In this chapter, we have examined how systemic, regulatory, and party-level variables can help to explain the different forms of DDC that we have cataloged in previous chapters. When it comes to the data that parties collect, the way data is analyzed, the technology deployed, or the personnel who play a role, we suggest that factors at each of these levels exert an influence on DDC. While in this chapter we have examined each of these variables in turn, it is of course the case that these factors overlap and interlink to result in the unique forms of campaigning this book has shown each party to engage in. While there are many similarities in the practices of parties with similar structures and levels of resources, the configuration of systemic, regulatory, and party-level factors surrounding any particular party can result in a distinctive form of DDC.

Applying these insights to think about the different practices we see in our countries, it is therefore clear that while the Labo(u)r parties in Australia and the United Kingdom possess many of the same characteristics, in terms of resource, structure, ideology, and attitudes toward campaigning, they exhibit different practices because of the distinct regulatory and systemic contexts in which they exist. Similarly, although the SPD and CDU in Germany have the same systemic and regulatory contexts, differences in party resources and structures result in alternative practices.

In pointing to these differences, our aim is not to determinatively predict the precise form that a data-driven campaign will take dependent on the particular systemic, regulatory, and party characteristics evident. However, the analysis in this chapter does point to broad and recurring tendencies between the dynamics evident at each of our levels and the form of DDC. As we will discuss further in the next chapter, these tendencies can offer important lessons when thinking about problematic practice and the form of regulation.

8
Conclusion

DDC is often depicted as a sinister, threatening activity, associated with particular practices most commonly found in the United States. Often driven by a focus on the sales pitches made by political consultants eager to secure a market for their latest data-driven technique, and the proclamations of political elites happy to assign success to the superiority of their data operation, a fairly uniform account of DDC has emerged. And yet, while widely depicted in these terms, it has previously been unclear whether these accounts of DDC resonate with campaign practice both within and, importantly, beyond the United States. As such, it has been difficult to pin down what exactly is meant by DDC, how it is manifest in different countries, and why practice varies.

Within this book, we have set out to demystify the practice of DDC, looking beyond the hyperbolic claims and sales pitches to examine how DDC is employed by political parties in five advanced democracies. Extending our focus beyond the US case, we have shown not only that DDC is by no means uniform, but also that data can be collected, analyzed, and deployed in different ways by different political parties. Indeed, our analysis has shown that while many parties do maintain large databases of personal information and engage in complex segmentation and modeling, many others draw on relatively simple forms of personal data that is simply sorted or filtered to identify broad target groups. This diversity has so far been overlooked in depictions of DDC, but is critical for attempts to understand what is happening within contemporary campaigns and to determine whether and how these activities pose a threat to democracy.

Within this concluding chapter, we focus on these democratic questions in more detail, reflecting on the implications of our findings for current debates about the need to regulate or curtail this activity. Specifically, we argue that future debates around the nature, impact, and regulation of DDC need to recognize:

- DDC is not a uniform practice, but can appear in a range of different forms;
- DDC is not inherently problematic, but can be used in ways that may be more or less acceptable to citizens;
- DDC is not new, but is the latest evolution of a long-standing practice of gathering and analyzing data in efforts to secure electoral success;
- Systemic, regulatory, and party-level factors affect the form of DDC.

These findings are vital in developing a less deterministic account of the democratic impact of DDC and need to be mirrored in any effort to develop a regulatory response. They also offer lessons for debates around new and emerging technologies, such as AI (Manheim & Kaplan 2019), suggesting a need to recast debates about the impact of technology on democracy more generally.

The Threat of DDC to Democracy

The claim that DDC and data use more broadly poses a serious threat to the effective functioning of liberal democracy has become a recurring feature of debates in the media and policymaking sphere. To cite just a few examples, in the United Kingdom, journalist Carole Cadwalladr proclaimed that "our personal data is being used to undermine democracy" (Taylor 2021, 5). In a report by the European Parliament (2021, 3) it has been claimed social media data provides:

> new and more effective ways to monitor people online, which can be used by governments to target politically active citizens and silence dissent (political surveillance). . . . The massive collection of data by social media creates privacy risks to users and may affect their capacity to form and express political opinions (loss of privacy and autonomy).

Civil society groups in the United States also claim that "big tech is using our data to poison our societies and imperil our democracies" (see, e.g., Pentzold & Fölsche 2020; Taylor 2021). These narratives offer vague and imprecise diagnoses of the threat that data use poses to democracy. It is therefore frequently unclear exactly why the use of personal data is problematic, if the use of all data is antithetical to democratic practice, or if concerns are context-specific and reflect the norms of local campaigning contexts. Despite these ambiguities, concerns about the democratic impact of DDC have begun to inform policy debates and efforts to pursue regulation. Indeed, the Council of Europe (2022, n.p.) recently proclaimed a need for action, asserting that:

> the use of online communications for electoral purposes may lead to an abusive use of personal data and techniques of microtargeting, use of opaque techniques and the inappropriate use of bots and algorithms to distribute information; and acknowledging that segmentation of the voters may boost the polarization of the debate and produce a shift from a public political debate to closed, personalized and targeted communication.

Other policymakers have voiced concerns around the growth of digital surveillance (Kuehn & Salter 2020, 2600–2601) and the use of political microtargeting (Parliament of Victoria 2021, 169), leading to calls for legislation to assuage democratic threats.

While these moves are in many ways laudable, given the findings of this book, we suggest they are grounded in an idealized and particular account of DDC. Reacting to this tendency, we argue that there is a need to revisit prevailing accounts of the impact of DDC, to reassess exactly what is meant by this term, and how and why it poses a threat to democracy.

The Practice of Data-Driven Campaigning

As this book has repeatedly made clear, when speaking about DDC, it is important not to envisage one set of practices or activities. As our chapters on data, analytics, technology, and personnel have shown, each element of a data-driven campaign can be enacted in different ways, reflecting the particular systemic, regulatory, and party-level context in which a campaign exists. In categorizing the different components of a data-driven campaign, we not only have provided a road map for understanding how and why data-driven campaigns may differ, but also have provided detailed empirical evidence that contradicts many of the claims seen to drive democratic concern.

In our discussions of data, we have shown not only that campaigns may rely on different types of data (i.e., publicly available, disclosed, inferential, or monitored), but also that the precise form of each type of data can vary between and even within a single case. Indeed, we have shown that publicly available information is not the same in Australia and Germany, and that even within the United States there is different information available to campaigns depending on the state. We have also shown that the data held by parties is not always extensive or highly personalized and that many parties' ability to collect, access, and integrate data is far less extensive and sophisticated than frequently depicted. Indeed, the data they do possess is often spread over many different systems and stored in different formats, meaning parties do not possess the comprehensive picture of individual voters that some accounts suggest. While we have therefore highlighted instances in which parties do gather significant amounts of canvassing data and append this with official statistics, polling data, and purchased insights from data brokers, we have also shown that many, often smaller parties have limited canvassing data and limited ability to finance the collection of polling or commercial data.

As our practitioners make clear in the perspectives they contributed, most data-collection practices are mundane and long-standing, originating from traditional door-to-door and phone-canvassing activities. We certainly found evidence of data coming from data brokers and social media, with services such as Facebook's "look-alike audiences" making it easier than ever before for parties to utilize information about voters, often without their knowledge or direct consent. These trends suggest that data collection and efforts to access data held by social media companies are increasingly normalized within contemporary party politics; however, this does not mean that this trend is inherently problematic. Indeed, one of our interviewees summed up the views of many people we spoke to when they said, "There is real value and there is a real democratic benefit in political parties trying to engage people on things that they're actually interested in." Hence, DDC could be viewed as not only non-problematic, but perhaps even as beneficial for democracy. To assess the democratic credentials of data collection, it is therefore necessary to introduce further considerations. For example, under what conditions should parties be able to access any form of data, to what degree is informed consent required, and does the goal of data collection affect what is democratically acceptable? Such questions are designed to show that the collection of data is not inherently problematic, and that there are important contextual considerations and conceptual questions to answer before passing judgment. These are questions that we argue any commentator or policymaker needs to answer in order to explain the cause for democratic concern and to evaluate the extent to which that concern is manifest in practice.

In our discussion of analytics, we confronted the idea that political parties are engaging new analytical campaign techniques, including forms of "big data" analysis, artificial intelligence, and the mass application of scientific testing (Issenberg 2012; Pons 2016; Römmele & Gibson 2020). Digging into the empirical practice of party activity in our five countries, we once again showed a spectrum of activity. Classifying three types of analytic practice—segmentation, targeting, and testing—we have shown that many techniques are long-standing. As one Canadian interviewee reflected:

> I think in some very, very key ways, and this I think kind of goes against the public perception, but politics with respect to data has changed very little in the last 70 years. We're essentially doing the same thing that we've always done and it's just the way we're doing it that has changed.

We saw evidence of this evolution in the tools and techniques utilized by many parties, seeing how in addition to established sorting and testing techniques, parties now have access to more complex modes of analysis, ranging from MRP to RCTs. They also have the capacity to target and contact smaller audiences more easily than ever before via social media.

While showing the potential for new forms of data analytics, our empirical cases suggested that actual usage of these methods is limited. Even in the United States, a country often lauded for its routine use of sophisticated data analytics, one interviewee suggested that:

> what gets written about in breathless anecdotes and books is so far from the truth. It's always absolute mayhem. People say to me, Ooh, how did you use data to do digital rapid response against Mitt Romney? The answer is, day-to-day, in the moment: we didn't. There's too much going on; you have to move way faster than you can if you're using data. And we didn't have the staff, and that was an American campaign; campaigns in other countries completely lack capacity.

The reality of much DDC therefore departs significantly from idealized accounts of slick, highly professionalized, scientific, and complex activity, as parties often lack the time and resources to invest in analytics. As Matthew McGregor outlined in the practitioner perspective he contributed, this means that "although the technical capacity does of course exist," in practice much campaign activity is far from complex. When it comes to most of the segmentation conducted by grassroots actors, the practices are often quite simple. We also saw, as McGregor outlined, that "when you look at the practice of campaigns, there isn't fine-grained micro-targeting." Although some of the larger, more resourced parties did deploy MRP and conduct randomized testing, these techniques are far from everyday common practice, often because of a lack of available resources or time.

These insights are important for debates around the democratic impact of analytics, and particularly for claims that parties are engaged in manipulation. Our analysis showed that while most parties use analytics to understand the electorate and engage in some form of testing to develop a resonant message, there is little evidence to suggest there are widespread attempts at manipulation. Changing voters' minds is no simple task, especially when it comes to partisan affiliation; hence it is important not to overstate the power of analytical techniques. Our cases also suggest that some concerns around political redlining (Kreiss 2016; Harker 2020, 155–156; Judge & Pal 2021) and concerns about the potential for parties to make Janus-faced promises to different audiences are not reflected in practice—as most of our parties focused on communicating broad messages to a wide audience, which are indicative of long-standing narrowcasting techniques (Kefford 2021).

These empirical findings suggest that while data analytics have continued to evolve and become more complex as technology and scientific knowledge advance, there is no automatic connection between the emergence of new techniques and evidence of democratically problematic behavior. Indeed, our cases suggest that relatively few parties are currently capable of utilizing the most complex tools routinely, and that where these are taken up there is limited evidence of problematic practice. These findings are important for those considering a potential regulatory response to DDC, as they suggest that regulation may address potential rather than actual practices.

When it comes to technology, we considered the idea that parties possess vast databases that enable large-scale and highly complex analysis to facilitate organization and communication. As our practitioner perspectives testify, we found that election campaigns are far from "well-oiled machines," and that it is often the case that parties are using old and temperamental systems which are not well integrated. We found that while larger parties often possess customized databases and CRMs—frequently adapting technology from a small number of international companies providing political systems for their purposes—some less resourced parties rely on off-the-shelf technology that was not built to advance their political goals, or they lack centralized databases entirely. The precise technology used was often determined by available resources and regulation (which can affect parties' ability to import internationally established software solutions).

When it comes to debates about democracy, these differences have potential implications for individual voters' privacy and data security. In contrast to fears around slick and sophisticated technologies that actors within parties can easily utilize to manipulate citizens, our empirical data suggests that much of the day-to-day use of data is clunky and mundane. As one of our interviewees noted, when reflecting on their parties' approach to technology:

> People do simple things because it's easier and because it's scalable to do simple things. Which is one of the things I think people often forget, that clever things are clever and effective, but if they're not much more effective than simple things, then do the simple thing if you're doing it at scale because simple things at scale succeed. Whereas clever things at scale break.

While assuaging some potential fears, our analysis did, however, raise some concerns that have so far been largely overlooked. Within our interviews we heard many stories of efforts to utilize technology in ways compliant with local stipulations, but also found some evidence of questionable data security practice and concerns about data breaches. Many of our parties exhibit strong practice, operating hierarchical access systems that limit data access and promote data security, but this was by no means uniform and was less common among those parties with limited resources and a lack of centrally overseen technology. Although we recognize the potential for even highly functional, tailored, and tested political technologies to be susceptible to data and security breaches—as in the case of the Russian hacking of the DNC or the data leak of sensitive member data from the German Christian Democratic canvassing app—smaller, untested, and untailored systems appeared in our analysis to be more vulnerable, suggesting that some technological concerns related to cyber-security require further investigation.

We also found evidence of an important distinction between parties' own infrastructure and the technology they are able to access and deploy. As Katie Harbath outlined in her practitioner perspective, "social media platforms have made it easier than ever before to be able to create targeted messages and connect with different audiences." Our analysis showed that such platforms have created significant loopholes through which parties can "outsource" critical marketing practices (for example, data collection and analysis) to bypass national privacy and electoral regulations. These insights raise important questions about the role and power of Facebook and other social networking platforms in democratic processes and suggest there is a need to consider the democratic vulnerabilities and oversight of externally provided technologies.

Finally, when it comes to personnel, we explored the emphasis placed on certain groups of actors as the source of data-driven interventions. Noting the focus on "geeks" and "nerds" who are seen to possess specialized scientific knowledge that allows them to execute complex analytics processes, we sought to show that a range of different actors often play a role in DDC. In doing so, we revealed that it is not just "nerds" and party officials who are responsible for each aspect of DDC, and that grassroots actors, party officials, and external actors can each play a role in data collection, analysis, and the use of technology.

For debates about democracy, this insight suggests that each potential actor should be seen as a potential source of more or less democratically problematic behaviors. Our cases illustrate that when it comes to data collection, analytics, and the use of technology, data-driven campaigns are assemblages in which a range of individuals play different roles (Nielsen 2012, 95). While, as our practitioners suggested, campaigns often have access to highly skilled professionals, they also call on a range of other actors to make a contribution. Grassroots activists and paid and unpaid external actors can therefore perform important roles, whether that be gathering data, conducting analytics, or developing new technology.

Although we found that it is most common for paid party staff and commercial companies to lead on the most complex forms of analytics and to utilize technology to its fullest capacity, other actors were able to access, alter, and utilize data within their campaigns. This suggests a need to not only focus on curtailing whom parties can employ to conduct data analysis (and how), but also consider the training and oversight that exist for the activities of other actors. In most of our parties, we found training schemes and central party oversight to try to guide the behavior of different actors and prevent problematic practices, but it's presently unclear how successful these interventions are. This suggests that those concerned about DDC need to not only consider expert data professionals, but also, as Amber MacIntyre observed in her perspective, appreciate "the huge variation" of people involved in campaigns. In part, this means looking beyond parties themselves, to consider the ecosystem that political parties operate in (Dommett et al. 2021), recognizing that it may be commercial companies or sister parties operating in different political contexts that are responsible for importing practices—problematic or otherwise—into different contexts. Indeed, while we found little evidence to prompt concern, it was notable that parties' knowledge of the data collection and analytics practices of some external providers was often thin—suggesting a potential area in which concerns may be uncovered in the future.

Rethinking DDC and Democracy

In considering the findings from our four central chapters, we suggest that three important points emerge that are critical to future debates around democracy and regulation. First, in showing there to be a spectrum of possible practices in the way data is used, it becomes important to understand exactly which practices are problematic. Whether thinking about DDC as an entire activity or looking more specifically at a particular component—such as data collection or analytics—our analysis suggests that data can be used in different ways that may be judged to be more or less problematic. It is therefore necessary to articulate how and why specific practices are not acceptable. This diagnostic process is likely to vary depending on context, as specific national norms and ideals shape what is deemed acceptable or not. Within our cases, for example, it is likely that German observers will find the collection of a wider array of personal data to be problematic, whereas in the United States or Australia, attitudes may be more permissive (Kozyreva et al. 2021). Similar variations are likely to be observed beyond our cases as well, with countries such as Sweden or Denmark, where personal data is more widely available, exhibiting different attitudes from a country like France, where attitudes to data sharing are more conservative.

In diagnosing what is and is not acceptable, it may be that attitudes vary in accordance with the degree to which certain practices are seen to be "new." In the case study countries we examined, there is a long-standing history of data collection and analysis (although doorstep canvassing is a more recent activity in Germany), and while new techniques and technologies are continually emerging, we found little evidence of a radical rupture with previous practice (Römmele & Gibson 2020). In these contexts, it is not, therefore, entirely clear why parties' attempts to collect personal data via a survey on a party website, or to target citizens using online advertisements, are less acceptable than the practice of gathering such insights through doorstep or telephone surveys or targeting through direct mail. Although digital media is often depicted as posing new and profound threats to democracy (Diamond 2019), this tendency toward "dystopian thinking" (Kundnani 2020) can result in what Jungherr et al. (2020) rightly describe as a moral panic. New technology does not automatically pose a distinct and novel threat to democracy, and it may be that attempts to curtail data collection via digital technology run counter to established precedent offline. This suggests a need to think carefully about what is problematic, in what contexts, and what regulatory levers would be most effective in eliminating such practices while minimizing effects on political participation and political competition.

In looking across our four key chapters on data, analytics, technology, and personnel, it is clear that those seeking to determine what is or is not acceptable need to ask a series of questions. When it comes to data, for example, it is important to reflect on the precise types of data that can or cannot be collected for use in each country, as well as to consider the conditions under which that data can be collected. It may, for example, be that so long as information is freely given there are no restrictions on what insights parties can collect. In other contexts, however, regulators may seek to impose limitations, arguing that only information gathered with fully informed consent is appropriate. Similarly, when it comes to analytics, it is important to reflect on whether segmentation, targeting, and testing are permissible, or whether only certain forms of these practices are acceptable. It could be, for example, that targeting in any form is not deemed acceptable, or that certain types of micro-targeting are not permissible. Cumulatively, therefore, our analysis suggests that DDC does not present an inherent threat to democracy; rather, different actors and national contexts can impose different understandings of the boundaries of acceptable practice.

Second, and building on the need for an appropriate diagnosis of the problem, it is vital to understand the prevalence of concerning practice more accurately. While spotlighting a range of potential threats posed by DDC and specific practices such as micro-targeting, we have found very little tangible evidence that these practices are being used as understood in popular commentary. It was notable that targeting was often not highly differentiated, and that the analytical techniques utilized were focused largely on segmenting voters and message testing, rather than developing highly granular personality profiles. Although our study did not involve scrutiny of the specific campaign interventions made by each of our 18 parties, we heard little evidence of attempts to profile, manipulate, or micro-target small groups of voters. While we acknowledge that these behaviors may be evident elsewhere (and note evidence of concerning practice: Dobber & Vreese 2022), we uncovered little cause for alarm. This is perhaps to be expected given our use of interviews with campaign practitioners, but it was notable that the additional sources we drew upon did not highlight concerns. In seeking to determine whether and what form of regulation (if any) is required, it is vital to consider the extent to which problems are realized. In doing so, it should be acknowledged, as Kusche (2020, 10) has argued, that negative practices are "neither inevitable nor likely to be uniform across all democratic settings." This links to our third and final argument: that it is vital to understand the conditions in which problematic behaviors emerge.

In seeking to understand why DDC looks different in different contexts, our analysis emphasized the potential for systemic, regulatory, and party-level factors to affect DDC. When it comes to the democratic impact of this activity, it is also the case that these factors inform the likelihood of problematic practices being evident. As shown across our cases, and discussed at length in Chapter 7, factors such as the electoral system, system of government, media regulation, and party-level factors can play an important role in driving country- and party-level differences. We therefore see apparently similar parties in different countries exhibiting different forms of DDC, with ideologically aligned organizations collecting subtly different forms of data and conducting alternative forms of analysis in Australia, the United Kingdom, and Germany. And parties in the same country—such as Canada—can vary dramatically in their technological infrastructure and approach to data collection because of party-level factors, such as different levels of resources and alternative ideological ideals and regulatory constraints (as mentioned by the information commissioner of British Columbia in their perspective). Understanding the relevance of these variables is not only helpful in mapping different behavior, but it can also help explain the conditions under which certain problematic behaviors are likely to emerge. In countries with majoritarian electoral systems, limited regulation, and high levels of party resources, it may, for example, be more likely that we will see higher levels of message differentiation, and more fine-grained segmentation and voter profiling. In contrast, in countries with proportional electoral systems and with high levels of privacy regulation and limited party resources, such issues are less likely to emerge. There are numerous configurations of these variables which will affect DDC; hence it is important to contextualize the phenomena within the institutional context that it is being employed.

These findings are important because to date much attention has been placed on data and privacy regulation as a mechanism for suppressing problematic practices. Though this is one important mechanism for altering the conditions of campaigning, our analysis suggests that it is not the only factor that affects how data-driven campaigns operate. Indeed, at the systemic level, we have shown that the electoral system can have a significant impact on the way that data is collected and utilized, while party-level factors such as ideology and resources can have similar effects. This suggests that attempts to counter problematic practices may need to look beyond one form of regulation to consider the different levers and influences that can be altered to change party behavior. It may, for example, be that regulation of party and campaign funding would curtail access to resources required for more complex practices (that could be viewed to be more problematic), or that larger systemic changes—such as voting system reform—could reduce the incentive to focus on narrow, target audiences. Efforts to regulate DDC can therefore benefit from appreciating the configuration of systemic, regulatory, and party-level factors that can be altered to induce certain types of DDC. One laboratory for how policy changes not designed to tackle DDC may end up altering practices is evident in Australia, where the attempt to reshape the relationship between "new" and "old" media with the introduction of the News Media and Digital Platforms Mandatory Bargaining Code (Fisher et al. 2021) is a case to follow. This attempt to make tech giants like Meta and Google pay to have media shared on their platforms imposes a new form of media regulation, but also has potential consequences for data-driven campaigns. In essence, DDC does not operate in a vacuum, meaning that changes to other forms of regulation, or to systemic and party-level considerations, should be seen to have the potential to exert as large an effect on DDC as data- and privacy-focused regulatory reforms.

These three lessons are particularly important for current debates around regulation. With high levels of public concern about data use, and a political discourse preoccupied with the threats posed by digital technology (Pentzold & Fölsche 2020), there is a danger that regulators look to respond to DDC without the necessary empirical evidence and fail to ask the appropriate questions needed to develop effective and proportionate responses to current data-driven practices.

There is also a need to consider the level at which any regulatory response should be made. At present, efforts are being pursued at national and international levels—with a notable attempt from the European Union to curtail targeting practice and data use through the Digital Services Act. Such efforts mark an important step in tackling global practices. However, our analysis suggests that such regulation may fail to take account of national-level differences that affect the ways in which data is collected and utilized. From this perspective, appreciating the universal and particular attributes of DDC across nations subject to regulation is crucial to ensuring that any rules which are developed are fit for the purpose.

Looking beyond Parties

Within this book, we have focused our attention on political parties, seeing these organizations as the principal agents of democratic engagement within advanced democracies. And yet, in exploring their practices we have also generated insights that resonate beyond this context. With civil society organizations (Macintyre 2020), governments (Etsy & Rushing 2007), trade unions (Hunt 2022), and many other groups increasingly utilizing data-driven techniques and insights, our study offers a range of useful insights for other contexts. First, in breaking down the components of a data-driven campaign and offering classifications of different activities, we provide a template for others to map the nature of DDC by other organizations. Our four key components—data, analytics, technology, and personnel—will remain constant across these other organizations, but the precise types of data, analytics, technology, and personnel will vary in accordance with the specific dynamics of the group. Recognizing this point, it will be interesting to look for points of commonality and divergence between different organizations, seeking to recognize when and where organizations exhibit similar practices and processes, and where radically different approaches or structures are found. In providing a framework to structure future studies, we hope to facilitate more extensive comparative work.

Beyond Our Five Cases

Our analysis also concentrated on the practices of 18 parties in five advanced democracies. As outlined in Chapter 1, we selected these cases to explore a range of systemic, regulatory, and party-level variables, but our case selection was necessarily narrow, and there is a pressing need to look beyond these cases to compare our findings with data-driven practices elsewhere. In examining five advanced democracies, we have looked at a particular set of campaigning practices, and we hope future work will look at alternative campaigning contexts. There is a need for further studies of countries with less established histories of data collection, and of parties that lack a membership or activist base and hence rely on alternative means and types of data acquisition. There is also an incentive to look at countries where attitudes to data collection may be more permissive. While attention is increasingly being paid to Germany as a site of stronger regulation (Kruschinski & Haller 2017), attention has not so far been paid to Scandinavian contexts in which attitudes to public data are more accepting. Likewise, currently unclear is what DDC looks like beyond the Anglo-American and European democracies. This is fertile ground for applying and re-examining our framework in other contexts.

Our study has also focused on national election campaigns. We did this for the principal reason that it is in these campaigns that we would expect to see the most significant investment in data-driven techniques. There is, however, a case for considering the uptake of these techniques in second-order or even internal party elections to build up a fuller picture of the extent to which these practices have become the norm. Our analysis suggests that many parties would like to invest in DDC year-round, yet are often prevented from doing so due to a lack of resources. Exploring the extent to which these emerging findings are borne out presents a fascinating avenue for further inquiry.

Beyond DDC

In this book we have focused on the particular phenomena of DDC, comparing prevailing narratives of concern to the actual practice of how data is being adopted by political parties. This approach to analysis is, we argue, insightful not only for studies of DDC, but for a range of new technologies emerging in politics. Most recently exemplified in coverage of AI, there is a recurring tendency to depict new technology as problematic and threatening for democracy. Indeed, recent headlines in Australia (Sky News Australia 2023), the United Kingdom (Milmo & Kiran 2023), and United States (Allen 2023) have claimed that AI poses a threat to democracy and electoral integrity. Such framing often leads to calls for regulation, and indeed there have already been moves by policy makers in countries such as Germany (Loh

2023) and the United States (Clarke 2023) to advance regulation of AI. Whilst this approach is to some extent understandable, as our analysis has shown, there is a danger that an emphasis on potential threats can lead to a misdiagnosis of the actual use and application of new technologies, potentially resulting in regulation that fails to address practice on the ground. For this reason we caution against sensationalized depictions of new technology and call instead for diagnoses rooted in observational insights.

Final Thoughts

DDC and the perceived threats associated with it have become a key debate of political communication in the twenty-first century. For those interested in political communication, elections, and democratic practice, early coverage of DDC offered a compelling and exciting story. It appeared that DDC challenged long-established democratic practices, setting new expectations for relations between parties and citizens. It also posed a set of challenging and important questions about the actual usage of these techniques, their impact on citizens, and effectiveness in securing desired goals. These conditions created a flurry of interest and swift attempts to outline potential threats and challenges, but as the reality of DDC becomes embedded within modern campaigns it appears that the transformational potential of this activity has not yet been realized. As such, there is a need to be wary of "game-changing" narratives. Instead, there is a need to view DDC as the latest iteration of a long-standing process of adaptation and change in response to media development (Blumler & Kavanagh 1999; Magin et al. 2017).

In understanding DDC in this way, we argue that there is a need to temper the claim that this practice poses an existential threat to democracy; nevertheless, we do recognize that it has the *potential* to manifest in problematic ways. Our failure to uncover evidence of concerning practice does not mean that DDC will always be unproblematic, and there is of course the potential that as this practice becomes more established it will be utilized in more problematic ways. This means that any move toward regulation needs to focus on creating the conditions in which acceptable and democratically positive manifestations of DDC can thrive, rather than focusing solely on mitigating perceived problems without solid empirical foundations. Moreover, any attempt to shape this activity needs to account for a range of variables which affect the configuration of DDC in each country. For this reason, a more sophisticated and reflective conversation is required that focuses not only on the threat and challenge of DDC, but also on how different countries around the globe envisage the positive use of this activity and define the boundaries of acceptable and unacceptable practice.

Finally, in this book, we have introduced a novel theoretical framework highlighting key explanatory variables across a multi-level framework to explain DDC variation cross-nationally. We hope this framework stimulates much discussion about its applicability to other case studies and actors beyond political parties, and encourages further qualitative work that builds rich descriptive accounts of the extent to which these practices are found in other contexts. This fine-grained descriptive work is essential in allowing scholars, regulators, and practitioners to better understand DDC, as it facilitates more grounded discussion of the threats and opportunities posed by the use of data in modern campaigning.

Notes

Chapter 1

1. The interview breakdown is as follows: Australia 183 (82 Labor, 48 Greens, 53 Liberal and Liberal National parties); United Kingdom 49 (31 Labour, 5 Conservative, 6 Liberal Democrat, 7 Green); Canada 9 (3 Liberal, 4 NDP, 2 Conservative); Germany 51 (13 Christian Democratic Union, 14 Social Democratic Party, 7 The Greens, 6 The Left, 8 Free Democratic Party, 2 Alternative for Germany, 1 Free Voters Bavaria). We also completed 37 interviews with digital marketing firms, campaign consultants, and data brokers. It is important to note that while the number of interviews with Australian parties far exceeds the others, this is necessary as there is almost no information available in the public domain about campaign spending and associated matters in Australia as parties are not required to provide almost any information on these matters. Hence, interviews are the only methods available to access information about campaigns in any detail.
2. Interviewees from the parties were drawn from across the population of those with knowledge of these practices, including those who sit at different points in the wider campaign assemblage. This includes those in party headquarters, such as campaign directors, data analysts, field directors, and digital operatives. But it also includes those at the state and regional level, those organizing and running campaigns in individual seats, as well as campaign volunteers, which included member and non-member activists. While it would be cumbersome to outline the roles of each individual interviewed, they represent a cross section of those within these parties. These varying perspectives are important as they reveal that views of data are not always consistent within single organizations, a point we illustrate within the chapters that follow.

Chapter 2

1. See also the work of Gauja (2017), who uses a multilevel framework to analyze party reform, as well as other similar frameworks from Barnea and Rahat (2007), who use a similar framework to understand candidate selection.

Chapter 3

1. Clearly, digital is a different medium or set of mediums, and there are a variety of channels that constitute digital. Nonetheless, most campaign messages are forms of

broadcast (sent to everyone on a list) or narrow-casted messages, to subgroups based on demographic or attitudinal variables. The granularity of targeting operations is what is often said to represent the difference between the previous era and the current one (Baldwin-Philippi 2017, 2019). Yet, how widespread targeting is at the individual level is an open question.
2. Facebook's custom audiences enable parties to connect with people who already have shown interest in the party and have interacted with it. For example, parties can re-target previous website visitors on Facebook or target users on the platform via their uploaded email addresses which were collected through canvassing or petitions. Facebook's lookalike audiences enable parties to reach new people who are similar to known audiences. For example, parties can target users on Facebook who are similar to the people who interacted with parties' Facebook pages, or to any of the parties' custom audiences.
3. Tracking cookies and pixels are text files from a website or an email which are stored on vistor's computers or mobile devices to track and remember information from them, such as their activity on a website, browsing history, geographic location, purchases, and more. Further, both enable the users' activity to be followed across multiple sites or services, continuing to stack data. This allows websites to display stored settings, information, or targeted content according to a specific users' previous behaviors. Parties can use this information not only to analyze user surf behavior, but also for targeted ads via Google or on Facebook.
4. The Representation of the People Act is not a unified piece of legislation for the entire UK, rather there are separate provisions in England and Wales (2001) and in Scotland (2001).
5. This refers to Daniel Kahneman and Amos Tversky, who conducted research on the psychology of judgment and decision-making. For more, see Thaler & Sunstein (2008).

Practitioner Perspectives on Analytics

1. For more information see: https://www.bluestate.co/eu/
2. For more information see: https://home.38degrees.org.uk/

Chapter 5

1. Our analysis focuses on the use of SNPs for external communication, but it should be noted that SNPs can also be used for internal party organization and management.
2. "Ad delivery" refers to the process by which Facebook shows paid content to users based on so-called ad auctions. They determine which paid content will be shown in which order for a specific search, user timeline, or feed from among all of the created paid content that includes the respective user in the target audience.

3. These figures were compiled by the authors through an analysis of the UK Electoral Commission's Political Finance Database.

Practitioner Perspectives on Technology

1. Software as a Service (SaaS) is a subsection of cloud computing. This is based on the principle that the software and IT infrastructure are operated by an external IT service provider and used by the customer as a service.

Chapter 6

1. Interestingly, elder statesmen were rarely involved in data collection (a trend found in each of our cases).
2. The depth of these ties extends beyond using C|T for cycle after cycle; for example, the private secretary of Prime Minister Morrison was a former CEO of C|T in Australia.
3. It is difficult to measure political party membership in Canada as there is no requirement for political parties to share their figures (Cross 2015).
4. In Australia, a booth is the voting place, and results are distributed at the electorate level as well as at the local booth level, allowing campaigners to segment up results at a more granular level.
5. Parties were hiring staff in competition with leading commercial companies, and many interviewees spoke about not being able to compete with wages in the commercial sector.
6. A Labour Party organogram detailing staffing at the 2019 General Election, for example, reports a director of Contact Creator, Targeting and Analysis overseeing a small team including a targeting and analysis manager, a targeting systems manager, targeting analysts, an electoral database and reporting administrator, a campaign and technology support team, and temp contract software engineers. For more information see: https://whimsical.com/labour-party-staff-M8tVcVzqDWX1GEZLpKxsVV.

Practitioner Perspectives on Personnel

1. For more information see: https://www.labourtogether.uk/.
2. For more information see: https://www.campaignlab.uk/.
3. For more information see: https://tacticaltech.org/.

Chapter 7

1. Of course, the United Kingdom and Canada do not elect members to their upper houses at the federal level, and in the United States there have been some states which use alternative electoral systems for electing representatives for local or sub-national elections.
2. These effects are accentuated by Australia's use of compulsory voting.
3. It is important to note that in Australia, the Liberal Party and the National Party are in a long-standing formal coalition at the federal level and in most sub-national jurisdictions, but in the state of Queensland the two parties have merged into the Liberal National Party.
4. Not all UK parties have a hierarchical structure; some are more decentralized and operate akin to federal parties. These differences reflect, however, not the dynamics of the system of government, but the ideological or historically determined structure of the party.
5. Until 2000, rules around donations allowed corporations and unions to give money to parties—and more than half of all donations to the Liberal and Conservative parties were from corporations, while more than a third of donations to the NDP were from unions. These rules, however, were changed in 2000 (Crandall & Roy 2020) to allow only individuals to donate to political parties.
6. Short money is the common name given to the financial assistance for Opposition parties in the House of Commons.
7. As per the Privacy Act (1988), a "registered political party"—defined as a political party registered under Part XI of the *Commonwealth Electoral Act*—is specifically excluded from the definition of "organization" and, therefore, is exempt from the operation of the Privacy Act.
8. This article extends the concept of "public interest" under Article 6(1)(e) GDPR to include "an activity that supports or promotes democratic engagement."
9. It should be noted that there has been some regulatory interest in the United Kingdom in parties' data-protection activity. Indeed, the UK Information Commission undertook an investigation in 2020, recommending improvements in data privacy notices, data processing, and social media data use (Information Commissioners Office 2018, 7).
10. It is worth noting that this interview was from 2017 and the granularity of targeting and analytics has improved since this time.

References

Chapter 1

Abrams, M. 1963. "Public Opinion Polls and Political Parties." *The Public Opinion Quarterly*, 27(1): 9–18.

Act Blue. n.d. "About Us." https://secure.actblue.com/about.

Baldwin-Philippi, J. 2019. "Data Campaigning: Between Empirics and Assumptions." *Internet Policy Review*, 8(4): 1–18.

Barnea, S., & Rahat, G. 2007. "Reforming Candidate Selection Methods: A Three-Level Approach." *Party Politics*, 13(3): 375–394.

Bartolini, S., & Mair, P. 1990. *Identity, Competition, and Electoral Availability*. New York: Cambridge University Press.

Bennett, C. J. 2016. "Voter Databases, Micro-Targeting, and Data Protection Law: Can Political Parties Campaign in Europe as They Do in North America?" *International Data Privacy Law*, 6(4): 261–275.

Berlin Data Commissioner for Data Protection and Freedom of Information. 2021. "Datenschutz und informationsfreiheit. Jahresbericht 2021 [Data protection and freedom of information. Annual report 2021]." https://www.datenschutz-berlin.de/fileadmin/user_upload/pdf/publikationen/jahresbericht/BlnBDI-Jahresbericht-2021-Web.pdf.

Bolleyer, N. 2012. "New Party Organization in Western Europe: Of Party Hierarchies, Stratarchies and Federations." *Party Politics*, 18(3): 315–336.

Bramston, T. 2016. "Labor's New Driver Noah Carroll May Be Antidote to Complacency." *The Australian*, October 3, 2016. https://www.theaustralian.com.au/commentary/opinion/labors-new-driver-noah-carroll-may-be-antidote-to-complacency/news-story/763aa352be673f87275f39fa0b68d72b.

Cadwalladr, C. 2017a. "The Great British Brexit Robbery: How Our Democracy Was Hijacked." *The Guardian*, May 7, 2017. https://www.theguardian.com/technology/2017/may/07/the-great-british-brexit-robbery-hijacked-democracy.

Cadwalladr, C. 2017b. "Revealed: Tory 'Dark' Ads Targeted Voters' Facebook Feeds in Welsh Marginal Seat." *The Guardian*, May 27, 2017. https://www.theguardian.com/politics/2017/may/27/conservatives-facebook-dark-ads-data-protection-election.

Campaign Live. 2007. "Direct Brief: The Labour Party Hires Experian." https://www.campaignlive.co.uk/article/direct-brief-labour-party-hires-experian/654302.

Carty, R. K. 2002. "The Politics of Tecumseh Corners: Canadian Political Parties as Franchise Organizations." *Canadian Journal of Political Science/Revue canadienne de science politique*, 35(4): 723–745.

Carty, R. K. 2004. "Parties as Franchise Systems: The Stratarchical Organizational Imperative." *Party Politics*, 10(1): 5–24.

Channel 4. 2020. "Revealed: Trump Campaign Strategy to Deter Millions of Black Americans from Voting in 2016." *Channel 4*, September 28, 2020. https://www.channel4.com/news/revealed-trump-campaign-strategy-to-deter-millions-of-black-americans-from-voting-in-2016.

Chester, J., & Montgomery, K. C. 2017. "The Role of Digital Marketing in Political Campaigns." *Internet Policy Review*, 6(4): 1–20.

Cicilline, D. 2020. "Cicilline Bill Will Crack Down on Spread of Misinformation in 2020 Elections." Washington, DC: United States House of Representatives.

Civis. n.d. Civis Analytics. https://www.civisanalytics.com/.

Coletto, D., Jansen, H. J., & Young, L. 2011. "Stratarchical Party Organization and Party Finance in Canada." *Canadian Journal of Political Science/Revue canadienne de science politique*, 44(1): 111–136.

C|T Group. n.d. "Expertise: We Are the Campaign Specialists." https://ctgroup.com/expertise/#research.

Dachwitz, I. 2017. "Wahlkampf in der Grauzone: Die Parteien, das Microtargeting und die Transparenz [Election campaigning in the legal gray zone: The parties, microtargeting and transparency]." https://netzpolitik.org/2017/wahlkampf-in-der-grauzone-die-parteien-das-microtargeting-und-die-transparenz/.

Data Council. 2019. "How Data Is Transforming Politics." *Data Council*. https://www.datacouncil.ai/talks/how-data-is-transforming-politics.

Data Trust. n.d. Data Trust. https://thedatatrust.com/.

Delacourt, S. 2012. "Political Parties in Legal Grey Zone When It Comes to Privacy Laws." *The Toronto Star*, September 29, 2012. https://www.thestar.com/news/canada/2012/09/29/political_parties_in_legal_grey_zone_when_it_comes_to_privacy_laws_delacourt.html.

Dommett, K. 2019. "Data-Driven Political Campaigns in Practice: Understanding and Regulating Diverse Data-Driven Campaigns." *Internet Policy Review*, 8(4): 1–18.

Dommett, K., & Power, S. 2021. "Studying Digital Parties: Methods, Challenges and Responses." In *Digital Parties: The Challenges of Online Organisation and Participation*, edited by O. Barberà, G. Sandri, P. Correa, & J. Rodríguez-Teruel, pp. 67–83. London: Routledge.

Dommett, K., Barclay, A. & Gibson, R., 2023. "Just What Is Data-Driven Campaigning? A Systematic Review." *Information, Communication & Society*: 1–22. https://www.tandfonline.com/doi/full/10.1080/1369118X.2023.2166794

Esser, F., & Strömbäck, J. 2012. "Comparing Election Campaign Communication." In *Handbook of Comparative Communication Research*, edited by F. Esser & T. Hanitzsch, pp. 289–307. London: Routledge

Gauja, A. 2017. *Party Reform: The Causes, Challenges, and Consequences of Organizational Change*. Oxford: Oxford University Press.

Harker, M. 2020. "Political Advertising Revisited: Digital Campaigning and Protecting Democratic Discourse." *Legal Studies*, 40(1): 151–171.

Hersh, E. D. 2015. *Hacking the Electorate: How Campaigns Perceive Voters*. Cambridge: Cambridge University Press.

Hersh, E. D., & Schaffner, B. F. 2013. "Targeted Campaign Appeals and the Value of Ambiguity." *The Journal of Politics*, 75(2): 520–534.

Information Commissioners Office. 2018. "Investigation into Data Analytics for Political Purposes." https://ico.org.uk/action-weve-taken/investigation-into-data-analytics-for-political-purposes/.

Jamieson, K. H. 2013. "Messages, Micro-Targeting, and New Media Technologies." *The Forum*, 11(3): 429–435.

Jamieson, K. H. 2018. *Cyberwar: How Russian Hackers and Trolls Helped Elect a President: What We Don't, Can't, and Do Know*. New York: Oxford University Press.

Jaursch, J. 2020. "Regeln für faire digitale Wahlkämpfe." *Stiftung Neue Verantwortung*. https://www.stiftung-nv.de/sites/default/files/regeln_fur_faire_digitale_wahlkampfe.pdf.

Jones, G., & Cinelli, A. 2017. "Hacking Attacks: A Pre-Election Setback for Italy's 5-Star Movement." *Reuters*, October 6, 2017. https://www.reuters.com/article/us-italy-politics-5star-idUSKBN1CA1TM.

Judge, E., & Pal, M. 2021. "Voter Privacy and Big-Data Elections." *Osgoode Hall Law Journal*, 58(1): 1–55.

Kearns, I., & Alexander, J. 2020. "Winning for Britain: Rebuilding the Liberal Democrats to Change the Course of Our Country." *Social Liberal*. https://www.socialliberal.net/winning_for_britain.

Kefford, G. 2021. *Political Parties and Campaigning in Australia: Data, Digital and Field*. London: Palgrave Macmillan.

Kefford, G., Dommett, K., Baldwin-Philippi, J., Bannerman, S., Dobber, T., Kruschinski, S., Kruikheimer, S., & Rzepecke, E. 2022. "Data-Driven Campaigning and Democratic Disruption: Evidence from Six Advanced Democracies." *Party Politics*, 39(3): 448–462.

Kim, Y. M. 2018. "Uncover: Strategies and Tactics of Russian Interference in US Elections." University of Wisconsin-Madison, April 9, 2018. https://www.brennancenter.org/our-work/analysis-opinion/voter-suppression-has-gone-digital.

Kolany-Raiser, D. B., & Radtke, T. 2018. "Microtargeting—Gezielte Wähleransprache im Wahlkampf [Microtargeting—Targeting voters in the election campaign]." *Abida*. https://www.abida.de/sites/default/files/16_Microtargeting.pdf.

Kreiss, D. 2012. *Taking Our Country Back: The Crafting of Networked Politics from Howard Dean to Barack Obama*. New York: Oxford University Press.

Kruschinski, S., & Bene, M. 2022. "*In varietate concordia*?! Political Parties' Digital Political Marketing in the 2019 European Parliament Election Campaign." *European Union Politics*, 23(1), 43–65.

Kruschinski, S., & Haller, A. 2017. "Restrictions on Data-Driven Political Micro-Targeting in Germany." *Internet Policy Review*, 6(4): 1–23.

Kuehn, K. M., & Salter, L. A. 2020. "Assessing Digital Threats to Democracy, and Workable Solutions: A Review of the Recent Literature." *International Journal of Communication*, 14(22): 2589–2610.

Labour Together. 2019. "Election Review 2019: The Ground Campaign." https://electionreview.labourtogether.uk/chapters/the-ground-campaign.

Lawson, K. 1980. *Political Parties and Linkage: A Comparative Perspective*. New Haven, CT: Yale University Press.

Mattoni, A., & Ceccobelli, D. 2018. "Comparing Hybrid Media Systems in the Digital Age: A Theoretical Framework for Analysis." *European Journal of Communication*, 33(5): 540–557.

Moore, M. 2018. *Democracy Hacked: Political Turmoil and Information Warfare in the Digital Age*. London: Oneworld.

Munroe, K. B., & Munroe, H. 2018. "Constituency Campaigning in the Age of Data." *Canadian Journal of Political Science/Revue canadienne de science politique*, 51(1): 135–154.

Murphy, K. 2019. "Australia's Major Political Parties Targeted by 'Sophisticated State Actor,' PM Says." *The Guardian*, February 17, 2019. 2019/02/18/T02:48:08.000Z.

Nadler, A., Crain, M., & Donovan, J. 2018. "Weaponizing the Digital Influence Machine." *Data & Society*, https://www.datasociety.net/wp-content/uploads/2018/10/DS_Digital_Influence_Machine.pdf.

National Democratic Party. 2021. "Campaign Debrief." https://xfer.ndp.ca/2022/Documents/Campaign_Debrief_Report_2021.pdf.

Nielsen, R. K. 2020. "Interview with Government vs the Robots Podcast." October 15, Episode 51. http://www.governmentvrobots.com/.

Office of the Privacy Commissioner of Canada. 2019. "Investigation Finds BC Firm Delivered Micro-Targeted Political Ads without Ensuring Consent." November 26, 2019. https://www.priv.gc.ca/en/opc-news/news-and-announcements/2019/nr-c_191126/.

Pasquino, G. 2005. "Italy and America: Politics and Culture: Americanization of Italian Politics?" *Journal of Modern Italian Studies*, 10(1): 3–9.

Phillips, J. M., Reynolds, T. J., & Reynolds, K. 2010. "Decision-based Voter Segmentation: An Application for Campaign Message Development." *European Journal of Marketing*, 44(3/4): 310–330.

Reed Awards. 2023. "2023 Reed Awards." *Campaigns and Elections Magazine*. https://reedawards.secure-platform.com/a/page/categories/all-categories.

Römmele, A., & Gibson, R. 2020. "Scientific and Subversive: The Two Faces of the Fourth Era of Political Campaigning." *New Media & Society*, 22(4): 595–610.

Rubinstein, I. S. 2014. "Voter Privacy in the Age of Big Data." *Wisconsin Law Review*, 5: 861–936.

Ryan-Mosley, T. 2020. "Data Should Enfranchise People, Says the Democrats' Head of Technology." *MIT Technology Review*, October 23, 2020. https://www.technologyreview.com/2020/10/23/1011092/data-should-enfranchise-people-says-the-democrats-head-of-technology/.

Scally, D. 2019. "Austrian People's Party Calls Alleged Hack an 'attack on democracy.'" *The Irish Times*, September 6, 2019. https://www.irishtimes.com/news/world/europe/austrian-people-s-party-calls-alleged-hack-an-attack-on-democracy-1.4010308.

SPD-Parteivorstand. 2021. "Acht Punkte für Fairness im digitalen Wahlkampf. [Eight points for a fair digital campaign]." https://www.spd.de/fileadmin/Dokumente/Beschluesse/Parteispitze/PV_2021/SPD-PV-Kodex-Fairness.pdf.

't Veld, S. 2017. "On democracy." *Internet Policy Review*, 6(4): 1–12.

Taylor, K. 2021. *The Little Black Book of Data and Democracy*. London: Byline Books.

US Senate. 2018. "Cambridge Analytica and the Future of Data Privacy." *US Senate*, May 16, 2018. https://www.judiciary.senate.gov/meetings/cambridge-analytica-and-the-future-of-data-privacy.

Vaccari, C. 2013. *Digital Politics in Western Democracies: A Comparative Study*. Baltimore, MD: Johns Hopkins University Press.

Völlinger, V. 2017. "Haustürwahlkampf: Klingeln bei alten Bekannten [Door-to-door campaign: ringing the doorbell of old acquaintances]." *Die Zeit*, September 20, 2017. https://www.zeit.de/politik/deutschland/2017-09/haustuerwahlkampf-cdu-spd-digitalisierung-filterblase/komplettansicht.

YouGov 2017. "Haustürwahlkampf bietet Parteien Chancen [Door-to-door canvassing offers opportunities for parties]." *YouGov*. https://yougov.de/news/2017/05/22/hausturwahlkampf-bietet-parteien-chancen.

Zuiderveen Borgesius, F., Möller, J., Kruikemeier, S., Ó Fathaigh, R., Irion, K., Dobber, T., Bodo, B., & de Vreese, C. H. 2018. "Online Political Microtargeting: Promises and Threats for Democracy." *Utrecht Law Review*, 14(1): 82–96.

Chapter 2

Anstead, N. 2017. "Data-Driven Campaigning in the 2015 United Kingdom General Election." *The International Journal of Press/Politics*, 22(3): 294–313.
Baldwin-Philippi, J. 2019. "Data Campaigning: Between Empirics and Assumptions." *Internet Policy Review*, 8(4): 1–18.
Bania, K. 2019. "The Role of Media Pluralism in the Enforcement of EU Competition Law." *Concurrences*. https://www.concurrences.com/en/all-books/the-role-of-media-pluralism-in-the-enforcement-of-eu-competition-law.
Barnea, S., & Rahat, G. 2007. "Reforming Candidate Selection Methods: A Three-Level Approach." *Party Politics*, 13(3): 375–394.
Bennett, C. 2015. "Trends in Voter Surveillance in Western Societies: Privacy Intrusions and Democratic Implications." *Surveillance and Society*, 13(3–4): 370–384.
Bennett, C. J. 2016. "Voter Databases, Micro-Targeting, and Data Protection Law: Can Political Parties Campaign in Europe as They Do in North America?" *International Data Privacy Law*, 6(4): 261–275.
Bimber, B. 2014. "Digital Media in the Obama Campaigns of 2008 and 2012: Adaptation to the Personalized Political Communication Environment." *Journal of Information Technology & Politics*, 11(2): 130–150.
Blumler, J. G. 1980. "Mass Communication Research in Europe: Some Origins and Prospects." *Media, Culture & Society*, 2(4): 367–376.
Bolleyer, N. 2012. "New Party Organization in Western Europe: Of Party Hierarchies, Stratarchies and Federations." *Party Politics*, 18(3): 315–336.
Bowler, S., Carter, E., & Farrell, D. M. 2001. *Studying Electoral Institutions and Their Consequences: Electoral Systems and Electoral Laws*. University of California, Irvine, CSD Working Papers.
Budge, I., Ezrow, L., & McDonald, M. 2010. "Ideology, Party Factionalism and Policy Change: An Integrated Dynamic Theory." *British Journal of Political Science*, 40(4): 781–804.
Cameron, S., & McAllister, I. 2019. "The 2019 Australian Federal Election: Results from the Australian Election Study." https://australianelectionstudy.org/wp-content/uploads/The-2019-Australian-Federal-Election-Results-from-the-Australian-Election-Study.pdf.
Chadwick, A. 2017. *The Hybrid Media System: Politics and Power*. Oxford: Oxford University Press.
Cross, W., & Pilet, J.-B. 2015. *The Politics of Party Leadership: A Cross-National Perspective*. Oxford: Oxford University Press.
Crotty, W. 2006. "Party Origins and Evolution in the United States." In *Handbook of Party Politics*, edited by R. Katz & W. Crotty, pp. 25–33. London: Sage.
Dobber, T., Trilling, D., & Helberger, N. 2017. "Two Crates of Beer and 40 Pizzas: The Adoption of Innovative Political Behavioural Targeting Techniques." *Internet Policy Review*, 6(4): 1–25.

Dodsworth, S., & Cheeseman, N. 2016. *More than Ideology, More than Elections: A Strategic Approach to Supporting Sister-Parties*. London: Westminster Foundation for Democracy.

Dommett, K. 2019. "Data-Driven Political Campaigns in Practice: Understanding and Regulating Diverse Data-Driven Campaigns." *Internet Policy Review*, 8(4): 1–18.

Dommett, K., Kefford, G., & Power, S. 2021. "The Digital Ecosystem: The New Politics of Party Organization in Parliamentary Democracies." *Party Politics*, 27(5), 847–857.

Dommett, K., Temple, L., & Seyd, P. 2020. "Dynamics of Intra-Party Organisation in the Digital Age: A Grassroots Analysis of Digital Adoption." *Parliamentary Affairs*, 74(2): 378–397.

Downs, A. 1957. "An Economic Theory of Political Action in a Democracy." *Journal of Political Economy*, 65(2): 135–150.

Elazar, D. J. 1997. "Contrasting Unitary and Federal Systems." *International Political Science Review*, 18(3): 237–251.

Eldersveld, S. J. 1964. *Political Parties: A Behavioral Analysis*. Chicago: Rand McNally.

Epstein, B. 2018. *The Only Constant Is Change: Technology, Political Communication, and Innovation over Time*. New York: Oxford University Press.

European Commission. 2020. "The Digital Services Act: Ensuring a Safe and Accountable Online Environment." https://ec.europa.eu/info/strategy/priorities-2019-2024/eur ope-fit-digital-age/digital-services-act-ensuring-safe-and-accountable-online-env ironment_en.

Farrell, D. M. 2006. "Political Parties in a Changing Campaign Environment." In *Handbook of Party Politics*, edited by R. Katz & W. Crotty, pp. 122–133. Thousand Oaks, CA: Sage.

Farrell, D. M. 2011. *Electoral Systems: A Comparative Introduction*. Basingstoke, UK: Palgrave Macmillan.

Freeden, M. 1996. *Ideologies and Political Theory: A Conceptual Approach*. Oxford: Clarendon Press.

Gauja, A. 2017. *Party Reform: The Causes, Challenges, and Consequences of Organizational Change*. Oxford: Oxford University Press.

Gibson, R., & Römmele, A. 2001. "Changing Campaign Communications: A Party-Centered Theory of Professionalized Campaigning." *The Harvard International Journal of Press/Politics*, 6(4): 31–43.

Gofas, A., & Hay, C. 2010. *The Role of Ideas in Political Analysis: A Portrait of Contemporary Debates*. Milton Park, UK: Routledge.

Hallin, D. C., & Mancini, P. 2017. "Ten Years after Comparing Media Systems: What Have We Learned?" *Political Communication*, 34(2): 155–171.

Harker, M. 2020. "Political Advertising Revisited: Digital Campaigning and Protecting Democratic Discourse." *Legal Studies*, 40: 151–171.

Hersh, E. D. 2015. *Hacking the Electorate: How Campaigns Perceive Voters*. Cambridge: Cambridge University Press.

Holcombe, R. G. 2021. "Elite Influence on General Political Preferences." *Journal of Government and Economics*, 3: 2667–3193.

Judge, E., & Pal, M. 2021. "Voter Privacy and Big-Data Elections." *Osgoode Hall Law Journal*, 58(1): 1–55.

Kaid, L., & Holtz-Bacha, C. 2006. *The Sage Handbook of Political Advertising*. Thousand Oaks, CA: Sage Publications.

Karvonen, L. 2007. "Legislation on Political Parties: A Global Comparison." *Party Politics*, 13(4): 437–455.

Katz, R. S., & Mair, P. 1995. "Changing Models of Party Organization and Party Democracy: The Emergence of the Cartel Party." *Party Politics*, 1(1): 5–28.

Kefford, G. 2018. "Digital Media, Ground Wars and Party Organisation: Does Stratarchy Explain How Parties Organise Election Campaigns?" *Parliamentary Affairs*, 71(3): 656–673.

Kefford, G. 2021. *Political Parties and Campaigning in Australia: Data, Digital and Field*. London: Palgrave Macmillan.

Kefford, G., Dommett, K., Baldwin-Philippi, J., Bannerman, S., Dobber, T., Kruschinski, S., Kruikheimer, S., & Rzepecke, E. 2022. "Data-Driven Campaigning and Democratic Disruption: Evidence from Six Advanced Democracies." *Party Politics*, 29(3): 448–462.

Kolodny, R., & Logan, A. 1998. "Political Consultants and the Extension of Party Goals." *Political Science and Politics*, 31(2): 155–159.

Kreiss, D. 2016. *Prototype Politics: Technology-Intensive Campaigning and the Data of Democracy*. New York: Oxford University Press.

Krewel, M. 2017. *Modernisierung deutscher Wahlkämpfe? [Modernization of German Election Campaigns?]*. Baden-Baden: Nomos Verlagsgesellschaft mbH & Co. KG.

Kruschinski, S., & Bene, M. 2022. "In Varietate Concordia?! Political Parties' Digital Political Marketing in the 2019 European Parliament Election Campaign." *European Union Politics*, 23(1): 43–65.

Kruschinski, S., & Haller, A. 2017. "Restrictions on Data-Driven Political Micro-Targeting in Germany." *Internet Policy Review*, 6(4): 1–23.

Lamprinakou, C. 2010. *The Party Evolution Framework: An Integrated Approach to Examining the Development of Party Communications and Campaigns*. School of Social Sciences Theses, Brunel University. http://bura.brunel.ac.uk/handle/2438/4404.

Laver, M. 1989. "Party Competition and Party System Change: The Interaction of Coalition Bargaining and Electoral Competition." *Journal of Theoretical Politics*, 1(3): 301–324.

Lilleker, D. 2016. "Comparing Online Campaigning: The Evolution of Interactive Campaigning from Royal to Obama to Hollandel." *French Politics*, 14: 234–253.

Lunt, P., & Livingstone, S. 2012. *Media Regulation: Governance and the Interests of Citizens and Consumers*. London: Sage.

Magin, M., Podschuweit, N., Haßler, J., & Russmann, U. 2017. "Campaigning in the Fourth Age of Political Communication: A Multi-Method Study on the Use of Facebook by German and Austrian Parties in the 2013 National Election Campaigns." *Information, Communication & Society*, 20(11): 1698–1719.

Martin, G., & Peskowitz, Z. 2018. "Agency Problems in Political Campaigns: Media Buying and Consulting." *American Political Science Review*, 112(2): 231–248.

Mattoni, A., & Ceccobelli, D. 2018. "Comparing Hybrid Media Systems in the Digital Age: A Theoretical Framework for Analysis." *European Journal of Communication*, 33(5): 540–557.

McKenna, E., & Han, H. 2014. *Groundbreakers: How Obama's 2.2 Million Volunteers Transformed Campaigning in America*. Oxford: Oxford University Press.

Mendilow, J., & Phélippeau, E. 2018. *Handbook of Political Party Funding*. London: Edward Elgar.

Michels, R. 1966. *Political Parties: A Sociological Study of the Oligarchical Tendencies of Modern Democracy*. New York: Free Press.

Plasser, F., & Plasser, G. 2002. *Global Political Campaigning: A Worldwide Analysis of Campaign Professionals and Their Practices.* Westport, CT: Greenwood.

Poguntke, T., Scarrow, S. E., & Webb, P. D. 2016. "Party Rules, Party Resources and the Politics of Parliamentary Democracies: How Parties Organize in the 21st Century." *Party Politics*, 22(6): 661–678.

Poguntke, T., & Webb, P. 2005. *The Presidentialization of Politics: A Comparative Study of Modern Democracies.* Oxford: Oxford University Press.

Power, S. 2020. *Party Funding and Corruption.* Basingstoke, UK: Palgrave MacMillan.

Puppis, M. 2010. "Media Governance: A New Concept for the Analysis of Media Policy and Regulation." *Communication, Culture and Critique*, 3(2): 134–149.

Rees, J. 1988. "Self Regulation: An Effective Alternative to Direct Regulation by OSHA?" *Policy Studies Journal*, 16(3): 602–614.

Renwick, A. 2010. *The Politics of Electoral Reform: Changing the Rules of Democracy.* Cambridge: Cambridge University Press.

Reuters. 2022. "Digital News Report 2022." *Reuters Institute*, https://reutersinstitute.politics.ox.ac.uk/digital-news-report/2022/dnr-executive-summary.

Riker, W. 1964. *Federalism: Origin, Operation, Significance.* Boston, MA: Little, Brown.

Samuels, D. J. 2002. "Presidentialized Parties: The Separation of Powers and Party Organization and Behavior." *Comparative Political Studies*, 35(4): 461–483.

Sartori, G. 2005. *Parties and Party Systems: A Framework for Analysis.* Colchester, UK: ECPR Press.

Scarrow, S. 2015. *Beyond Party Members: Changing Approaches to Partisan Mobilization.* Oxford: Oxford University Press.

Schoen, H. 2015. "Wahlkampfforschung" [Campaign Research]. In *Handbuch Wahlforschung* [Handbook of Campaign Research], edited by J. W. Falter & H. Schoen, pp. 489–522. Wiesbaden: Springer VS.

Sheingate, A. D. 2016. *Building a Business of Politics: The Rise of Political Consulting and the Transformation of American Democracy.* Oxford: Oxford University Press.

Stromer-Galley, J. 2019. *Presidential Campaigning in the Internet Age.* Oxford: Oxford University Press.

Swanson, D., & Mancini, P. 1996. *Politics, Media, and Modern Democracy: An International Study of Innovations in Electoral Campaigning and Their Consequences.* Westport, CT: Greenwood.

United Kingdom Electoral Commission. n.d. "Public Funding for Political Parties." https://www.electoralcommission.org.uk/who-we-are-and-what-we-do/financial-reporting/donations-and-loans/public-funding-political-parties.

Vaccari, C. 2013. *Digital Politics in Western Democracies: A Comparative Study.* Baltimore, MD: Johns Hopkins University Press.

Van Biezen, I., & Borz, G. 2012. "Models of Party Democracy: Patterns of Party Regulation in Post-War European Constitutions." *European Political Science Review*, 4(3): 327–359.

Van Biezen, I., & Rashkova, E. R. 2014. "Deterring New Party Entry? The Impact of State Regulation on the Permeability of Party Systems." *Party Politics*, 20(6): 890–903.

Ware, A. 1996. *Political Parties and Party Systems.* Oxford: Oxford University Press.

Zipkin, S. 2010. "The Election Period and Regulation of the Democratic Process." *William & Mary Bill of Rights Journal*, 18(3): 533–594.

Chapter 3

Anstead, N. 2017. "Data-Driven Campaigning in the 2015 United Kingdom General Election." *The International Journal of Press/Politics*, 22(3): 294–313.

Anstead, N. 2018. "Data and Election Campaigning." *Political Insight*, 9(2): 32–35.

Baldwin-Philippi, J. 2017. "The Myths of Data-Driven Campaigning." *Political Communication*, 34(4): 627–633.

Baldwin-Philippi, J. 2019. "Data Campaigning: Between Empirics and Assumptions." *Internet Policy Review*, 8(4): 1–18.

Barberá, P. 2021. "Voter files." https://github.com/pablobarbera/voter-files.

Bartlett, J., Smith, J., & Acton, R. 2018. "The Future of Political Campaigning." *Demos*, July. https://ico.org.uk/media/2259365/the-future-of-political-campaigning.pdf.Barocas, S. 2012. "The Price of Precision: Voter Microtargeting and Its Potential Harms to the Democratic Process." *Proceedings of the First Edition Workshop on Politics, Elections and Data*, 2012, 31–36.

Benle, N., & Papatla, P. 2021. "The 2020 Campaign: Candidates in a New World." In *Political Marketing in the 2020 U.S. Presidential Election*, edited by J. Gillies, pp. 41–63. Basingstoke, UK: Palgrave Macmillan.

Bennett, C. 2015. "Trends in Voter Surveillance in Western Societies: Privacy Intrusions and Democratic Implications." *Surveillance and Society*, 13(3–4): 370–384.

Bennett, C., & Bayley, R. 2018. *The Influence Industry in Canada*. Berlin: Tactical Tech. https://cdn.ttc.io/s/ourdataourselves.tacticaltech.org/ttc-influence-industry-canada.pdf.

Bennett, C. J. 2016. "Voter Databases, Micro-Targeting, and Data Protection Law: Can Political Parties Campaign in Europe as They Do in North America?" *International Data Privacy Law*, 6(4): 261–275.

Bennett, C. J., & Lyon, D. 2019. "Data-Driven Elections: Implications and Challenges for Democratic Societies." *Internet Policy Review*, 8(4): 1–16.

Bimber, B. 2014. "Digital Media in the Obama Campaigns of 2008 and 2012: Adaptation to the Personalized Political Communication Environment." *Journal of Information Technology & Politics*, 11(2): 130–150.

Black, J. 2022. "Voter Data as a Utility." Produced by E. Wilson. *The Business of Politics Podcast*. https://www.businessofpoliticspodcast.com/episode/voter-data-as-a-utility-jon-black-data-trust.

Bogle, A. 2019. "How the Australian Federal Election Invaded Your Inbox with Email Tracking Tools." *ABC*. May 2, 2019. https://www.abc.net.au/news/science/2019-05-02/email-tracking-parties-lobby-groups-australian-federal-election/11056186.

Bundestag. 1994. "Political Parties Act." https://www.bmi.bund.de/SharedDocs/downloads/DE/gesetzestexte/Parteiengesetz_PartG_engl_042009.pdf?__blob=publicationFile&v=1.

Butler, D. 1995. *British General Elections since 1945*, 2nd edition. Oxford: John Wiley & Sons.

Cadwalladr, C. 2017a. "The Great British Brexit Robbery: How Our Democracy Was Hijacked." *The Guardian*, May 7, 2017. https://www.theguardian.com/technology/2017/may/07/the-great-british-brexit-robbery-hijacked-democracy.

Cadwalladr, C. 2017b. "Revealed: Tory 'Dark' Ads Targeted Voters' Facebook Feeds in Welsh Marginal Seat." *The Guardian*, May 27, 2017. https://www.theguardian.com/politics/2017/may/27/conservatives-facebook-dark-ads-data-protection-election.

Cadwalladr, C., & Graham-Harrison, E. 2018. "Revealed: 50 Million Facebook Profiles Harvested for Cambridge Analytica in Major Data Breach." *The Guardian*. March 18, 2018. https://www.theguardian.com/news/2018/mar/17/cambridge-analytica-facebook-influence-us-election.

Campaign Monitor. 2019. "Email Tracking Pixel: Learning about Your Audience." April 2, 2019. https://www.campaignmonitor.com/blog/email-marketing/2019/04/email-tracking-pixel-learning-about-your-audience/.

Castleman, D. 2016. "Essentials of Modeling and Microtargeting." In *Data and Democracy: How Political Data Science Is Shaping the 2016 Elections*, edited by A. Therriault, pp. 1–6. Sebastopol, CA: O'Reilly Media.

Clemens, C. 2018. "The CDU/CSU's Ambivalent 2017 Campaign." *German Politics and Society*, 36(2): 55–75.

Delacourt, S. 2012. "Political Parties in Legal Grey Zone When It Comes to Privacy Laws." *Toronto Star*, September 29, 2012. https://www.thestar.com/news/canada/2012/09/29/political_parties_in_legal_grey_zone_when_it_comes_to_privacy_laws_delacourt.html?rf.

Delacourt, S. 2013. *Shopping for Votes: How Politicians Choose Us and We Choose Them*. Madeira Park, BC: Douglas and McIntyre.

Delacourt, S. 2019. "How the Liberals Won—An Inside Look at the Targeting and Tactics That Got Trudeau Re-elected." *Toronto Star*. November 23, 2019. https://www.thestar.com/politics/2019/11/23/how-the-liberals-won-an-inside-look-at-the-targeting-and-tactics-that-got-trudeau-re-elected.html.

Dommett, K. 2019. "Data-Driven Political Campaigns in Practice: Understanding and Regulating Diverse Data-Driven Campaigns." *Internet Policy Review*, 8(4): 1–18.

Dommett, K., Kefford, G., & Power, S. 2020. "The Digital Ecosystem: The New Politics of Party Organization in Parliamentary Democracies." *Party Politics*, 27(5): 847–857.

Federal Ministry of the Interior and Community. "Funding of Political Parties." https://www.bmi.bund.de/EN/topics/constitution/funding-of-political-parties/funding-of-political-parties-node.html.

Gibson, R. K., & McAllister, I. 2015. "Normalising or Equalising Party Competition? Assessing the Impact of the Web on Election Campaigning." *Political Studies*, 63(3): 529–547.

Gorton, W. A. 2016. "Manipulating Citizens: How Political Campaigns' Use of Behavioral Social Science Harms Democracy." *New Political Science*, 38(1): 61–80.

Hankey, S., Marrison, J., & Naik, R. 2018. *Data and Democracy in the Digital Age*. London: The Constitution Society.

Hersh, E. D. 2015. *Hacking the Electorate: How Campaigns Perceive Voters*. Cambridge: Cambridge University Press.

Hessian Commissioner for Data Protection and Freedom. 2023. "Datenschutz bei Wahl- und Abstimmungswerbung [Data protection regarding election and voting advertisement]." https://datenschutz.hessen.de/sites/datenschutz.hessen.de/files/2023-02/datenschutz_bei_wahl-_und_abstimmungswerbung_langfassung.pdf.

Information Commissioner's Office. 2018. "Investigation into Data Analytics for Political Purposes." https://ico.org.uk/action-weve-taken/investigation-into-data-analytics-for-political-purposes/.

Issenberg, S. 2012b. *The Victory Lab: The Secret Science of Winning Campaigns.* New York: Broadway Books.

Johnston, R., Cutts, D., Pattie, C., & Fisher, J. 2012. "We've Got Them on the List: Contacting, Canvassing and Voting in a British General Election Campaign." *Electoral Studies*, 31(2), 317–329.

Judge, E., & Pal, M. 2021. "Voter Privacy and Big-Data Elections." *Osgoode Hall Law Journal*, 58(1): 1–55.

Jungherr, A. 2016. "Datengestützte Verfahren im Wahlkampf [Data-driven methods in election campaigns]." *Zeitschrift für Politikberatung (ZPB) [Journal for Policy Advice and Political Consulting]*, 8(1): 3–14.

Jungherr, A., Rivero, G., & Gayo-Avello, D. 2020. *Retooling Politics: How Digital Media Are Shaping Democracy.* Cambridge: Cambridge University Press.

Kalla, J. L., & Broockman, D. E. 2018. "The Minimal Persuasive Effects of Campaign Contact in General Elections: Evidence from 49 Field Experiments." *American Political Science Review*, 112(1): 148–166.

Karpf, D. 2012. *The MoveOn Effect: The Unexpected Transformation of American Political Advocacy.* Oxford: Oxford University Press.

Karpf, D. 2019. "On Digital Disinformation and Democratic Myths." *Mediawell, Social Science Research Council*, December 10, 2019. https://mediawell.ssrc.org/expert-refl ections/on-digital-disinformation-and-democratic-myths/.

Katz, R. S., & Mair, P. 1995. "Changing Models of Party Organization and Party Democracy: The Emergence of the Cartel Party." *Party Politics*, 1(1): 5–28.

Kefford, G. 2021. *Political Parties and Campaigning in Australia: Data, Digital and Field.* London: Palgrave Macmillan.

Kreiss, D. 2012. *Taking Our Country Back: The Crafting of Networked Politics from Howard Dean to Barack Obama.* New York: Oxford University Press.

Kreiss, D. 2016. *Prototype Politics: Technology-Intensive Campaigning and the Data of Democracy.* New York: Oxford University Press.

Kreiss, D. 2017. "Micro-Targeting, the Quantified Persuasion." *Internet Policy Review*, 6(4): 1–14.

Kreiss, D., & Howard, P. N. 2010. "New Challenges to Political Privacy: Lessons from the First US Presidential Race in the Web 2.0 Era." *International Journal of Communication*, 4(19): 1032–1050.

Kruschinski, S., & Haller, A. 2017. "Restrictions on Data-Driven Political Micro-Targeting in Germany." *Internet Policy Review*, 6(4): 1–23.

Kusche, I. 2020. "The Old in the New: Voter Surveillance in Political Clientelism and Datafied Campaigning." *Big Data & Society*, 7(1): 1–17.

Lapowsky, I. 2016. "Here's How Facebook Actually Won Trump the Presidency." *Wired*, November 15, 2016. https://www.wired.com/2016/11/facebook-won-trump-election-not-just-fake-news/.

Lapowsky, I. 2022. "The DNC Has a New Secret Weapon for Finding Voters." *The Protocol*, June 23, 2022. https://www.protocol.com/policy/dnc-data-midterms.

Margetts, H. 2017. "The Data Science of Politics." *Political Studies Review*, 15(2): 201–209.

McGregor, G. 2014. "The Big Data Election: Political Parties Building Detailed Voter Records." *Ottawa Citizen*, October 18, 2014. https://ottawacitizen.com/news/politics/the-big-data-election-political-parties-building-detailed-voter-records.

McGregor, G. 2017. "Liberal Party's Exclusive Deal with Data Company Benefits Trudeau Friend." *CTV News*, March 29, 2017. https://www.ctvnews.ca/politics/liberal-party-s-exclusive-deal-with-data-company-benefits-trudeau-friend-1.3346830.

Mills, S. 2014. *The Professionals: Strategy, Money and the Rise of the Political Campaigner in Australia*. Collingwood: Black.

Munroe, K. B., & Munroe, H. 2018. "Constituency Campaigning in the Age of Data." *Canadian Journal of Political Science/Revue canadienne de science politique*, 51(1): 135–154.

Naik, R. 2019. "Political Campaigning: The Law, the Gaps and the Way Forward." *Oxford Technology and Elections Commission*. https://oxtec.oii.ox.ac.uk/wp-content/uploads/sites/10/2019/10/OxTEC-The-Law-The-Gaps-and-The-Way-Forward.pdf.

Newman, B. 1994. *The Marketing of the President: Political Marketing as Campaign Strategy*. London: Sage.

Nickerson, D. W., & Rogers, T. 2014. "Political Campaigns and Big Data." *Journal of Economic Perspectives*, 28(2): 51–74.

Nielsen, R. K. 2012. *Ground Wars: Personalized Communication in Political Campaigns*. Princeton, NJ: Princeton University Press.

Panebianco, A. 1988. *Political Parties: Organization and Power*. Cambridge; New York: Cambridge University Press.

Patten, S. 2017. "Databases, Microtargeting, and the Permanent Campaign: A Threat to Democracy?" In *Permanent Campaigning in Canada*, edited by A. Marland, T. Giasson, & A. L. Esselment, pp. 47–64. Vancouver: UBC Press.

Reuters. 2020. "How Political Campaigns Use Your Data." October 12, 2020. https://graphics.reuters.com/USA-ELECTION/DATA-VISUAL/yxmvjjgojvr/

Representation of the People Act. 2001. (Scotland) Regulations 2001/497.

Representation of the People Act. 2001. (England and Wales) Regulations 2001/341.

Rubinstein, I. S. 2014. "Voter Privacy in the Age of Big Data." *Wisconsin Law Review*, 5: 861–936.

Ruffini, P. 2016. "How Technology Is Changing the Polling Industry." In *Data and democracy: How political data science is shaping the 2016 elections*, edited by A. Therriault, pp. 13–18. Sebastopol, CA: O'Reilly Media.

Schleifer, T. 2019. "A New Way 2020 Candidates Want to Win Your Vote: Tracking Your Phone's Location." *Vox*, December 11, 2019. https://www.vox.com/recode/2019/12/11/20986682/trump-democrats-phone-location-data-collection-campaigns.

Stratton, N. 2020. "First-hand Insights on Data Governance in the World of Politics." *The UCOVI Blog*, https://ucovi-data.com/BlogPosts/Blog21DatainPoliticsP1.html.

Stromer-Galley, J. 2019. *Presidential Campaigning in the Internet Age*. Oxford: Oxford University Press.

Tactical Tech. 2019. *Personal Data: Political Persuasion. Inside the Influence Industry. How It Works*. Berlin: Tactical Tech. https://cdn.ttc.io/s/tacticaltech.org/methods_guidebook_A4_spread_web_Ed2.pdf.

Thaler, R., & Sunstein, R. 2008. *Nudge: Improving Decisions about Health, Wealth, and Happiness*. New Haven: Yale University Press.

The Economist. 2017. "The World's Most Valuable Resource Is No Longer Oil, but Data." May 6, 2017. https://www.economist.com/leaders/2017/05/06/the-worlds-most-valuable-resource-is-no-longer-oil-but-data.

Therriault, A. 2016. *Data and Democracy: How Political Data Science Is Shaping the 2016 Elections*. Sebastopol, CA: O'Reilly Media.

Tunnl. n.d. "Prebuilt Audience Library." https://www.tunnldata.com/prebuilt-audience-library.
Van Duyn. E. 2021. *Democracy Lives in the Darkness*. Oxford: Oxford University Press.
Voigt, M. 2018. "Digital Trump-Card? Digitale Transformation in der Wähleransprache [Digital Trump-Card? Digital Transformation in Voter Contact.]." In *Fallstudien zur Digitalen Transformation [Case Studies in Digital Transformation]*, edited by, C. Gärtner, & C. Heinrich, pp. 149–172. Wiesbaden: Springer Fachmedien.
Walker, D., & Nowlin, E. L. 2021. "Data-Driven Precision and Selectiveness in Political Campaign Fundraising." *Journal of Political Marketing*, 20(2): 73–92.
Wallace, M. 2017. "The Rusty Machine: Part One." *Conservative Home*, September 5, 2017. https://conservativehome.com/majority_conservatism/2017/09/our-cchq-election-audit-the-rusty-machine-part-one-why-the-operation-that-succeeded-in-2015-failed-in-2017.
Weitbrecht, v. D. 2019. "Parteien kaufen Personen-Daten [Parties are buying personal data]." *Mitteldeutscher Rundfunk*, March 20, 2019. https://www.mdr.de/medien360g/medienpolitik/wahlen-datenhandel-partei-100.html.
Wielhouwer, P. W. 1995. "Strategic Canvassing by Political Parties, 1952–1990." *American Review of Politics*, 16: 213–238.
Wong, J. C. 2020. "One Year Inside Trump's Monumental Facebook Campaign." *The Guardian*, January 29, 2020. https://www.theguardian.com/us-news/2020/jan/28/donald-trump-facebook-ad-campaign-2020-election.
Zax, D. 2011. "Is Personal Data the New Currency?." *MIT Technology Review*, November 30, 2011. https://www.technologyreview.com/2011/11/30/20993/is-personal-data-the-new-currency/
Zeng, E., Wei, M., Gregersen, T., Kohno, T., & Roesner, F. 2021. "Polls, Clickbait, and Commemorative $2 Bills: Problematic Political Advertising on News and Media Websites around the 2020 U.S. Elections." In *Proceedings of the 21st ACM Internet Measurement Conference (IMC '21)*, pp. 507–525. New York: Association for Computing Machinery.

Practitioner Perspectives on Data

McEvoy, M. 2019. *Investigation Report P19-01 Full Disclosure: Political Parties, Campaign Data, and Voter Consent*. https://www.oipc.bc.ca/investigation-reports/2278, accessed April 7, 2022.
Webber, R., & Burrows, R. 2018. *The Predictive Postcode, the Geodemographic Classification of British Society*. London: Sage.

Chapter 4

Ali, M., Sapiezynski, P., Korolova, A., Mislove, A., & Rieke, A. 2021. "Ad Delivery Algorithms: The Hidden Arbiters of Political Messaging." *Proceedings of the 14th ACM International Conference on Web Search and Data Mining*, pp. 13–21. https://arxiv.org/abs/1912.04255.
Andreou, A., Silva, M., Benevenuto, F., Goga, O., Loiseau, P., & Mislove, A. 2019. "Measuring the Facebook Advertising Ecosystem." In *NDSS 2019—Proceedings of the*

Network and Distributed System Security Symposium, pp. 1–15. https://dx.doi.org/10.14722/ndss.2019.23280.

Anstead, N. 2017. "Data-Driven Campaigning in the 2015 United Kingdom General Election." *The International Journal of Press/Politics*, 22(3): 294–313.

Baldwin-Philippi, J. 2016. "The Cult(ure) of Analytics in 2014." In *Communication and Midterm Elections*, edited by D. Schill & J. Hendricks, pp. 25–42. London: Springer.

Baldwin-Philippi, J. 2017. "The Myths of Data-Driven Campaigning." *Political Communication*, 34(4): 627–633.

Castleman, D. 2016. "Essentials of Modeling and Microtargeting." In *Data and Democracy: How Political Data Science Is Shaping the 2016 Elections*, edited by A. Therriault, pp. 1–6. Sebastopol, CA: O'Reilly Media.

Chester, J., & Montgomery, K. C. 2017. "The Role of Digital Marketing in Political Campaigns." *Internet Policy Review*, 6(4): 1–20.

Crain, M., & Nadler, A. 2019. "Political Manipulation and Internet Advertising Infrastructure." *Journal of Information Policy*, 9: 370–410.

Davidson, S., & Binstock, R. H. 2011. "Political Marketing and Segmentation in Aging Democracies." In *Routledge Handbook of Political Marketing*, edited by J. Lees-Marshment, pp. 20–33. London: Routledge.

Elgendy, N., & Elragal, A. 2014. "Big Data Analytics: A Literature Review Paper." In *Advances in Data Mining. Applications and Theoretical Aspects*, edited by P. Perner, pp. 214–227. Cham: Springer.

Epstein, B. 2018. *The Only Constant Is Change: Technology, Political Communication, and Innovation Over Time*. New York: Oxford University Press.

Farrell, D. M. 2006. "Political Parties in a Changing Campaign Environment." In *Handbook of Party Politics*, edited by R. Katz & W. Crotty, pp. 122–133. Thousand Oaks, CA: Sage.

Gelman, A., Lax, J., Philipps, J., Gabry, J., & Trangucci, R. 2018. "Using Multilevel Regression and Poststratification to Estimate Dynamic Public Opinion." August 28, 2018. http://www.stat.columbia.edu/~gelman/research/unpublished/MRT(1).pdf.

Ghitza, Y., & Gelman, A. 2013. "Deep Interactions with MRP: Election Turnout and Voting Patterns among Small Electoral Subgroups." *American Journal of Political Science*, 57(3): 762–776.

Gibson, R., & Römmele, A. 2001. "Changing Campaign Communications: A Party-Centered Theory of Professionalized Campaigning." *The Harvard International Journal of Press/Politics*, 6(4): 31–43.

Gorton, W. A. 2016. "Manipulating Citizens: How Political Campaigns' Use of Behavioral Social Science Harms Democracy." *New Political Science*, 38(1): 61–80.

Green, D. P., & Gerber, A. S. 2019. *Get Out the Vote: How to Increase Voter Turnout*, 4th edition, Washington, DC: Brookings Institution Press.

Hanretty, C. 2020. "An Introduction to Multilevel Regression and Post-Stratification for Estimating Constituency Opinion." *Political Studies Review*, 18(4): 630–645.

Harker, M. 2020. "Political Advertising Revisited: Digital Campaigning and Protecting Democratic Discourse." *Legal Studies*, 40(1): 151–171.

Harrison, N. 2007. "Data Giant Launches Ethnic Segmentation Tool." *Campaign Live*, March 9, 2007. https://www.campaignlive.co.uk/article/data-giant-launches-ethnic-segmentation-tool/642791?DCMP=ILC-SEARCH&preferredformat=mobile.

Hersh, E. D. 2015. *Hacking the Electorate: How Campaigns Perceive Voters*. Cambridge: Cambridge University Press.

Hersh, E. D., & Schaffner, B. F. 2013. "Targeted Campaign Appeals and the Value of Ambiguity." *The Journal of Politics*, 75(2): 520–534.

Hutchinson, A. 2020. "Analysis Reveals Key Facebook Ad Strategies of Trump Campaign." *Social Media Today*, January 30, 2020. https://www.socialmediatoday.com/news/analysis-reveals-key-facebook-ad-strategies-of-trump-campaign/571346/.

International Institute for Democracy and Electoral Assistance. 2018. "Digital Microtargeting." Stockholm: International IDEA. https://www.idea.int/sites/default/files/publications/digital-microtargeting.pdf.

Issenberg, S. 2012a. "How Obama's Team Used Big Data to Rally Voters." *MIT Technology Review*, December 19, 2012. https://www.technologyreview.com/s/509026/how-obamas-team-used-big-data-to-rally-voters/.

Issenberg, S. 2012b. *The Victory Lab: The Secret Science of Winning Campaigns*. New York: Broadway Books.

Jungherr, A. 2016. "Four Functions of Digital Tools in Election Campaigns: The German Case." *The International Journal of Press/Politics*, 21(3): 358–377.

Jungherr, A., Rivero, G., & Gayo-Avello, D. 2020. *Retooling Politics: How Digital Media Are Shaping Democracy*. Cambridge: Cambridge University Press.

Kearns, I., & Alexander, J. 2020. "Winning for Britain." https://www.socialliberal.net/winning_for_britain.

Kefford, G. 2021. *Political Parties and Campaigning in Australia: Data, Digital and Field*, London: Palgrave Macmillan.

Kreiss, D. 2012. *Taking Our Country Back: The Crafting of Networked Politics from Howard Dean to Barack Obama*. New York: Oxford University Press.

Kreiss, D. 2016. *Prototype Politics: Technology-Intensive Campaigning and the Data of Democracy*, New York: Oxford University Press.

Kreiss, D. 2017. "Micro-Targeting, the Quantified Persuasion." *Internet Policy Review*, 6(4): 1–14.

Kruschinski, S., & Bene, M. 2022. "*In varietate concordia*?! Political Parties' Digital Political Marketing in the 2019 European Parliament Election Campaign." *European Union Politics*, 23(1): 43–65.

Mattinson, D. 2011. *Talking to a Brick Wall: How New Labour Stopped Listening to the Voter and Why We Need a New Politics*. London: Biteback.

Nadler, A., Crain, M., & Donovan, J. 2018. *Weaponizing the Digital Influence Machine*. New York: Data & Society Research Institute. https://datasociety.net/library/weaponizing-the-digital-influence-machine/.

Negrine, R. 2007. "The Professionalisation of Political Communication in Europe." In *The Professionalisation of Political Communication*, edited by R. Negrine, C. Holtz-Bacha, & S. Papathanassopoulos, pp. 27–45. Bristol: Intellect Books.

Negrine, R., & Papathanassopoulos, S. 1996. "The 'Americanization' of Political Communication: A Critique." *Harvard International Journal of Press/Politics*, 1(2): 45–62.

New York Times. 2020. "Lord of the Rings, 2020 and Stuffed Oreos: Read the Andrew Bosworth Memo." *New York Times*, January 7, 2020. https://www.nytimes.com/2020/01/07/technology/facebook-andrew-bosworth-memo.html.

Nickerson, D. W., & Rogers, T. 2014. "Political Campaigns and Big Data." *Journal of Economic Perspectives*, 28(2): 51–74.

Nielsen, R. K. 2012. *Ground Wars: Personalized Communication in Political Campaigns*. Princeton, NJ: Princeton University Press.

Norris, P. 2000. *A Virtuous Circle: Political Communications in Postindustrial Societies.* Cambridge: Cambridge University Press.

Panebianco, A. 1988. *Political Parties: Organization and Power.* Cambridge; New York: Cambridge University Press.

Pons, V. 2016. "Has Social Science Taken Over Electoral Campaigns and Should We Regret It?" *French Politics, Culture & Society,* 34(1): 34–47.

Pons, V. 2018. "Will a Five-Minute Discussion Change Your Mind? A Countrywide Experiment on Voter Choice in France." *American Economic Review,* 108(6): 1322–1363.

Römmele, A., & Gibson, R. 2020. "Scientific and Subversive: The Two Faces of the Fourth Era of Political Campaigning." *New Media & Society,* 22(4): 595–610.

Scarvalone, D. 2016. "Digital Advertising in the Post-Obama Era." In *Data and Democracy: How Political Data Science Is Shaping the 2016 Elections,* edited by A. Therriault, pp. 31–37. Sebastopol, CA: O'Reilly Media.

Shor, D. 2021. "Toronto Data Workshop." YouTube, May 21, 2021. https://www.youtube.com/watch?v=_IEPKapa9_0.

Sides, J., & Vavreck, L. 2014. "Obama's Not So Big Data." *Pacific Standard,* January 21, 2014. https://psmag.com/social-justice/obamas-big-data-inconclusive-results-political-campaigns-72687.

Tufekci, Z. 2014. "Engineering the Public: Big Data, Surveillance and Computational Politics." *First Monday,* https://firstmonday.org/article/view/4901/4097.

Tunnl. n.d. "Prebuilt Audience Library." https://www.tunnldata.com/prebuilt-audience-library.

Vaccari, C. 2013. *Digital Politics in Western Democracies: A Comparative Study.* Baltimore, MD: Johns Hopkins University Press.

Voigt, M. 2018. "Digital Trump-Card? Digitale Transformation in der Wähleransprache [Digital Trump-Card? Digital Transformation in Voter Contact.]." In *Fallstudien zur Digitalen Transformation [Case Studies in Digital Transformation],* edited by C. Gärtner & C. Heinrich, pp. 149–172. Wiesbaden: Springer Fachmedien.

Waters, T. 2019. "2019-09-18 Key Seats Strategy—An Update and Appraisal of Our Strategy PDF." *Scribd.* https://www.scribd.com/document/473454110/2019-09-18-Key-seats-strategy-an-update-and-appraisal-of-our-strategy-pdf#.

Webber, R. 2006. "How Parties Used Segmentation in the 2005 British General Election Campaign." *Journal of Direct, Data and Digital Marketing Practice,* 7(3): 239–252.

Webber, R., & Burrows, R. 2018. *The Predictive Postcode: The Geodemographic Classification of British Society.* London: Sage.

Wong, J. C. 2020. "One Year Inside Trump's Monumental Facebook Campaign." *The Guardian,* January 29, 2020. https://www.theguardian.com/us-news/2020/jan/28/donald-trump-facebook-ad-campaign-2020-election.

Wong, S. 2019. "What Is MRP and Can It Predict the Result of the UK General Election?." *New Scientist,* November 27, 2019. https://www.newscientist.com/article/2224783-what-is-mrp-and-can-it-predict-the-result-of-the-uk-general-election/.

Chapter 5

Ali, M., Sapiezynski, P., Korolova, A., Mislove, A., & Rieke, A. 2021. "Ad Delivery Algorithms: The Hidden Arbiters of Political Messaging." In *Proceedings of the 14th*

ACM International Conference on Web Search and Data Mining, pp. 13–21. https://arxiv.org/abs/1912.04255.

Antrobus, B. 2022. "Research Reveals Massive Figures Parties Spent on Social Media Ads in Election's Final Months." *News.com.au*, June 23, 2022. https://www.news.com.au/national/federal-election/research-reveals-massive-figures-parties-spent-on-social-media-ads-in-elections-final-months/news-story/f03efbfe1c51bf733964e6cb5267919b.

Baldwin-Philippi, J. 2017. "The Myths of Data-Driven Campaigning." *Political Communication*, 34(4): 627–633.

Barberà, O., Sandri, G., Correa, P., & Rodríguez-Teruel, J. 2021. *Digital Parties: The Challenges of Online Organisation and Participation*. Cham: Springer.

Becker, B. n.d. "Becker Digital Strategies." https://beckerdigitaltraining.com/.

Bennett, C., & Bayley, R. 2018. *The Influence Industry in Canada*. Berlin: Tactical Tech. https://cdn.ttc.io/s/ourdataourselves.tacticaltech.org/ttc-influence-industry-canada.pdf.

Bennett, C. J., & Gordon, J. 2021. "Understanding the "micro" in Political Microtargeting: An Analysis of Facebook Digital Advertising in the 2019 Federal Canadian Election." *Canadian Journal of Communication*, 46(3): 431–459.

Bennett, W. L., Segerberg, A., & Knüpfer, C. B. 2018. "The Democratic Interface: Technology, Political Organization, and Diverging Patterns of Electoral Representation." *Information, Communication & Society*, 21(11): 1655–1680.

Bimber, B. 1998. "The Internet and Political Transformation: Populism, Community, and Accelerated Pluralism." *Polity*, 31(1): 133–160.

Bimber, B. 2014. "Digital Media in the Obama Campaigns of 2008 and 2012: Adaptation to the Personalized Political Communication Environment." *Journal of Information Technology & Politics*, 11(2): 130–150.

Bimber, B., & Davis, R. 2003. *Campaigning Online: The Internet in US Elections*. New York: Oxford University Press.

Boutilier, A. 2022. "Conservatives' Post-election Report Gives Mixed Reviews on O'Toole's Performance." *Global News*, January 27, 2022. https://globalnews.ca/news/8542416/conservatives-post-election-mixed-reviews/.

Chester, J., & Montgomery, K. C. 2019. "The Digital Commercialisation of US Politics: 2020 and Beyond." *Internet Policy Review*, 8(4): 1–23.

CNBC. 2020. "How Presidential Campaigns Use Apps for Data Collection." October 18, 2020. https://www.youtube.com/watch?v=-tzyDB48LDQ.

Crain, M., & Nadler, A. 2019. "Political Manipulation and Internet Advertising Infrastructure." *Journal of Information Policy*, 9: 370–410.

Delacourt, S. 2012. "Political Parties in Legal Grey Zone When It Comes to Privacy Laws." *The Toronto Star*, September 29, 2012. https://www.thestar.com/news/canada/2012/09/29/political_parties_in_legal_grey_zone_when_it_comes_to_privacy_laws_delacourt.html.

Dommett, K. 2019. "Data-Driven Political Campaigns in Practice: Understanding and Regulating Diverse Data-Driven Campaigns." *Internet Policy Review*, 8(4): 1–18.

Dommett, K., & Power, S. 2021. "Studying Digital Parties: Methods, Challenges and Responses." In *Digital Parties: The Challenges of Online Organisation and Participation*, edited by O. Barberà, G. Sandri, P. Correa, & J. Rodríguez-Teruel, pp. 67–83. London: Routledge.

Dommett, K., Power, S., Barclay, A., & MacIntyre, A. 2022. "Regulating the Business of Election Campaigns." *International IDEA*. https://www.idea.int/publications/catalogue/regulating-business-election-campaigns.

Dubois, E., & Owen, T. 2019. "Understanding the Digital Ecosystem: Findings from the 2019 Federal Election." *Centre for Media, Technology and Democracy*, June 24, 2019. https://techlaw.uottawa.ca/news/digital-ecosystem-research-challenge-launched-ahead-2019-election.

Epstein, B. 2018. *The Only Constant Is Change: Technology, Political Communication, and Innovation over Time*. New York: Oxford University Press.

Farrell, D. M. 1998. "Political Consultancy Overseas: The Internationalization of Campaign Consultancy." *PS: Political Science & Politics*, 31(2): 171–178.

Farrell, D. M., & Schmitt-Beck, R. 2003. *Do Political Campaigns Matter? Campaign Effects in Elections and Referendums*. Abingdon, UK: Routledge.

Gerbaudo, P. 2019. *The Digital Party: Political Organisation and Online Democracy*. London: Pluto Press.

Giasson, T., & Small, T. A. 2017. "Objectives of Canadian Opposition Parties." In *Permanent Campaigning in Canada*, edited by A. Marland, T. Giasson, & A. L. Esselment, pp. 109–126. Vancouver: UBC Press.

Gibson, R. K. 2015. "Party Change, Social Media and the Rise of 'Citizen-Initiated' Campaigning." *Party Politics*, 21(2): 183–197.

Gibson, R. K. 2020. *When the Nerds Go Marching in: How Digital Technology Moved from the Margins to the Mainstream of Political Campaigns*. New York: Oxford University Press.

Gómez-García, S., Gil-Torres, A., Carrillo-Vera, J., & Navarro-Sierra, N. 2019. "Constructing Donald Trump: Mobile Apps in the Political Discourse about the President of the United States." *Comunicar: Media Education Research Journal*, 27(59): 49–59.

Groß, A. 2021. "The CDU's Leaky Campaign App." *Berliner Zeitung*, August 10, 2021. https://www.berliner-zeitung.de/en/the-cdus-leaky-campaign-app-li.176310.

Halpern, S. 2020. "How the Trump Campaign's Mobile App Is Collecting Huge Amounts of Voter Data." *The New Yorker*, September 13, 2020. https://www.newyorker.com/news/campaign-chronicles/the-trump-campaigns-mobile-app-is-collecting-massive-amounts-of-voter-data.

Hayman, P. 2021. "The Development of Field Campaigning in the Australian Greens Party." Master's thesis, Melbourne: La Trobe.

Heine, C. 2016. "Trump's Campaign Just Quietly Launched a Mobile App Called America First." *AdWeek*, August 19, 2016. https://www.adweek.com/performance-marketing/trumps-campaign-just-quietly-launched-mobile-app-called-america-first-173044/.

Hennewig, S. 2013. "Die Graswurzel-Aktivitäten der CDU [The grassroots activities of the CDU]." In *Grassroots-Campaigning*, edited by R. Speth, pp. 159–169. Wiesbaden: Springer.

Hersh, E. D. 2015. *Hacking the Electorate: How Campaigns Perceive Voters*. Cambridge: Cambridge University Press.

Higher Ground Labs. 2021. "Political Tech Landscape Report 2021." May 19, 2021. https://highergroundlabs.com/political-tech-landscape-2021/.

Hindman, M. 2005. "The Real Lessons of Howard Dean: Reflections on the First Digital Campaign." *Perspectives on Politics*, 3(1): 121–128.

Issenberg, S. 2012b. *The Victory Lab: The Secret Science of Winning Campaigns.* New York: Broadway Books.

Jungherr, A., Rivero, G., & Gayo-Avello, D. 2020. *Retooling Politics: How Digital Media Are Shaping Democracy.* Cambridge: Cambridge University Press.

Jungherr, A., & Schoen, H. 2013. *Das Internet in Wahlkämpfen: Konzepte, Wirkungen und Kampagnenfunktionen [The Internet in Election Campaigns: Concepts, Effects and Campaign Functions].* Wiesbaden: Springer.

Jürgens, P., & Stark, B. 2022. "Mapping Exposure Diversity: The Divergent Effects of Algorithmic Curation on News Consumption." *Journal of Communication*, 72(3): 322–344.

Karpf, D. 2012. *The MoveOn Effect: The Unexpected Transformation of American Political Advocacy.* Oxford: Oxford University Press.

Karpf, D. 2016. *Analytic Activism: Digital Listening and the New Political Strategy.* Oxford: Oxford University Press.

Kefford, G. 2021. *Political Parties and Campaigning in Australia: Data, Digital and Field.* London: Palgrave Macmillan.

Kreiss, D. 2012. *Taking Our Country Back: The Crafting of Networked Politics from Howard Dean to Barack Obama.* New York: Oxford University Press.

Kreiss, D. 2016. *Prototype Politics: Technology-Intensive Campaigning and the Data of Democracy.* New York: Oxford University Press.

Kreiss, D., & Howard, P. N. 2010. "New Challenges to Political Privacy: Lessons from the First US Presidential Race in the Web 2.0 Era." *International Journal of Communication*, 4(19): 1032–1050.

Kreiss, D., Lawrence, R. G., & McGregor, S. C. 2018. "In Their Own Words: Political Practitioner Accounts of Candidates, Audiences, Affordances, Genres, and Timing in Strategic Social Media Use." *Political Communication*, 35(1): 8–31.

Kreiss, D., & McGregor, S. C. 2018. "Technology Firms Shape Political Communication: The Work of Microsoft, Facebook, Twitter, and Google with Campaigns during the 2016 US Presidential Cycle." *Political Communication*, 35(2): 155–177.

Kreiss, D., & McGregor, S. C. 2019. "'The 'Arbiters of What Our Voters See': Facebook and Google's Struggle with Policy, Process, and Enforcement around Political Advertising." *Political Communication*, 36(4): 499–522.

Kruschinski, S., & Bene, M. 2022. "In varietate concordia?! Political Parties' Digital Political Marketing in the 2019 European Parliament Election Campaign." *European Union Politics*, 23(1): 43–65.

Labour Party. n.d. "Tools for Activists." https://labour.org.uk/members/activist-area/tools-for-activists/.

Liberal Democrats. n.d. "Connect." https://www.libdems.org.uk/connect.

Magin, M., Podschuweit, N., Haßler, J., & Russmann, U. 2017. "Campaigning in the Fourth Age of Political Communication. A Multi-Method Study on the Use of Facebook by German and Austrian Parties in the 2013 National Election Campaigns." *Information, Communication & Society*, 20(11): 1698–1719.

Manthorpe, R. 2019. "General Election: Labour Launches New Phone Canvassing App with 'Badges' to Motivate Campaigners." *Sky News*, November 13, 2019. https://news.sky.com/story/labour-launches-new-phone-canvassing-app-with-badges-to-motivate-campaigners-11860363.

Margetts, H., John, P., Hale, S., & Yasseri, T. 2015. *Political Turbulence: How Social Media Shape Collective Action.* London: Princeton University Press.

McKelvey, F. 2015. "Battling Political Machines: Coming to a Riding Near You!" *Canadian Centre for Policy Alternatives Monitor*, 22(3): 38–39.

McKelvey, F., & Piebiak, J. 2018. "Porting the Political Campaign: The NationBuilder Platform and the Global Flows of Political Technology." *New Media & Society*, 20(3): 901–918.

McKenna, E., & Han, H. 2014. *Groundbreakers: How Obama's 2.2 Million Volunteers Transformed Campaigning in America*. New York: Oxford University Press.

National Democratic Party. 2021. *2021 Campaign Debrief*. https://xfer.ndp.ca/2022/Documents/Campaign_Debrief_Report_2021.pdf.

Newman, B. I. 1999. *Handbook of Political Marketing*, 1st edition, Thousand Oaks, CA: SAGE Publications.

Nickerson, D. W., & Rogers, T. 2014. "Political Campaigns and Big Data." *Journal of Economic Perspectives*, 28(2): 51–74.

Nielsen, R. K. 2011. "Mundane Internet Tools, Mobilizing Practices, and the Coproduction of Citizenship in Political Campaigns." *New Media & Society*, 13(5): 755–771.

Nielsen, R. K. 2012. *Ground Wars: Personalized Communication in Political Campaigns*. Princeton, NJ: Princeton University Press.

Norris, P. 2000. *A Virtuous Circle: Political Communications in Postindustrial Societies*. Cambridge: Cambridge University Press.

Open Secrets. n.d. "Vendor/Recipient Profile: Gop Data Trust." https://www.opensecrets.org/campaign-expenditures/vendor?cycle=2020&vendor=Gop+Data+Trust.

Patel, V. 2018. "The 2018 United States Congressional Midterm Elections: A Case Study of Third-Party Tracking Scripts on Candidate Websites." *Ghostery*. https://cdn.ghostery.com/website/wp-content/uploads/2018/10/08153356/Ghostery_Election_Study.pdf.

Ridout, T. N., Fowler, E. F., & Franz, M. M. 2021a. "The Influence of Goals and Timing: How Campaigns Deploy Ads on Facebook." *Journal of Information Technology & Politics*, 18(3): 293–309.

Ridout, T. N., Fowler, E. F., & Franz, M. M. 2021b. "Spending Fast and Furious: Political Advertising in 2020." *The Forum*, 18(4): 465–492.

Righetti, N., Giglietto, F., Kakavand, A. E., Kulichkina, A., Marino, G., & Terenzi, M. 2022. *Political Advertisement and Coordinated Behavior on Social Media in the Lead-Up to the 2021 German Federal Elections*. Düsseldorf: Media Authority of North Rhine-Westphalia.

Römmele, A., & Gibson, R. 2020. "Scientific and Subversive: The Two Faces of the Fourth Era of Political Campaigning." *New Media & Society*, 22(4): 595–610.

Ryan-Mosley, T. 2020. "The Technology That Powers the 2020 Campaigns, Explained." *MIT Technology Review*, September 28, 2020. https://www.technologyreview.com/2020/09/28/1008994/the-technology-that-powers-political-campaigns-in-2020-explained/.

Sheingate, A. 2016. *Building a Business of Politics: The Rise of Political Consulting and the Transformation of American Democracy*, 1st edition. New York: Oxford University Press.

Shirky, C. 2008. *Here Comes Everybody: The Power of Organizing without Organizations*. London: Allen Lane.

Stromer-Galley, J. 2019. *Presidential Campaigning in the Internet Age*. Oxford: Oxford University Press.

Tactical Tech. 2019. "Personal Data: Political Persuasion. Inside the Influence Industry. How It Works." https://ourdataourselves.tacticaltech.org/posts/inside-the-influence-industry.

Vaccari, C. 2013. *Digital Politics in Western Democracies: A Comparative Study*, Baltimore, MD: Johns Hopkins University Press.

Voigt, M. 2018. "Digital Trump-Card? Digitale Transformation in der Wähleransprache [Digital Trump-Card? Digital Transformation in Voter Contact.]." In *Fallstudien zur Digitalen Transformation [Case Studies in Digital Transformation]*, edited by, C. Gärtner, & C. Heinrich, pp. 149–172. Wiesbaden: Springer Fachmedien.

Watters, H. 2015. "Conservative App Puts Voter Identification in Campaign Workers' Hands." *CBC News*, June 12, 2015. https://www.cbc.ca/news/politics/conservative-app-puts-voter-identification-in-campaign-workers-hands-1.3104470.

Whittaker, Z. 2020. "A Bug in Joe Biden's Campaign App Gave Anyone Access to Millions of Voter Files." *Tech Crunch*, September 14, 2020. https://techcrunch.com/2020/09/14/biden-app-voter-files/.

Williamson, A., Miller, L., & Fallon, F. 2010. "Behind the Digital Campaign." *Hansard Society*. https://www.astrid-online.it/static/upload/protected/HANS/HANSARD_Digital-campaign_04_2010.pdf.

Wired. 2018. "Democrats Are Busting Their 2016 Mobile Canvassing Records," September 24, 2018. https://www.wired.com/story/2018-midterms-democrats-mobile-canvassing-records/.

Zuboff, S. 2019. *The Age of Surveillance Capitalism: The Fight for a Human Future at the New Frontier of Power*. London: Profile Books.

Chapter 6

Baldwin-Philippi, J. 2020. "Data Ops, Objectivity, and Outsiders: Journalistic Coverage of Data Campaigning." *Political Communication*, 37(4): 468–487.

Bale, T., Webb, P., & Poletti, M. 2019. *Footsoldiers: Political Party Membership in the 21st Century*. Abingdon, UK: Routledge.

Barberà, O., Sandri, G., Correa, P., & Rodríguez-Teruel, J. 2021. *Digital Parties: The Challenges of Online Organisation and Partocipation*. Cham: Springer.

Barrett, B. 2022. "Commercial Companies in Party Networks: Digital Advertising Firms in US Elections from 2006–2016." *Political Communication*, 39(2): 147–165.

Bartlett, J., Smith, J., & Acton, R. 2018. "The Future of Political Campaigning." Demos, July. https://ico.org.uk/media/2259365/the-future-of-political-campaigning.pdf.

Bennett, C. J., & Lyon, D. 2019. "Data-Driven Elections: Implications and Challenges for Democratic Societies." *Internet Policy Review*, 8(4): 1–16.

Bennett, C. J., & McDonald, M. 2020. "From the Doorstep to the Database: Political Parties, Campaigns, and Personal Privacy Protection in Canada." In *Big Data, Political Campaigning and the Law*, edited by N. Witzleb, M. Paterson, & J. Richardson, pp. 141–163. London: Routledge.

Bodó, B., Helberger, N. & de Vreese, C. H. 2017. "Political Micro-targeting: A Manchurian Candidate or Just a Dark Horse?" *Internet Policy Review*, 6(4). https://policyreview.info/articles/analysis/political-micro-targeting-manchurian-candidate-or-just-dark-horse

Bolleyer, N. 2012. "New Party Organization in Western Europe: Of Party Hierarchies, Stratarchies and Federations." *Party Politics*, 18(3): 315–336.

Bureau of Labor Statistics. 2020. "Employment in Political Organizations." https://www.bls.gov/opub/ted/2020/employment-in-political-organizations.htm.

Campaigns and Elections. 2019. "The Rise of Scientifically Optimized Creative." August 20, 2019. https://campaignsandelections.com/creative/the-rise-of-scientifically-optimized-creative/.

Carty, R. K. 2004. "Parties as Franchise Systems: The Stratarchical Organizational Imperative." *Party Politics*, 10(1): 5–24.

Carty, R. K., & Eagles, M. 1999. "Do Local Campaigns Matter? Campaign Spending, the Local Canvass and Party Support in Canada." *Electoral Studies*, 18(1): 69–87.

Carty, R. K., Young, L., & Cross, W. P. 2000. *Rebuilding Canadian Party Politics*. Vancouver: UBC Press.

Coletto, D., Jansen, H. J., & Young, L. 2011. "Stratarchical Party Organization and Party Finance in Canada." *Canadian Journal of Political Science/Revue canadienne de science politique*, 44(1): 111–136.

Commissioner of Canadian Elections. 2014. "Investigation Report on Robocalls." https://www.cef-cce.ca/rep/rep2/roboinv_e.pdf.

Common Knowledge. 2020. "Labour Election Review 2019." Labour Together. https://docs.labourtogether.uk/Labour%20Together%202019%20Election%20Review.pdf.

Cross, W. 2015. "Party Membership in Canada." In *Party Members and Activists*, edited by E. v. Haute & A. Gauja, pp. 50–65. London: Routledge.

Cross, W., & Pilet, J.-B. 2015. *The Politics of Party Leadership: A Cross-National Perspective*. Oxford: Oxford University Press.

Dalton, R. J., & Wattenberg, M. P. 2000. *Parties Without Partisans: Political Change in Advanced Industrial Democracies. Comparative Politics*. Oxford: Oxford University Press.

Data Sciences. n.d. https://datasciences.ca/.

Davies, A. 2020. "Party Hardly: Why Australia's Big Political Parties Are Struggling to Compete with Grassroots Campaigns." *The Guardian*, December 13, 2020. https://www.theguardian.com/australia-news/2020/dec/13/party-hardly-why-australias-big-political-parties-are-struggling-to-compete-with-grassroots-campaigns?CMP=Share_AndroidApp_Other.

Delacourt, S. 2013. *Shopping for Votes: How Politicians Choose Us and We Choose Them*. Madeira Park, BC: Douglas and McIntyre.

Dennis, J. 2020. "A Party within a Party Posing As A Movement? Momentum as a Movement Faction." *Journal of Information Technology & Politics*, 17(2): 97–113.

Dommett, K., & Bakir, M. E. 2020. "A Transparent Digital Election Campaign? The Insights and Significance of Political Advertising Archives for Debates on Electoral Regulation." *Parliamentary Affairs*, 73(Suppl 1): 208–224.

Dommett, K., Kefford, G., & Power, S. 2020. "The Digital Ecosystem: The New Politics of Party Organization in Parliamentary Democracies." *Party Politics*, 27(5): 847–857.

Dommett, K., Power, S., Barclay, A., & Macintyre, A. 2022. *The Business of Election Campaigns*, International IDEA. https://www.idea.int/publications/catalogue/regulating-business-election-campaigns.

Dommett, K., & Temple, L. 2018. "Digital Campaigning: The Rise of Facebook and Satellite Campaigns." *Parliamentary Affairs*, 71(Suppl 1): 189–202.

Duverger, M. 1967. *The Idea of Politics: The Uses of Power in Society*. London: Methuen.

Engage. 2018. "Inside the Cave: An In-Depth Look at the Digital, Technology and Analytics Operations of Obama for America." https://enga.ge/wp-content/uploads/2018/01/Inside_the_Cave-1.pdf.

Farrell, D. M., Kolodny, R., & Medvic, S. 2001. "Parties and Campaign Professionals in a Digital Age: Political Consultants in the United States and Their Counterparts Overseas." *Harvard International Journal of Press/Politics*, 6(4): 11–30.

Gauja, A. 2013. *The Politics of Party Policy: From Members to Legislators*. Basingstoke, UK: Palgrave Macmillan.

Gauja, A. 2015. "The State of Democracy and Representation in Australia." *Representation*, 51(1): 23–34.

Gauja, A., & Jackson, S. 2016. "Australian Greens Party Members and Supporters: Their Profiles and Activities." *Environmental Politics*, 25(2): 359–379.

Gibson, R. 2020. *When the Nerds Go Marching In*. Oxford: Oxford University Press.

Grassia, A. 2016. "Data Management for Political Campaigns." In *Data and Democracy: How Political Data Science Is Shaping the 2016 Elections*, edited by A. Therriault, pp. 7–12. Sebastopol, CA: O'Reilly Media.

Grossmann, M. 2009. "Going Pro? Political Campaign Consulting and the Professional Model." *Journal of Political Marketing*, 8(2): 81–104.

Hankey, S., Marrison, J., & Naik, R. 2018. *Data and Democracy in the Digital Age*. London: The Constitution Society.

Hatch, R. S. 2016. "Party Organizational Strength and Technological Capacity: The Adaptation of the State-Level Party Organizations in the United States to Voter Outreach and Data Analytics in the Internet Age." *Party Politics*, 22(2): 191–202.

Hayman, P. 2021. *The Development of Field Campaigning in the Australian Greens Party*. Master's thesis, Melbourne: La Trobe.

HM Government. 2022. *Elections Act*. https://www.legislation.gov.uk/ukpga/2022/37/contents/enacted.

Issenberg, S. 2012a. "How Obama's Team Used Big Data to Rally Voters." *MIT Technology Review*, December 19, 2012. https://www.technologyreview.com/s/509026/how-obamas-team-used-big-data-to-rally-voters/.

Karpf, D. 2012. *The MoveOn Effect: The Unexpected Transformation of American Political Advocacy*. Oxford: Oxford University Press.

Katz, R. S., & Mair, P. 1993. "The Evolution of Party Organizations in Europe: The Three Faces of Party Organization." *American Review of Politics*, 14(4): 593–617.

Kefford, G. 2016. "Agency, Institutional Stretch and Structural Adjustment: The Australian Labor Party 2006–2013." *Party Politics*, 22(4): 512–521.

Kefford, G. 2021. *Political Parties and Campaigning in Australia: Data, Digital and Field*. London: Palgrave Macmillan.

Kreiss, D. 2012. *Taking Our Country Back: The Crafting of Networked Politics from Howard Dean to Barack Obama*. New York: Oxford University Press.

Kreiss, D. 2016. *Prototype Politics: Technology-Intensive Campaigning and the Data of Democracy*. New York: Oxford University Press.

Kreiss, D., & Howard, P. N. 2010. "New Challenges to Political Privacy: Lessons from the First US Presidential Race in the Web 2.0 Era." *International Journal of Communication*, 4(19): 1032–1050.

Kreiss, D., & McGregor, S. C. 2018. "Technology Firms Shape Political Communication: The Work of Microsoft, Facebook, Twitter, and Google with Campaigns during the 2016 US Presidential Cycle." *Political Communication*, 35(2): 155–177.

Kusche, I. 2020. "The Old in the New: Voter Surveillance in Political Clientelism and Datafied Campaigning." *Big Data & Society*, 7(1): 1–17.

Lees-Marshment, J., & Pettitt, R. T. 2014. "Mobilising Volunteer Activists in Political Parties: The View from Central Office." *Contemporary Politics*, 20(2): 246–260.

Loft, P., Dempsey, N., & Audickas, L. 2019. "Membership of UK Political Parties." House of Commons Library. https://researchbriefings.files.parliament.uk/documents/SN05125/SN05125.pdf.

Mazzoleni, O., & Voerman, G. 2017. "Memberless Parties: Beyond the Business-Firm Party Model?" *Party Politics*, 23(6): 783–792.

McGrane, D. 2019. *The New NDP: Moderation, Modernization, and Political Marketing*. Vancouver: UBC Press.

McGregor, G. 2017. "Liberal Party's Exclusive Deal with Data Company Benefits Trudeau Friend." *CTV News*. March 29, 2017. https://www.ctvnews.ca/politics/liberal-party-s-exclusive-deal-with-data-company-benefits-trudeau-friend-1.3346830.

McKenna, E., & Han, H. 2014. *Groundbreakers: How Obama's 2.2 Million Volunteers Transformed Campaigning in America*. New York: Oxford University Press.

Medvic, S. K. 2003. "Professional Political Consultants: An Operational Definition." *Politics*, 23(2): 119–127.

Meta. n.d. "How to Boost a Post from Your Facebook Page." https://www.facebook.com/business/help/347839548598012?id=352109282177656.

Mie Kim, Y., Hsu, J.,Neiman, D., Kou, C., Bankston, L., Yun Kim, S., Heinrich, R., Baragwanath, R., & Raskutti, G. 2018. "The Stealth Media? Groups and Targets behind Divisive Issue Campaigns on Facebook." *Political Communication*, 35(4): 515–541.

Miller, S. 2022. "Startup Caucus Raises $500k For Second Investment Round." *Campaigns and Elections*, March 3, 2022.https://campaignsandelections.com/campaigntech/startup-caucus-raises-500k-for-second-investment-round/.

Morris, J. 2018. "Introducing Conservative Academy, Our New Training Tool for Members." Conservative Home. https://www.conservativehome.com/platform/2018/10/james-morris-introducing-conservative-academy-our-new-training-tool-for-members.html.

Munroe, K. B., & Munroe, H. 2018. "Constituency Campaigning in the Age of Data." *Canadian Journal of Political Science/Revue canadienne de science politique*, 51(1): 135–154.

National Post. 2014. "If the 2011 Vote Was the 'Twitter Election,' Then 2015 Will Be the 'Big Data Election.'" October 18, 2014. https://nationalpost.com/news/if-the-2011-vote-was-the-twitter-election-then-2015-will-be-the-big-data-election.

Newman, B. I. 1999. *Handbook of Political Marketing*, 1st edition, Thousand Oaks, CA: SAGE Publications.

Niedermayer, O. 2013. "Die Analyse von Parteiensystemen [The Analysis of Party Systems]." In *Handbuch Parteienforschung [Handbook of Party Research]*, edited by O. Niedermayer, pp. 83–117. Wiesbaden: Springer.

Niedermayer, O. 2020. *Parteimitglieder in Deutschland: Version 2020 [Party members in Germany: Version 2020]*. Workbooks from the Otto Stammer Center No. 31. Freie Universität Berlin.

Nielsen, R. K. 2011. "Mundane Internet Tools, Mobilizing Practices, and the Coproduction of Citizenship in Political Campaigns." *New Media & Society*, 13(5): 755–771.

Nielsen, R. K. 2012. *Ground Wars: Personalized Communication in Political Campaigns*. Princeton, NJ: Princeton University Press.

Ormiston, S. 2015. "Federal Election 2015: How Data Mining Is Changing Political Campaigns." *CBC News*. September 3, 2015. https://www.cbc.ca/news/politics/federal-election-2015-how-data-mining-is-changing-political-campaigns-1.3211895.

Patten, S. 2017. "Databases, Microtargeting, and the Permanent Campaign: A Threat to Democracy?" In *Permanent Campaigning in Canada*, edited by A. Marland, T. Giasson, & A. L. Esselment, pp. 47–64. Vancouver: UBC Press.

Papakyriakopoulos, O., Hegelich, S., Shahrezaye, M. & Serrano, J. 2018. "Social Media and Microtargeting: Political Data Processing and the Consequences for Germany." *Big Data and Society*, 5(2): 1–15.

Pettitt, R. 2020. *Recruiting and Retailing Party Activists*. Basingstoke, UK: Palgrave Macmillan.

Radwanski, A. 2015. "Game on: Each Party's Final Push to Get Voters to the Polls." *Globe and Mail*, October 16, 2015. https://www.theglobeandmail.com/news/politics/game-on-each-partys-final-push-to-get-voters-to-thepolls/article26843129/.

Richterich, A. 2018. "How Data-Driven Research Fuelled the Cambridge Analytica Controversy." *Partecipazione e conflitto*, 11(2): 528–543.

Rhodes, A. 2019. "Movement-Led Electoral Campaigning: Momentum in the 2017 General Election." In *Political Communication in Britain: Campaigning, Media and Polling in the 2017 General Election*, edited by D. Wring, D. Mortimore, & S. Atkinson, Basingstoke, UK: Palgrave Macmillan: pp. 171–186.

Römmele, A., & Gibson, R. 2020. "Scientific and Subversive: The Two Faces of the Fourth Era of Political Campaigning." *New Media & Society*, 22(4): 595–610.

Rubenstein, J. 2022. "Small Money Donating as Democratic Politics." *Perspectives on Politics*, 20(3): 965–982.

Rudzio, W. 2015. *Das politische System Deutschlands [The political system of Germany]*. Oldenburg: Springer VS.

Scarrow, S. 2015. *Beyond Party Members: Changing Approaches to Partisan Mobilization*. Oxford: Oxford University Press.

Scottish National Party v. Information Commissioner. 2006. *Information Tribunal EA/2005/0021*.

Sheingate, A. 2016. *Building a Business of Politics: The Rise of Political Consulting and the Transformation of American Democracy*, 1st edition, New York: Oxford University Press.

Simon, F. M. 2019. "We Power Democracy: Exploring the Promises of the Political Data Analytics Industry." *The Information Society*, 35(3): 158–169.

Sparrow, N., & Turner, J. 2001. "The Permanent Campaign: The Integration of Market Research Techniques in Developing Strategies in a More Uncertain Political Climate." *European Journal of Marketing*, 35(9–10): 984–1002.

Vromen, A. 2016. *Digital Citizenship and Political Engagement: The Challenge from Online Campaigning and Advocacy Organisations*. London: Springer.

Washington, J. 2019. "Mike Bloomberg Exploited Prison Labor to Make 2020 Presidential Campaign Phone Calls." *The Intercept*, December 24, 2019. https://theintercept.com/2019/12/24/mike-bloomberg-2020-prison-labor/.

Webb, P., Poletti, M., & Bale, T. 2017. "So Who Really Does the Donkey Work in 'Multi-Speed Membership Parties'? Comparing the Election Campaign Activity of Party Members and Party Supporters." *Electoral Studies*, 46, 64–74.

Chapter 7

Andreou, A., Silva, M., Benevenuto, F., Goga, O., Loiseau, P., & Mislove, A. 2019. "Measuring the Facebook Advertising Ecosystem." In *NDSS 2019—Proceedings of the Network and Distributed System Security Symposium*, pp. 1–15. https://dx.doi.org/10.14722/ndss.2019.232.

Bayley, R. M., & Bennett, C. J. 2012. "Privacy Impact Assessments in Canada." In *Privacy Impact Assessment. Law, Governance and Technology Series 6*, edited by D. Wright & P. De Hert, pp. 161–185. Dordrecht: Springer.

Bundestag. 1994. "Political Parties Act." https://www.bmi.bund.de/SharedDocs/downloads/DE/gesetzestexte/Parteiengesetz_PartG_engl_042009.pdf?__blob=publicationFile&v=1.

Crandall, E., & Roy, M. 2019. "New Generation of Party Fundraisers Are Multi-skilled Innovators." *Policy Options Politiques*, June 4, 2020. https://policyoptions.irpp.org/magazines/june-2020/new-generation-of-party-fundraisers-are-multi-skilled-innovators/.

Crotty, W. 2006. "Party Origins and Evolution in the United States." In *Handbook of Party Politics*, edited by R. Katz & W. Crotty, pp. 25–33. London: Sage.

Dachwitz, I. 2017. "Wahlkampf in der Grauzone: Die Parteien, das Microtargeting und die Transparenz [Election campaigning in the legal gray zone: The parties, microtargeting and transparency]." https://netzpolitik.org/2017/wahlkampf-in-der-grauzone-die-parteien-das-microtargeting-und-die-transparenz/.

Dommett, K., & Power, S. 2019. "The Political Economy of Facebook Advertising: Election Spending, Regulation and Targeting Online." *The Political Quarterly*, 90(2): 257–265.

Dommett, K., & Zhu, J. 2022. "The Barriers to Regulating the Online World: Insights from UK Debates on Online Political Advertising." *Policy & Internet*, 14(4): 772–787.

Elections Canada. 2022. "Expenses Limits." https://www.elections.ca/content.aspx?section=pol&dir=limits&document=index&lang=e.

Electoral Commission UK. n.d. "Public Funding for Political Parties." https://www.electoralcommission.org.uk/who-we-are-and-what-we-do/financial-reporting/donations-and-loans/public-funding-political-parties.

Fisher, J. 2002. "Next Step: State Funding for the Parties?." *The Political Quarterly*, 73(4): 392–399.

Fowler, E., Franz, M., Martin, G., Pekowitz, Z., & Ridout, T. 2021. "Political Advertising Online and Offline." *American Political Science Review*, 115(1): 130–149.

Fridkin, K., Kahn, K., & Kenney, P. J. 2004. *No Holds Barred: Negativity in US Senate Campaigns*. Upper Saddle River, NJ: Pearson.

German Party Law. 2021. https://www.bundeswahlleiter.de/en/dam/jcr/1aedeb82-9067-4321-acce-880ba22ddc28/parteiengesetz.pdf.

Hankey, S., Marrison, J., & Naik, R. 2018. *Data and Democracy in the Digital Age*. London: The Constitution Society. Harker, M. 2020. "Political Advertising Revisited: Digital Campaigning and Protecting Democratic Discourse." *Legal Studies*, 40(1): 151–171.

Hessian Commissioner for Data Protection and Freedom. 2023. "Datenschutz bei Wahl- und Abstimmungswerbung [Data protection regarding election and voting advertisements]." https://datenschutz.hessen.de/sites/datenschutz.hessen.de/files/2023-02/datenschutz_bei_wahl-_und_abstimmungswerbung_langfassung.pdf.

Information Commissioners Office. 2018. "Investigation into Data Analytics for Political Purposes." https://ico.org.uk/action-weve-taken/investigation-into-data-analytics-for-political-purposes/.

Institute for Government. 2022. "Rules for Funding for Political Parties." https://www.instituteforgovernment.org.uk/explainers/political-party-funding.

Iyengar, S., & Ansolabehere, S. 2010. *Going Negative*. New York: Simon & Schuster.

Kölln, A.-K. 2014. "Party Decline and Response: The Effects of Membership Decline on Party Organisations in Western Europe, 1960–2010." University of Twente. https://research.utwente.nl/en/publications/party-decline-and-response-the-effects-of-membership-decline-on-p.

Kreiss, D. 2016. *Prototype Politics: Technology-Intensive Campaigning and the Data of Democracy*. New York: Oxford University Press.

Kreiss, D., & McGregor, S. C. 2018. "Technology Firms Shape Political Communication: The Work of Microsoft, Facebook, Twitter, and Google with Campaigns during the 2016 US Presidential Cycle." *Political Communication*, 35(2): 155–177.

Kruschinski, S., & Bene, M. 2022. "*In varietate concordia*?! Political Parties' Digital Political Marketing in the 2019 European Parliament Election Campaign." *European Union Politics*, 23(1): 43–65.

Kruschinski, S., & Haller, A. 2017. "Restrictions on Data-Driven Political Micro-Targeting in Germany." *Internet Policy Review*, 6(4): 1–23.

Lidberg, J. 2019. "The Distortion of the Australian Public Sphere: Media Ownership Concentration in Australia." *AQ-Australian Quarterly*, 90(1): 12–20.

McKenna, E., & Han, H. 2014. *Groundbreakers: How Obama's 2.2 Million Volunteers Transformed Campaigning in America*. New York: Oxford University Press.

Pal, M. 2021. "Constitutional Design of Electoral Governance in Federal States." *Asian Journal of Comparative Law*, 16(S1): S23–S39.

Patten, S. 2017. "Databases, Microtargeting, and the Permanent Campaign: A Threat to Democracy?" In *Permanent Campaigning in Canada*, edited by A. Marland, T. Giasson, & A. L. Esselment, pp. 47–64. Vancouver: UBC Press.

Poguntke, T., Scarrow, S. E., & Webb, P. D. 2016. "Party Rules, Party Resources and the Politics of Parliamentary Democracies: How Parties Organize in the 21st Century." *Party Politics*, 22(6): 661–678.

Privacy Act. 1988. "Privacy Act." *Parliament of Australia*. https://www.legislation.gov.au/Details/C2014C00076.

Reuters. 2022. "Digital News Report." *Reuters Institute*. https://reutersinstitute.politics.ox.ac.uk/sites/default/files/2022-06/Digital_News-Report_2022.pdf.

Seely, A. 2017. "Media Ownership & Competition Law: The BSkyB Bid in 2010–11." https://commonslibrary.parliament.uk/research-briefings/sn06028/.

Statista. 2021. "Leading TV Broadcasters in the United Kingdom (UK) 2020, by Audience Share." *Statista*. https://www.statista.com/statistics/269983/leading-tv-broadcasters-in-the-uk-by-audience-share/.

Stromer-Galley, J. 2019. *Presidential Campaigning in the Internet Age*. Oxford: Oxford University Press.

The Federal Returning Officer. 2022. "Electoral System." https://www.bundeswahlleiter.de/en/bundestagswahlen/2021/informationen-waehler/wahlsystem.html.

Thomas, P., Susan, E. S., & Paul, D. W. 2020. "PPDB_Round1a_1b_consolidated_v1." Harvard Dataverse. https://dataverse.harvard.edu/dataset.xhtml?persistentId=doi:10.7910/DVN/NBWDFZ.

Van Biezen, I. 2004. "Political Parties as Public Utilities." *Party Politics*, 10(6): 701–722.
Van Biezen, I., & Kopecký, P. 2007. "The State and the Parties: Public Funding, Public Regulation and Rent-Seeking in Contemporary Democracies." *Party Politics*, 13(2): 235–254.

Chapter 8

Allen, D. 2023. "The Next Level of AI Is Approaching. Our Democracy Isn't Ready." *Washinton Post*, April 26, 2023. https://www.washingtonpost.com/opinions/2023/04/26/artificial-intelligence-democracy-danielle-allen/.
Barrett, B., Dommett, K., & Kreiss, D. 2021. "The Capricious Relationship between Technology and Democracy: Analyzing Public Policy Discussions in the UK and US." *Policy & Internet*, 13(4): 522–543.
Blumler, J. G., & Kavanagh, D. 1999. "The Third Age of Political Communication: Influences and Features." *Political Communication*, 16(3): 209–230.
Clarke, E. 2023. "Require the Exposure of AI-Led Political Advertisements Act." *Congress.gov*. https://www.congress.gov/bill/118th-congress/senate-bill/1596/text?s=1&r=5.
Council of Europe. 2022. "Recommendation CM/Rec(2022)12 of the Committee of Ministers to Member States on Electoral Communication and Media Coverage of Election Campaigns." https://search.coe.int/cm/pages/result_details.aspx?objectid=0900001680a6172e.
Diamond, L. 2019. "The Road to Digital Unfreedom: The Threat of Postmodern Totalitarianism." *Journal of Democracy*, 30(1): 20–34.
Dobber, T., & Vreese, C. d. 2022. "Beyond Manifestos: Exploring How Political Campaigns Use Online Advertisements to Communicate Policy Information and Pledges." *Big Data & Society*, 9(1): 1–12.
Dommett, K., Kefford, G., & Power, S. 2021. "The Digital Ecosystem: The New Politics of Party Organization in Parliamentary Democracies." *Party Politics*, 27(5), 847–857.
Etsy, D., & Rushing, R. 2007. "The Promise of Data-Driven Policymaking." *Issues in Science and Technology*, 23(4): 67–72.
European Parliament. 2021. *Key Social Media Risks to Democracy*. https://www.europarl.europa.eu/RegData/etudes/IDAN/2021/698845/EPRS_IDA(2021)698845_EN.pdf.
Fisher, C., McCallum, K., & Park, S. 2021. "Is the News Media Bargaining Code Fit for Purpose?" *The Conversation*, November 29, 2021. https://theconversation.com/is-the-news-media-bargaining-code-fit-for-purpose-172224.
Harker, M. 2020. "Political Advertising Revisited: Digital Campaigning and Protecting Democratic Discourse." *Legal Studies*, 40(1): 151–171.
Hunt, T. 2022. "Using Data to Build Strong Unions." https://unions21.org.uk/ideas/using-data-to-build-strong-unions.
IDEA. 2018. "Digital Microtargeting." *International Institute for Democracy and Electoral Assistance*. https://www.idea.int/sites/default/files/publications/digital-microtargeting.pdf.
Issenberg, S. 2012b. *The Victory Lab: The Secret Science of Winning Campaigns*. New York: Broadway Books.
Judge, E., & Pal, M. 2021. "Voter Privacy and Big-Data Elections." *Osgoode Hall Law Journal*, 58(1): 1–55.
Jungherr, A., Rivero, G., & Gayo-Avello, D. 2020. *Retooling Politics: How Digital Media Are Shaping Democracy*. Cambridge: Cambridge University Press.

Kefford, G. 2021. *Political Parties and Campaigning in Australia: Data, Digital and Field*. London: Palgrave Macmillan.

Kreiss, D. 2016. *Prototype Politics: Technology-Intensive Campaigning and the Data of Democracy*. New York: Oxford University Press.

Kozyreva, A., Lorenz-Spreen, P., & Hertwig, R. 2021. "Public Attitudes towards Algorithmic Personalization and Use of Personal Data Online: Evidence from Germany, Great Britain, and the United States." *Humanities and Social Science Communication*, 8(117): 1–11.

Kruschinski, S., & Haller, A. 2017. "Restrictions on Data-Driven Political Micro-Targeting in Germany." *Internet Policy Review*, 6(4): 1–23.

Kuehn, K. M., & Salter, L. A. 2020. "Assessing Digital Threats to Democracy, and Workable Solutions: A Review of the Recent Literature." *International Journal of Communication*, 14(22): 2589–2610.

Kundnani, H. 2020. "The Future of Democracy in Europe: Technology and the Evolution of Representation." *Chatham House*, March 3, 2020. https://www.chathamhouse.org/2020/03/future-democracy-europe.

Kusche, I. 2020. "The Old in the New: Voter Surveillance in Political Clientelism and Datafied Campaigning." *Big Data & Society*, 7(1): 1–17.

Loh, T. 2023. "German President Steinmeier Warns of AI's Risk to Democracies." *Bloomberg*, June 11, 2023. https://www.bloomberg.com/news/articles/2023-06-11/german-president-steinmeier-warns-of-ai-s-risk-to-democracies#xj4y7vzkg.

Macintyre, A. 2020. "Adaption to Data-Driven Practices in Civil Society Organizations: A Case Study of Amnesty International." *Journal of Information Technology & Politics*, 17(2): 161–173.

Magin, M., Podschuweit, N., Haßler, J., & Russmann, U. 2017. "Campaigning in the Fourth Age of Political Communication; A Multi-Method Study on the use of Facebook by German and Austrian Parties in the 2013 National Election Campaigns." *Information, Communication & Society*, 20(11): 1698–1719.

Manheim, K., & Kaplan, L. 2019. "Artificial Intlligence: Risks to Privacy and Democracy." *The Yale Journal of Law and Technology*, 21: 106–188.

Meaker, M. 2022. "Australia's Standoff against Google and Facebook Worked—Sort of." *Wired*, February 25, 2022. https://www.wired.com/story/australia-media-code-facebook-google/.

Milmo, D. & Kiran, S. 2023. "AI-enhanced Images a 'threat to democratic processes', Experts Warn." *The Guardian*, August 3, 2023. https://www.theguardian.com/technology/2023/aug/03/ai-enhanced-images-a-threat-to-democratic-processes-experts-warn#:~:text=Experts%20have%20warned%20that%20action,Rishi%20Sunak%20pouring%20a%20pint.

Nielsen, R. K. 2012. *Ground Wars: Personalized Communication in Political Campaigns*. Princeton, NJ: Princeton University Press.

Parliament of Victoria. 2021. "Inquiry into the Impact of Social Media on Victorian Elections and Victoria's Electoral Administration." https://www.parliament.vic.gov.au/emc/inquiries/inquiry/998.

Pentzold, C., & Fölsche, L. 2020. "Data-Driven Campaigns in Public Sensemaking: Discursive Positions, Contextualization, and Maneuvers in American, British, and German Debates around Computational Politics." *Communications*, 45(s1): 535–559.

Pons, V. 2016. "Has Social Science Taken over Electoral Campaigns and Should We Regret It?" *French Politics, Culture & Society*, 34(1): 34–47.

Römmele, A., & Gibson, R. 2020. "Scientific and Subversive: The Two Faces of the Fourth Era of Political Campaigning." *New Media & Society*, 22(4): 595–610.

Sky News Australia. 2023. "AI Misinformation Poses an 'enormous threat' to Democracy." May 26, 2023. https://www.skynews.com.au/opinion/piers-morgan/ai-misinformation-poses-an-enormous-threat-to-democracy/video/a31dde91de17105dc16c170b270be5bc.

Taylor, K. 2021. *The Little Black Book of Data and Democracy*. London: Byline Books.

Index

For the benefit of digital users, indexed terms that span two pages (e.g., 52–53) may, on occasion, appear on only one of those pages.

Tables and figures, are indicated by *t* and *f* following the page number

A/B testing, 73, 77, 92, 93–94, 100–1, 107, 128–29, 130, 150
America First app, 120
analytics. *See* data analytics
Australia
    Broadcasting Services Act in, 180–81
    canvassing, 142, 144
    compulsory voting in, 27, 55–56, 59, 79, 169–70
    data and privacy regulation in, 178
    databases and CRM software in, 112–13, 156
    disclosed data in, 55–56, 142
    electoral system in, 169–70
    hybrid media system in, 174
    inferential data in, 62, 142
    media regulation in, 180–81
    monitoring data in, 59, 142–43
    party personnel, technology and, 156
    party personnel for data analysis in, 149–50, 171–72
    party personnel for data collection in, 142–43
    party regulation in, 175
    party structure in, 185–86
    party system in, 172
    party websites in, 122–23, 156
    publicly available data in, 50–51, 142
    segmentation in, 78–79, 149
    SNPs used by parties in, 126, 156
    system of government in, 170–72
    targeting in, 85–86
    testing in, 92–93

Baldwin-Philippi, J., 34–35, 73, 136
Bale, T., 143
Barocas, S., 44
Barrett, B., 159–60
Bartlett, J., 138
Becker, Beth, 134
Bene, M., 34–35
Bennett, C., 34–35
Biden campaign, 116, 120, 128
big data, 6–7, 43, 67, 72
Bosworth, Andrew, 90
British Election Study, 52, 151
Broadcasting Services Act of 1992, 180–81

Cadwalladr, Carole, 192
Cambridge Analytica, 9, 17–18, 134, 165–66
Campaign Central system, 112, 118–19
campaign finance, 33–34, 176–77
campaign finance rules, 33–34, 176–77
campaigning, attitudes to, 40–41, 188–89
campaigning apps, 109, 118–22
campaign regulation, 32, 33–34, 176–77, 200–1
Canada
    campaigning apps in, 119
    campaign regulation in, 176–77
    canvassing, 63, 119, 144
    data and privacy regulation in, 178, 180
    databases and CRM software in, 115, 158
    data in campaigns in, 2–3, 68–70
    disclosed data in, 57
    electoral system in, 168–69
    inferential data in, 63
    media regulation in, 181
    monitoring data in, 60, 145
    party ideology in, 187–88
    party personnel, technology and, 158
    party personnel for data analysis in, 152–53, 154–55
    party personnel for data collection in, 144–46

Canada (*cont.*)
  party regulation in, 175, 176
  party structure in, 184–85, 186
  party websites in, 124
  PIPEDA in, 178
  privacy law in, 69–70
  publicly available data in, 52–53, 145
  segmentation in, 81–82
  SNPs used by parties in, 127–28, 158
  system of government in, 170–72
  targeting in, 88–89
  testing in, 94–95
canvassing, 44–46, 55–58, 109, 143–48, 171, 193–95, 199–200
  practitioner perspectives on, 69, 100, 131, 132, 163
  variations in uses of, 171, 185, 186
Castleman, Dan, 83, 89
Chester, J., 7
CIMS. *See* Constituent Information Management System
Citizen Relationship Management software, 116–17
CiviCRM, 112–13, 114–15
commercial data, 37–38, 62, 63, 146–47, 193–94
communication technologies and tools, 109–11, 122–29, 156, 157, 158, 159–61
Connect App, 121, 185
Constituent Information Management System (CIMS), 115, 119
constructivism, 21
Contact Creator system, 113–14
Council of Europe, 192–93
CRM software. *See* customer relationship management software
Crosby, Lynton, 9, 171–72
Cross, W., 145
C|T Group, 9, 79, 142–43, 171–72
customer relationship management (CRM) software, 108, 109–10, 111–18, 122–23, 156, 158–59

Dandelion app, 119
data, 7
  commercial, 37–38, 62, 63, 146–47, 193–94
  in elections and democracy, 1, 43
  practitioner perspectives on, 66–70
  privacy and, 12, 34–35, 49–50, 62, 178–80
  types, sources, and utility, 46*f*, 46–50, 48*t*, 64–65, 141–43, 193–94
  variations in use by advanced democracies, 50–64
data analytics, 97–98
  data and privacy regulation in, 180
  in DDC, 71, 72–73, 85, 195–96
  hybrid media system and, 173–74
  by party personnel, 148–55, 171–72
  party structure in, 185–86
  party system in, 172–73
  practitioner perspectives on, 99–103
  processes, 74–77, 75*t*
  scholarship on, 72–73
  segmentation in, 74–76, 78–85, 148–49, 150
  in subversive campaign practices, 73, 100
  system of government in, 171–72
  targeting in, 74–75, 76–77, 85–92
  testing in, 74–75, 77, 92–97, 100–1, 148–49, 150
data and privacy regulation, 34–35, 178–80, 202–3
databases
  CRM software and, 108, 111–18, 142, 156–57, 158–59
  in data analytics, 150
  voter, 7–8, 45–46, 63–64, 178
data brokers, 45–47, 49–50, 52, 69, 137–38, 193–95
data collection, 64, 69, 194–95
  by canvassing, 55–58
  census data in, 54
  data and privacy regulation in, 180
  disclosed data in, 55–58
  in electoral politics, 43
  monitoring data, 60, 141–44
  by party personnel, 141–48
  party resources in, 184
  party structure in, 185
  party system in, 172–73
  regulation of, 200
  system of government in, 171
data-driven campaigning (DDC), 3–7, 20, 203–4, 205–6
  analytics in, 71, 72–73, 85, 195–96

companies selling services, 9, 17–18
comparative international analysis of, 4,
    6, 8, 9–10, 11, 13–17, 167, 191
data collection in, 43, 44–46
data use in, academic scholarship on,
    44–46
defining, 10–11
democracy and, 1, 11–12, 192–93, 196,
    197–98, 199–203, 205
external actors in, 138, 140
grassroots actors in, 139
party personnel in, 136–37, 138–40,
    141–62, 198–99
party structure in, 38–39, 184–87
party variables and parties in cases
    analysed, 13–17, 15t, 37t
party websites in, 109–10
practice of, 193–99
regulating, 12–13
systemic and regulatory variables in
    cases analysed, 13, 14t
technology for organization and
    communication, 104–6, 107f
technology in, 104, 106, 107–8, 129–30,
    196–99
theoretical foundations of, 21–24
in US, 1–2, 7, 8, 12, 45–46, 191
data-driven campaigning (DDC), theoretical
    framework for, 23f, 24, 41–42, 190
attitudes to campaigning in, 40–41,
    188–89
campaign regulation in, 33–34, 176–77
data and privacy regulation in, 34–35,
    178–80
electoral system in, 26–27, 168–70
hybrid media system in, 30–31, 173–74
media regulation in, 35–36, 180–81
party ideology in, 39–40, 187–88
party-level variables in, 36–41, 182–90
party regulation in, 32–33, 175–76
party resources in, 37–38, 182–84
party system in, 29–30, 172–73
regulatory-level variables in, 31–36, 32t,
    175–82
system-level variables in, 24–31, 32t,
    167–74
system of government in, 27–29, 170–72
three-layered model of, 22–24, 23f

data points, 44, 47–50, 48t, 54, 55–56, 62,
    64–65, 80–81, 85
data protection law, in Germany, 3–4, 64,
    84, 129, 130, 155
data regulation, 12, 34–35, 58, 61, 84, 85,
    155
Data Sciences Inc., 82
DDC. *See* data-driven campaigning
DDx. *See* Democratic Data Exchange
democracy, DDC and, 1, 11–12, 192–93,
    196, 197–98, 199–203, 205
Democratic Data Exchange (DDx), 116
door-to-door canvassing, *See* canvassing
disclosed data, 47–48, 49, 55–58, 141–42, 147
Dommett, K., 140

Elections Canada, 52–53
electoral systems, 26–27, 168–70
Elgendy, N., 72
Elragal, A., 72
Enterprise Act of 2020, 180–81
European Union (EU), GDPR in, 49–50,
    52, 178–80
Experian, 75–76, 79
external actors, in party personnel, 138, 140,
    141–42, 145–48, 149–50, 151–52, 153–
    54, 155, 157–58, 159–60, 161, 183–84

Facebook, 34–35, 50, 59
A/B testing on, 100–1, 150
Ad Library, 127–28
advertising archive, 58, 157–58
Australian parties using, 126
ban on political advertising on, 181
Canadian parties using, 127–28
data and privacy regulation and, 180
German parties using, 129
look-alike audience tool, 69, 194–95
parties advertising on, 126–28, 134
regulations, 36
targeted advertising on, 85–87, 88, 90,
    91–92, 128, 130, 134, 150, 160
tracking cookies, 59, 61, 122–23
tracking pixels from, 60, 61, 125–26, 128
in Trump digital campaign, 90, 128
UK parties using, 126–27, 157–58
US parties using, 128
Farrell, D. M., 138

federal government systems, 27–28
Feedback system, 112
Frankenfield, J., 72
fundraising, 94, 95

General Data Protection Regulation (GDPR), EU, 49–50, 52, 178–80
Germany, 131–33
　campaigning apps in, 120–22
　campaign regulation in, 176–77
　canvassing, 58, 61, 90, 120–22, 147–48
　data and privacy regulation in, 178–80
　databases and CRM software in, 116–18
　data protection law in, 3–4, 64, 84, 129, 130, 155
　disclosed data in, 58, 147
　electoral system in, 169
　inferential data in, 64
　monitoring data in, 61
　party ideology in, 187
　party personnel, technology and, 160–61
　party personnel for data analysis in, 154–55
　party personnel for data collection in, 147–48
　party regulation in, 175
　party resources in, 183–84
　party structure in, 185–86
　party system in, 173
　party websites in, 125–26
　publicly available data in, 54–55
　segmentation in, 78, 83–84
　SNPs used by parties in, 128–29
　system of government in, 185
　targeting in, 90–92
　television in, 174
　testing in, 96–97
get-out-the-vote (GOTV), 59, 75t, 81, 116
Giasson, T., 124
Gibson, R., 40–41, 137, 138–39
Google, 59, 122–23, 126, 130, 134, 181
GOP Data Center, 115–16
GOTV, See get-out-the-vote (GOTV)
Gorton, W. A., 60
Grassia, Audra, 154, 158–59

Hankey, S., 137–38
Harbath, Katie, 131, 133–35, 197–98
Hayman, P., 112–13
Hersh, E. D., 7, 37–38

Howard, P. N., 138
hybrid media system, 25t, 30–31, 173–74

inferential data, 49, 62–64, 141–42
institutionalism, 21
interactive voice response (IVR) polls, 55–56
IVR polls. See interactive voice response polls

Jungherr, A., 104–5, 199–200

Karpf, D., 60
Kefford, G., 59
König, Jochen, 131–33
Kreiss, D., 138, 146–47
Kruschinski, S., 34–35
Kusche, I., 200–1

Lamprinakou, C., 40
Liberal Democrat Connect system, 114
Liberalist database, 119

Macintyre, Amber, 163, 165–66, 198–99
majoritarian electoral systems, 26
MAVIS software, 117
McAllister, Jenny, 192
McEvoy, Michael, 66, 68–70
McGregor, Matthew, 99–101, 195–96
media regulation, 35–36, 180–81, 202
Merlin database, 113
Messina Group, 117–18
micro-targeting, 72–73, 85, 90, 100, 200–1
MiniVAN app, 119, 120
mobile apps, for campaigning, 109, 118–22
monitoring data, 48–49, 59–61, 109–10, 141–44, 145, 146–47
Montgomery, K. C., 7
MRP model. See multilevel regression and poststratification model
multilevel regression and poststratification (MRP) model, 3–4, 33–34, 76, 78, 79, 81, 92, 102–3, 171–72
Munroe & Munroe, 154–55

NationBuilder system, 112–14, 170
Nielsen, R. K., 12, 146
NPG VAN database, 120

Obama campaigns, 21–22, 95, 100–1, 116, 136, 137, 155

organizational technologies, 107–9, 111–12, 156
O'Rourke, Hannah, 163–65

parliamentary government systems, 28–29, 171–72
parties, SNPs and, 126–29
party campaigning apps, 109, 118–22
party databases and CRM software, 108, 112–18, 119–20, 129–30, 142
party grassroots actors, 41, 139, 141–43, 145, 146–47, 148–49, 150, 154–55, 156–59, 160, 189
party ideology, 39–40, 187–88
party officials, 140, 141–42, 143–44, 145, 146–47, 149–50, 151, 154–55, 156–59, 160
party organization, 136, 137, 139–40, 141*t*, 147, 170–85
party personnel, 136–37
    data analysis by, 148–55, 171–72
    data collection by, 141–48
    in DDC, 136–37, 138–40, 141–62, 198–99
    external actors in, 138, 140, 141–42, 145–48, 149–50, 151–52, 153–54, 155, 157–58, 159–60, 161, 183–84
    grassroots actors, 41, 139, 141–43, 145, 146–47, 148–49, 150, 154–55, 156–59, 160, 189
    party officials, 140, 141–42, 143–44, 145, 146–47, 149–50, 151, 154–55, 156–59, 160
    party resources and, 183–84
    practitioner perspectives on, 163–66
    scholarship on, 137–40
    targeting by, 148–49, 150–51
    technology and, 156–61, 198–99
    types of actors, 139–40, 141*t*, 148–49
party regulation, 32–33, 175–76, 201
party resources, 37–38, 182–84
party structure, 38–39, 184–87
party systems, 29–30, 172–73
party websites, 109–10, 122–26, 156, 160
Patten, S., 178
PIPEDA. *See* Privacy Act and the Personal Information Protection and Electronic Documents Act
political elites, 21, 40–41, 191

polling, 55–57, 101, 102, 147–48
Populus system, 115
predictive modeling, 76, 79, 85–86, 154–55
presidential government systems, 28–29
Privacy Act and the Personal Information Protection and Electronic Documents Act of 2000 (PIPEDA), 178
publicly available data, 47, 50–55, 65, 141–42, 145

randomized controlled trials (RCTs), 33–34, 77, 92, 94
Rashkova, E. R., 32–33
rational choice approach, 21
RCTs. *See* randomized controlled trials
Reuters Digital News Report, 25*t*, 31
Römmele, A., 40–41, 137, 138–39

Samuels, D. J., 28–29
Sartori, G., 29–30
segmentation, 74–76, 78–85, 148–49, 150
Shor, David, 82–83
Sides, J., 95
Small, T. A., 124
SNPs. *See* social networking platforms
social media, 31, 46–47, 58, 59, 61, 86–87, 94, 194–95
social networking platforms (SNPs), 34–35, 49, 58, 94, 110–11, 126–29, 130, 133–35, 156, 157–58, 159–60, 197–98. *See also* Facebook
Stromer-Galley, J., 38–39
systems of government, 27–29, 170–72

targeted advertising, on Facebook, 85–87, 88, 90, 91–92, 128, 130, 134, 150, 160
targeting, 7
    in analytics, 74–75, 76–77, 85–92
    micro-targeting, 72–73, 85, 90, 100, 200–1
    by party personnel, 148–49, 150–51
Tarsney, Catherine, 2
technology
    for campaign organization and communication, 104–7
    communication, 109–11, 122–29, 156, 157, 158, 159–61
    in DDC, 104, 106, 107–8, 129–30, 196–99
    electoral system and, 170

technology (cont.)
　organizational, 107–9, 111–12, 156
　party personnel and, 156–61, 198–99
　party structure and, 186
　practitioner perspectives on, 131–35
　variations in uses of, 111–22
　testing, 74–75, 77, 92–97, 100–1, 148–49, 150
tracking cookies, 48–49, 59, 61, 122–23
tracking pixels, 60, 61, 125–26, 128
Trump campaign, 63–64, 90, 120, 128
Tunnl, 63–64

unitary government systems, 28
United Kingdom (UK)
　attitudes to campaigning in, 189
　campaigning apps in, 119
　campaign regulation in, 176–77
　canvassing, 63, 86–87, 119, 143–44
　data and privacy regulation in, 178–79
　databases and CRM software in, 113–15, 156–57
　data in campaigns in, 3–4, 67–68
　disclosed data in, 56–57
　electoral system in, 168–69, 170
　Enterprise Act in, 180–81
　inferential data in, 62–63
　media regulation in, 180–81
　monitoring data in, 59–60, 143–44
　party ideology in, 188
　party personnel, technology and, 156–58
　party personnel for data analysis in, 150–52
　party personnel for data collection in, 142–44
　party regulation in, 175, 176
　party resources in, 182–83
　party structure in, 184
　party system in, 172
　party websites in, 123–24
　publicly available data in, 51–52
　segmentation in, 80–81, 150
　SNPs used by parties in, 126–27, 157–58
　system of government in, 171–72, 185
　targeting in, 86–88, 150–51
　television in, 174
　testing in, 93–94, 150
United States (US)
　campaigning apps in, 120
　canvassing, 58, 61, 89–90, 120, 146
　data and privacy regulation in, 178
　databases and CRM software in, 115–16, 129–30, 158–59
　DDC in, 1–2, 7, 8, 12, 45–46, 191
　disclosed data in, 58
　inferential data in, 63–64
　media platform companies in, 173–74
　media regulation in, 181
　monitoring data in, 60–61, 146–47
　party personnel, technology and, 158–60
　party personnel for data analysis in, 154
　party personnel for data collection in, 146–47
　party regulation in, 175–76
　party resources in, 183–84
　party system in, 172
　party websites in, 124–25
　publicly available data in, 53–54, 65
　segmentation in, 82–83
　SNPs used by parties in, 126, 128, 159–60
　system of government in, 171
　targeting in, 89–90
　television in, 174
　testing in, 95

Vaccari, C., 13
VAN. See Voter Activation Network
Van Biezen, I., 32–33
Vavreck, L., 95
Voigt, M., 63–64
Vote Builder database, 116
Voter Activation Network (VAN), 114
voter databases, 7–8, 45–46, 63–64, 178
Voter Vault database, 115–16
VoteSource database, 113
voting laws, 27

Ware, A., 37
Webber, Richard, 66, 67–68
White, Campbell, 99, 101–3